Twenty Over Eighty

—

Conversations on a Lifetime in Architecture and Design

Aileen Kwun and Bryn Smith

PRINCETON ARCHITECTURAL PRESS · NEW YORK

Published by
Princeton Architectural Press
A McEvoy Group Company
37 East Seventh Street
New York, New York 10003

Visit our website at www.papress.com

Editors: Megan Carey, Jenny Florence
Editorial Assistance: Marielle Suba

Book Design: Paul Wagner
Design Assistance: Mia Johnson
Typeset in Plantin and Super Grotesk

Special thanks to: Nicola Bednarek Brower, Janet Behning,
Erin Cain, Tom Cho, Barbara Darko, Benjamin English,
Jan Cigliano Hartman, Lia Hunt, Mia Johnson, Valerie Kamen,
Simone Kaplan-Senchak, Stephanie Leke, Diane Levinson,
Jennifer Lippert, Sara McKay, Jaime Nelson Noven, Rob Shaeffer,
Sara Stemen, Joseph Weston, and Janet Wong of
Princeton Architectural Press —Kevin C. Lippert, publisher

Library of Congress Cataloging-in-Publication Data
available upon request

Contents

Foreword

The annals of architecture and design are filled with those who never called it quits. Legends who worked into their eighties and nineties: Frank Lloyd Wright, Massimo Vignelli, and Charlotte Perriand.

From where does this fountain of youth spring? The question intrigued me as I traded design chat with Princeton Architectural Press publisher Kevin Lippert one day last year. I mused about the *New Yorker*'s occasional showcase of younger writers, *20 Under 40*. It's an idea used to tip us off to the up-and-coming of the literary world. What about the other side of that equation? Those, say, *over eighty* who still punch in day after day, year after year? It was with this in mind that we conceived of the book's central intention: to celebrate the legacies our greatest, oldest architects, designers, and thinkers have given the world.

The editorial brain trust at Princeton enlisted Aileen Kwun and Bryn Smith, two multifaceted writer-critic-designers, to develop the all-star roster of architecture and design veterans to interview for this book. The prospect of having Kwun and Smith, cohorts of a contemporary generation of designers and writers, take on the editorial content fascinated me and, I thought, would make this book appealing to a younger audience as well.

When I studied design in the late 1960s, most of the women and men profiled here were approaching middle age. Some had established reputations and were exemplars to me. Others were not as well known outside the precincts of their craft. It was an era when design news was gleaned from books, magazines and newspapers, and TV. We didn't have the surplus of information we have today. Instead, it seeped slowly from those media sources, and from the mouths of our professors.

The term "starchitect" did not exist, nor the means—the personal computer and the Internet—to actively disseminate the concept. Possibly the first person closest to acquiring that distinction might be Eero Saarinen, whose portrait appeared on a 1956 cover of *TIME* magazine, the litmus test for having arrived.

Design practitioners began to achieve name recognition by signing their work, a tradition more rooted in the illustration field. And so, designers such as Milton Glaser and his Push Pin Studios partner, Seymour Chwast, became known not only to design students but to a consumer public. This trend of signed work created an awareness of design that otherwise might not have developed. The practice also established a value for design as a business and marketing tool. Because of that, and because of their persistence and passion, many of these pioneers of design are still working today.

If there is a thread that weaves its way through the lives and times of the octogenarians and nonagenarians in this book, it is this: keep working. It seems to prove Newton's law—a body in motion tends to stay in motion. Some claim that under the circumstances of advanced age, denial is useful. Perhaps. But sift through their reasons for pressing on in their careers; it is simply their love of working. Work reveals the motivations—the joy of discovery, the tease of curiosity, the satisfaction of learning that only comes with ongoing work. There's little that surprises them. They've seen it all, or enough to know what makes the world tick. That's knowledge. And once they have that knowledge, they learn there is always more to learn. Paradoxically, the work then becomes a form of play in the minds and hands of these old masters.

Even with these decades of experience and day-to-day working, the following twenty figures claim they don't feel any older. Working, learning, discovering: it's a way of life.

—*Michael Carabetta*

Introduction

When the editors at Princeton Architectural Press first approached us to research, shape, and ultimately author this book, we were overjoyed. For two young design writers, it has been a dream project—to meet and speak with the most prominent minds in architecture and design— and yet, as we began, the weight of responsibility quickly settled in. How does one presume to capture the essence of twenty legends, let alone any single one? To delve beyond familiar territory and truly engage these influential figures in a conversation worth their time, and yours?

For many, after all, the impulse to create has not waned since the start of their careers as twenty-somethings. From his longtime Manhattan studio—where the phrase "Art is Work" is stenciled above the front door—Milton Glaser, eighty-six, suggests that retirement was a concept invented to stimulate the economy, describing blissful non-work in old age as an outdated American conceit. Jane Thompson, who runs an urban planning firm in Cambridge, Massachusetts, is likely to agree. She was once profiled in a book about retirement entitled *The Third Act*, now ironic in retrospect. It was published more than ten years ago, and the thought of stopping has never since crossed Thompson's mind, then or now.

As goes the trajectory of many of our interviewees, Thompson began working in one discipline, as a museum curator, then went on to embark on several others: writing and editing, retail, consulting, education, architecture; the list goes on. Any of the twenty creatives in the following pages could easily be the topic of a comprehensive monograph. Many, in fact, are—for Bob Gill, the number of books enters the double digits, his prolific output testament to a relentless drive found in the most successful, independent practitioners. (He even pitched us to design the cover of this title during our interview, to near persuasion.)

For all, work is not a burden but a necessity, and for each their daily labor is an abundant source of pride, passion, and identity. Ricardo Scofidio, born to a musical family, found his calling in architecture's compelling mix of art and science (though he nearly left the field mid career). Seymour Chwast discovered drawing at the age of six, after a screening of Disney's *Snow White and the Seven Dwarfs* filled him with awe. Ingo Maurer's passion came to light while he was lying in bed one afternoon, after a heavy lunch of spaghetti and red wine led him to contemplate the bare bulb hanging above his head—since then, he's never looked back from the artistry of the incandescent.

Maestros they may be, but the urgency of this project and the delicacy of this age group were never far from our minds. Michael Graves, an enigmatic presence in the architecture community, passed away at age eighty, just a month after our meeting. Deborah Sussman, who ran Sussman/Prejza with her husband and longtime partner, Paul Prejza, had recently witnessed a renewed interest in her early work, with a retrospective exhibition the year before our discussion; she passed away just weeks after we spoke.

For all our cultural obsession with the new and the next—talents, trends, paradigms of thought— it seemed novel, and indeed overdue, to turn our focus to those who have managed to exceed the accomplishments of their debut with an enduring level of dedication and talent. Nearly all of those profiled in this book have careers that span half a century, and sometimes more—such as Jens Risom, who's been at work for more than seventy years. In spite of our own nerves and nerdish adoration for this coterie of creatives in their ninth decade (and beyond), we tried our best to set our pedestals aside during each of these tête-à-têtes. Our inquiries are heavily informed by each of our subjects' illustrious achievements, yet in another sense, are distinctly general. Perhaps naively, we were brashly unafraid to ask the obvious and the mundane—*When did you first discover your interest in design?*—and were surprised by the insights we received in response. As members of the same community, we also indulged our curiosities in order to learn what we might apply to our own careers as they unfold in the years ahead. While we didn't discover one answer to staying relevant and creatively fulfilled, we're excited to share with you twenty.

Throughout the process, a handful of epicenters emerged—the usual suspects, New York, London, and Milan, among them, in addition to Munich, Los Angeles, Philadelphia, Chicago, and Montreal. And yet, for all of the diversity we've tried to reflect across disciplines, backgrounds, geography, and gender, certain conditions presented themselves: there were simply not as many women as men working in design in the midcentury years, and even fewer with whom we could secure an interview (our subjects count six women among twenty— a proportion far from equal, but one we feel fortunate to include). As two writers based in New York and with limited resources, this book also represents some degree of regional bias. There were dozens of names we drafted at the outset; access and availability narrowed down that list quite significantly. Some of the conversations lasted thirty minutes; others ran upwards of three hours. One, with Richard Hollis, occurred over a series of email exchanges.

The resulting text, edited and condensed with care, presents some stories that may be familiar— those persistent tales that have long since passed from first telling to near-myth—along with a series of warm revelations that could hardly be gleaned from textbooks or museum catalogs (or so we'd like to think). In gathering these oral histories, we've provided some brief context on the careers of these well-known figures, and for the more involved reader, have also annotated brief, abridged timelines of each in the back matter. These are by no means exhaustive, but rather meant to offer an additional roadmap for the series of portraits at present.

The most revealing observation, however, came from confirming our suspicion that the world of design was and continues to be a pretty damn small one. To follow but one thread, Lora Lamm and Richard Sapper worked together in Milan, at the department store La Rinascente; Sapper was also well acquainted with Sussman, a longtime collaborator of the Eames Office, as was Ralph Caplan, who, in turn, was hired at *Industrial Design* by Thompson, the magazine's founding editor. The connections are dizzying. And yet, there are also several who broke from the pack to challenge prevailing ideas and upend the status quo. Denise Scott Brown, for example, placed the vernacular design of the Las Vegas Strip under an academic lens, and forever changed the path of architectural discourse.

Tellingly, and to our relief, none of these legendary forces needed much coaxing to speak openly, just some clarity. Caplan, a longtime design critic and former teacher of ours, earnestly wondered what drew our interest to this particular demographic to begin with. Did we intentionally allude to the "80 over 20 rule," he asked, referring to the Pareto principle, which posits that there is a small but powerful twenty percent of just about any population. While the idea, otherwise known as the "law of the vital few," had not played a direct role in our approach, the thought posed an intriguing analogy. The following twenty conversations— shared with Ralph Caplan, Seymour Chwast, Bob Gill, Milton Glaser, Michael Graves, Charles Harrison, Richard Hollis, Phyllis Lambert, Lora Lamm, Jack Lenor Larsen, Ingo Maurer, Alessandro Mendini, Jens Risom, Richard Sapper, Ricardo Scofidio, Denise Scott Brown, Deborah Sussman, Jane Thompson, Stanley Tigerman, and Beverly Willis—collect some of the most compelling voices in architecture and design from the past century. Though a small sampling of a larger whole, these individuals wield great and enduring influence.

We've collected their stories with the hope that you'll not only enjoy reading them but also feel a part of the conversation; that you, too, will feel the flicker of inspiration, the generosity of spirit, and, in turn, pass these histories along.

Here's to the vital few.

—*Aileen Kwun and Bryn Smith*

Conversations

Ralph Caplan

—

Writer, Editor, Educator
b. 1925

Ralph Caplan is a man who takes chairs seriously. At his apartment on Manhattan's Upper West Side, a venerable collection of designs by Charles and Ray Eames peppers the space, coupled in the living room and arranged in communion around the dining table with seeming affection. Among the framed images hanging in his study is a series of photographs originally published in the 1978 book *Chair*, showing Caplan alternately observing and adoring an Eames Lounge Chair.

A poet and design writer, Caplan has been navigating the complex, sprawling world of design for more than fifty years, with an infectious sense of humor, a penchant for storytelling, and a keen ability to combine the analytic and the literary. He landed in the field at age thirty-two, with a move to New York and a serendipitous offer from *I.D.* magazine (then called *Industrial Design*) to work on its editorial staff under Jane Thompson. He was one of the first writers to bring a critical eye to the budding profession, pioneering discourse on emerging trends and acting as a guidepost to its collective conscious. Eventually rising to the position of editor in chief, Caplan left the magazine in 1963 to author a novel, *Say Yes!* (Doubleday), based partly on his experience studying and teaching English literature at liberal arts schools in Indiana.

Design drew him back to teaching, as well as to new endeavors as a board member and director of the International Design Conference in Aspen (now the Aspen Design Summit) and as a consultant to dozens of design firms and companies. Working with Herman Miller, IBM, and the Eames Office, he collaborated on a wide range of exhibitions, films, and publications, including the IBM Pavilion at the 1964 New York World's Fair and the book *The Design of Herman Miller* (Watson-Guptill, 1976). The author of two collections of essays, Caplan has contributed to numerous publications and has lectured and taught in many important design programs, including the Design Criticism MFA at the School of Visual Arts in New York. In 2010 he was named a Design Mind at the National Design Awards.

These days, Caplan does most of his writing at home, and likes to read from his favorite armchair, which—unexpectedly—is not a design classic, but a reupholstered secondhand rocker. Much like his writing, his manner of speaking is insightful, often surprising, candid, and full of self-deprecating charm.

Ralph Caplan photographed with an Eames Lounge Chair in *Chair: The Current State of the Art, with the Who, the Why, and the What of It* (Crowell, 1978).

What projects are you currently working on?
I'm doing what I've always done, which is to write. Occasionally I do a lecturing gig, but mostly I'm writing. During my career, I've mainly done things that I was asked to do; I've initiated very little. What's changed for me now is that I'm initiating projects that I want to do. They're various. One is a collection of essays that I wrote several years ago. Another is either a long article or a small book on why this is such an exciting and promising time to be in design. I'm not usually that sanguine, but the field of design has changed so much since it began.

How has design changed, in your opinion?
I recently gave a talk to the Products of Design department at the School of Visual Arts (SVA). I

went to their website first, and it explains that design is no longer about merely designing products, but rather a series of consequences involving sustainability, impoverished areas, and design for the handicapped—all very lofty ideals. I went to other websites for design schools that I hadn't looked at in a while, and they're pretty much all in line with that kind of thinking, which is surprising. When I spoke to the students, they pointed out that everything design is about now has never been done before.

For example, the Industrial Designers Society of America (IDSA), in collaboration with IBM, Eastman, and Autodesk, recently made a pamphlet all about ecological design. It has a number of design guides for green buildings in architecture and so forth—it's such a leap for the IDSA. When it started in the 1960s, the organization didn't have any interest in ecology. Nobody even used the term. These are ideals I actually crusaded for, or ended up crusading for, at first because I didn't know anything about design.

How did you get involved at *Industrial Design*?
Jane Thompson hired me. I was in New York, working for a humor magazine that folded. A friend of mine told me that a woman he knew was leaving her job at *I.D.* I had never heard of the magazine, and I had scarcely heard of the field. I'd only read an article in *TIME* on Raymond Loewy that had just come out.

So, I knew nothing about design, but I needed a job, and I applied. To my astonishment, they hired me—or at least offered me a job. The first time they offered it to me, I didn't take it because a spot opened up at an arts magazine, which I thought I knew more about, or at least something about. I took that job, but then discovered the position mostly involved selling advertising, which I was absolutely unfit for. *I.D.* hadn't found anybody yet, so I went there.

How did you relate to industrial design, coming into it uninitiated?
I had never taken an art course, nor an engineering course. I knew that I had absolutely no aptitude

for making things. I didn't build boats in my basement, or even play with model airplanes, and I had never taken courses related to design. I had gone to a small Quaker college and was an English major. I came to *I.D.* not intending to stay there longer than it took to find a suitable job doing something I knew something about. I thought I had no interest in the field, but I had a lot of experience writing. So from the start, everything I did in design depended on the background I had.

I.D. had just published George Nelson's first book, *Problems of Design* (1957). Because there was no distribution lined up, we had cartons of books stacked up in the office hallways. So I took one. I began reading it, and couldn't stop. I thought, wow, is this what design is? Do designers think like this? I hadn't even imagined. And then, of course, I discovered that designers *didn't* think like this—this was how George thought—but that was enough.

Years later, at the International Design Conference in Aspen, I had the same feeling, like, "God, this is what designers talk about. This is something worth pursuing." But again, that wasn't what designers generally talked about. What they talked about was far more prosaic: how to get clients, materials, and manufacturers, and how to make things. I discovered that I really was interested in design, but in the way that George was talking about it, and the way that people at Aspen

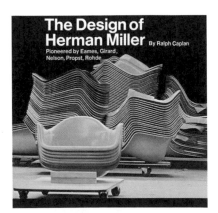  

Covers of *The Design of Herman Miller* (Whitney Library of Design, 1976); *By Design: Why There Are No Locks on the Bathroom Doors in the Hotel Louis XIV and Other Object Lessons* (McGraw-Hill, 1982); and *Cracking the Whip: Essays on Design and Its Side Effects* (Fairchild Publications, 2005).

were discussing it. But I still didn't know anything about it, or what design meant. Or so I thought.

What did you write about at *I.D.*?
My first articles were based on what I knew as an English major, on topics that could be based on anything else. Then when I became editor, I had to write editorials. I wrote about things that designers are thinking about today: sustainability, design for the handicapped (which I have a special interest in), the peace movement.

How did Aspen affect your view of design?
The first time I ever went there, in the 1960s, I was invited to speak on a panel. One of the things we were asked to talk about was the quintessential design of the twentieth century. The chosen designs were pretty predictable: Le Corbusier's chapel (Notre Dame du Haut in Ronchamp, France), the Eameses' molded plywood chair, Saarinen's plastic Tulip chair, Knoll, and other things considered important. When it came to my turn, I surprised everyone on the panel, including myself, when I said the quintessential twentieth-century design was the sit-in.

Nobody had heard of a famous design called the "sit-in." I defended it because I knew that the Civil Rights movement wasn't successful because some people from Montgomery, Alabama, suddenly got fed up, but because they knew what to do. Their aim wasn't to get a hamburger or service, their aim was to close the restaurant until it was integrated. They sat there because the strategy had been designed long before, and they had been trained and taken courses in it. It was all premeditated. The whole Civil Rights movement was based on that: a design strategy. I realized at the time that for a lot of my life, I had known and recognized that the sit-in was a design. But it was hard to explain.

The sit-in presented a decisive moment for you. What were some seminal texts or episodes from your youth that also influenced you in your later years?
We didn't have a lot of books around when I was a kid, but one of the few we had was called *The Rise of David Levinsky*, by Abraham Cahan. I must have read it at least three times when I was twelve or thirteen years old. It's about the development of the US garment industry by Jewish immigrants, but for me it was also a story about the relationship between design and business.

Many years later, I wrote an editorial for *I.D.* on the subject, as it was something that all designers were campaigning for by that time: the idea that a designer should be called in at the inception of a project, not at the end. But they never were. Manufacturers always had designers come in at the end of the process, and designers always wanted to be in from the beginning. Designing was seen mainly as a marketing tool.

What led to your departure from *I.D.*?
I left *I.D.* because I had planned to write a novel, *Say Yes!*, and I realized I would never finish the book if I stayed at a job. It was a satire of self-help books, but many people thought it was a satire of Norman Vincent Peale, the forefather of positive thinking. To some extent, the main villainous character *was* based somewhat on Peale. I had some bad breaks: the week it came out, there was a newspaper strike. Also that year, Sammy Davis Jr. wrote a book called *Yes I Can*, and people got them confused.

After it was published, Charles Eames, whom I knew through *I.D.*, asked me to work on the IBM Pavilion for the 1964 World's Fair in New York. I didn't know him well, and our last contact had been a fairly bitter argument over the phone. He had done an exhibition called *Mathematica: A World of Numbers…and Beyond*, and one of our writers, Judith Ransom Miller, had reviewed it rather unfavorably. Charles was furious and called me, very angry, and I told him we couldn't second-guess our writer's review. She saw the exhibition, I didn't. Before he hung up on me, he either said, "I'll forgive this, but I'll never forget it," or, "I'll forget this, but I'll never forgive it." [*Laughs*] Which was a shame, because I had always wanted to know him better.

And then about a year later, he asked me to work for him on the pavilion. He said he really needed a writer, and I was fascinated with the idea. I had never worked in a design office before, though I had visited many of them to do interviews. I went in with serious trepidation: here I had been writing about design with authority for several years, and I figured as soon as I got into a design office, they'd see me pick up an X-acto knife the wrong way, or something, and I'd completely blow my cover. [*Laughs*] I had no idea what I'd do for them.

This was in California?
Yes, in Venice. Charles had arranged for a motel, the Surfrider, and in those days I went to the Eames Office on the jitney. It was the best commute I ever had. My first day there, I arrived at 8 in the morning. When I left, it was 2 a.m. I arrived terrified, and left thinking, "How will they ever get along without me?" There was so much to do.

And that was the beginning of my relationship with the Eames Office. I did a lot of projects with them, and it became a kind of thing for me, working with design offices. I got to see a lot. I knew that in another part of the building, somebody was developing chairs. I had nothing to do with that, but I was interested in learning more about the process.

Aside from working with the Eameses, I started to do other things: exhibitions with Chermayeff & Geismar, and consulting with corporate clients. I got over my fear of working in design offices. By that time I felt—and designers were beginning to understand—that they needed more minds, more writers, for exhibitions.

Working with designers in their studios must have been instrumental to your understanding of design. Are there any figures you would consider mentors?
The most important, by far, was Charles Eames, though I was very close with both him and Ray. Charles was an incredible mind, and open to so many things. He had so many ideas, and wrote almost nothing. He was very nervous about lecturing, and so he had a reputation that was narrower than his gifts, by far.

The year my novel came out, *Library Journal* did a special issue on first-time novelists—I think there were four or five of us. They sent us a questionnaire, and one of the things they asked

was, "Who is your most important inspiration, mentor, etc.?" I knew the answer was probably supposed to be Tolstoy, or Norman Mailer, maybe. I probably did mention some of them, but I said that my most important model for working was Charles Eames. I got a call from the magazine and they said, "Well, this is embarrassing. We're the *Library Journal*—we have the best research facilities there are—and the only Charles Eames we can find is a furniture designer. We can't find a writer by that name." And I said, "No, no, that's the right Charles."

You've always taken a cross-disciplinary approach to the fields of design and writing. What inspires this?
In the long run, they really aren't disparate.

If you could go back, what advice would you give yourself at the beginning of your career?
Pay more attention to how much you know that you aren't aware of knowing. I've decided that I did know what I know now. What I didn't know was how to act on it; I didn't even know you were supposed to act on it. When you are in your eighties, you sometimes get credited for wisdom— especially if your hair goes white—but you have to be careful not to take it seriously. It seems to me that mainly you're wiser in the sense of rediscovering things that, in one way or another, you already knew.

What would you consider your greatest professional triumph?
I suppose my greatest triumph was when *By Design* (1982) came out—after it had been rejected by eleven publishers. My agent at the time, John Brockman, was very enthusiastic about the book, and was going to auction it. No agent would show a publisher anything that another publisher had seen before it was rejected once, and auctioning was just becoming acceptable. So Jean had them all come to lunch and they all turned it down. But three of them came back and said they would be interested if I wrote a non-technical book about design. I said, "I don't know enough to write a technical book about design. [*Laughs*] This is

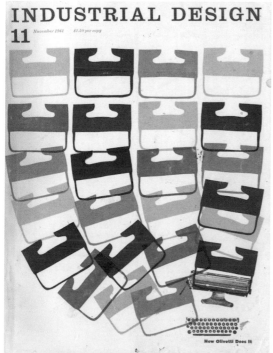

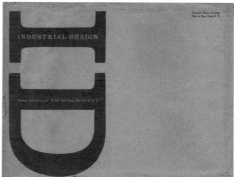

Top: Caplan (right) working on a puppet show for the IBM Pavilion at the 1964–65 New York World's Fair, alongside Glen Fleck at the Eames Office, 1963.

Left: Cover of the bimonthly magazine *Industrial Design*, issue 11, November 1961.

Above: Custom mailing envelope for *Industrial Design* designed by Alvin Lustig, c. 1954.

Clockwise from top left:
Caplan with Ray Eames at the Walker Art
Center in Minneapolis, 1970s.

Caplan with British design critic Reyner
Banham at the International Design
Conference in Aspen, 1965.

Caplan speaking on a panel alongside
writer Cleveland Amory, at Berko Studio
in Aspen, Colorado, 1965.

Caplan with Charles Eames in a polaroid
taken by Ray Eames, early 1970s.

about as non-technical as you can get." But the prejudice, at least then, was that if something was called design, it could only be understood by engineers.

How has the public's understanding— or even your understanding—of design changed since you first began working in the field?

I think the public understanding is not where you wish it were; it's not total. But design is understood much more broadly now. There's not the fear of the term. I think that's been enlarged a lot, to designers' credit, because much of design is so different now.

Design education has evolved as the discipline itself has changed. As both a writer and a teacher, how would you say things have grown over the years?

Professional design is much more idealistic than it ever was. The only idealism you found when I got started was in schools, among faculty and students. Student projects were dismissed as "blue sky"—design that means well but will never get anything done. At that time, the curriculum in design schools was very different. Everyone took a course called Materials and Methods. Now, in classes like Allan Chochinov's at SVA, the students have access to 3D printers.

I used to think that the ideal education for a designer was to go to a liberal arts college first, and then to design school. Nobody did that. But then as design schools got better, more and more articulate designers started appearing. As designers became more professional, they became more like architects, who in the beginning were the only "real" professionals; they were the only ones who professed anything, had a developed philosophy, and generally went to school. To be an architect, you had to have gone to college; to be a designer, you didn't have to. So the profession matured, but I also think society changed. A lot of it has had to do with technology—many more opportunities for designers opened up. Not only in areas where they hadn't been before, but in areas that hadn't *existed* before.

What topics do you speak about when lecturing to or teaching design students?

One exercise that I still do from time to time involves asking design students to write sonnets. You have to assume that if they're in design school, they don't know what a sonnet is, and most don't. A sonnet is a very rigid form. It has fourteen lines, but it can't be any fourteen lines, it has to be fourteen lines of iambic pentameter. *Duh-da, duh-da, duh-da, duh-da, duh-da.* The exercise makes a point—and this is another thing that I learned from the Eameses—about the importance of constraints. A sonnet is a good example because it is nothing but constraints. You can't design anything without them. And it's absolutely essential that you know what they are as soon as possible.

Do you still write poetry yourself?

Very seldom, and only occasionally. When I was a young poet, I accomplished the thing that every poet wanted to do, which was get into *Poetry* magazine. It was my first year teaching at Penn State. I wrote a few poems and submitted them to *Poetry*. All three were accepted. And then I stopped writing poetry; I wasn't very good.

It *sounds* like you were quite good.

Enough to get into *Poetry* once. I once gave a reading at the Bread Loaf Writers' Conference in Vermont and was invited to have an audience with Robert Frost, who lived in the area. I was told when to come, and who would meet me, and I was escorted up to the house. Frost was very congenial, but he didn't like my poems. He said they were all negative, and I was surprised he'd wanted to have a meeting. But he was very charming.

As a poet, writer, educator, lecturer, consultant, and nationally ordained "Design Mind," how would you define design now?

Broadly, as using whatever resources are available to improve situations that need improving. Because it's not always a problem; sometimes it's just a circumstance.

Seymour Chwast

—

Graphic Designer, Illustrator
b. 1931

Seymour Chwast has been sketching, drawing, and obsessing for more than seventy-five years. A self-described "designer who illustrates," he has worked between and across the two traditionally separate disciplines with masterful fluency, altering the course of American visual culture in the process. A postmodern pioneer, Chwast borrowed freely from the past—Victoriana, art nouveau, art deco—to create new works that wholly integrated type and art. In the 1950s and 1960s, his vivid poster, book, and packaging designs championed individual expression, often in direct contrast to both Swiss modernism's rational, rectilinear grids and the narrative realism of golden-age illustrators such as Norman Rockwell and J. C. Leyendecker.

Born in New York, Chwast (pronounced "kwast") cut his teeth watching animated Walt Disney classics. Boyhood days were spent filling notebooks with hand-drawn comics and delving into imaginative worlds of his own making. Introduced to graphic design by his high school art teacher, Chwast published his first illustration for *Seventeen* in 1948 and graduated from the Cooper Union School of Art and Architecture three years later. After a slew of short, unfulfilling stints in the publishing industry, he joined forces with college classmates Edward Sorel, Reynold Ruffins, and (later) Milton Glaser to produce a promotional mailer called *The Push Pin Almanack*. Sent to three thousand art directors, it quickly developed a steady following. It led to numerous freelance assignments and the birth of Push Pin Studios in 1954. Their sometimes-monthly publication, *Push Pin Graphic* (launched in 1957), combined visual experimentation with political subject matter, literary themes, and irreverent humor—a deft showcase of their ambitions and various talents. A 1970 retrospective of the studio's work, *The Push Pin Style*, was the first exhibition of graphic design at the Musée des Arts Décoratifs, Paris, and signaled the growing influence of American design abroad.

Since parting ways with Glaser in 1975, Chwast has quietly led Push Pin to further acclaim, adding representation services for illustrators, an audio visual arm, and a product line, while producing books on art and design through the Push Pin Press and Push Pin Editions. The firm was later renamed the Pushpin Group, with Chwast as the sole director. His work has been the subject of two monographs, a book devoted to all eighty-six issues of *Push Pin Graphic*, and numerous exhibitions worldwide. His posters reside in the permanent collections of the Museum of Modern Art, New York; the Cooper Hewitt, Smithsonian Design Museum, New York; the Philadelphia Museum of Art; and the Library of Congress. Unsurprisingly, his eclectic oeuvre continues to expand tirelessly, populated by a cast of recurring subjects and objects rooted in the everyday: cars, shoes, hats, food, sex, politics, and war. Fluent in any number of styles, from primitive folk art to surrealism, Chwast's work is often transcendent and customarily entertaining, each indelible mark following the last.

What projects are you currently working on?
A book called *Shoes, Shoes, Shoes,* with about a hundred fanciful shoes I've done: surreal, whimsical, a few straight ones, all in black and white for kids to color. I've also proposed a book on the whole body—*Fantasy Fashion*—to do the same thing with clothes. And I'm finishing up a children's book, *The Adventures of Dr. Dolittle,* as sort of a graphic novel. Right now, what's been occupying my time is getting a lot of things together for an auction. I'm dividing my work into different categories: prints, illustration, contemporary art.

Do you work every day?
Yes. And I paint on weekends. I've done many paintings of battle scenes, mostly airplanes fighting. Recently, I started a new series of paintings on the subject of war, using diagrams. Some were mock, some were real. Four-by-six-foot pieces—one was a bomb exploding in London. Others are cross-sections of submarines, tanks, or military rifles—that was the last thing I worked on. I'm taking them apart, indicating that these things kill people. It's antiwar. The absurdity of war is perfect material.

How do you balance your independent projects with your professional design work? How do you differentiate the two?
I always have to feel like I'm accomplishing something. If there's no deadline, I still have to work. It's always something—an idea in my head that I have to get out—even if I'm not working on an assignment.

If there's an assignment, you find out what's required. You do a sketch and expect there to be some changes. The front page of the *New York Times Book Review* that I just finished, for example, involved a lot of time. It was sort of a panorama, lots of details to pick apart. I was happy with the way it came out. Much of the work I generate—other stuff like paintings, a lot of books, especially children's books, where I come up with ideas and do a couple of spreads—gets rejected. Those are the things I start by myself.

Seymour Chwast in his studio, New York, 2014.

Do you identify more as a designer, an illustrator, or an artist? And has this changed during the course of your career?
I'm a designer because I'm concerned with how my work is used, or the environment—what it's around. If it's a drawing in a magazine, I have no control over it, but there are other things that I can do. If I do a poster, I can handle the type and present the whole thing. Or a book. So that takes design. I'm more interested in concept than rendering, but I'm a designer who illustrates. It really is fascinating how design has evolved.

What fascinates you about that evolution?
What attracts people, how the styles have changed to go along with the culture. A lot of it is governed by the technology of a given time. During Victorian times, typography was very ornate; publications used wood engravings to be more illustrative. And then with art nouveau and art deco, it became simpler, sort of streamlined. Now it's sort of eclectic. There's more hand-lettering than there used to be. I've done four graphic novels all in hand-lettering, and other people are doing it, too; it's not a novelty anymore. It's a shame we don't have more design magazines. But illustration seems to be flourishing.

Do you remember when you first became interested in drawing?

When I saw *Snow White and the Seven Dwarfs*. It was 1937. Then, I wanted to become an animator. I was sure after I saw *Pinocchio*.

What about design? Did that come later?

When I was in high school in Brooklyn, my teacher Leon Friend taught design, which was unusual. He'd emigrated from Germany and had written a book called *Graphic Design*. He was very charismatic; you had to go along with him. The Art Squad was an elite group of students, mostly from Mr. Friend's class, who had a special role: we were asked to do banners, posters, and other stuff around the school. We were allowed to leave class, and had special permission to violate the rules. To get into the Art Squad, you had to show a portfolio and be examined by the other students who were already in. You'd get to school at six in the morning and be expected to work very hard. If you didn't, you would fall by the wayside, discarded. So I worked hard. We learned about all the great poster designers. And modernism.

Do you remember others who were in the Art Squad?

Jay Maisel is a terrific photographer, very well known. Alex Steinweiss, who invented album cover art, was in that class in the late 1930s. Gene Federico was a terrific advertising art director—he helped to bring design to advertising.

From there, you studied design more formally at the Cooper Union. Did you ever consider other creative disciplines?

I took a painting class, but I was no fine artist. There was nothing like that in my head. I appreciated some fine artists—George Grosz, Ben Shahn, Saul Steinberg, who tend to be sort of graphic; Goya, very graphic; Picasso was okay, but he made paintings. What was great to me was a piece of graphic work that had meaning; when there was a message there.

How did Push Pin Studios come about?

Ed [Sorel] and I started producing a promotion piece called *The Push Pin Almanack*. Milton [Glaser] was in Europe on a Fulbright scholarship. We had jobs and started getting freelance work. Then Milton came back, and at one point, Ed and I were both getting fired, left and right, and we decided nobody would hire us again, so we'd freelance and call ourselves Push Pin Studios. So that was Milton, Ed, and me. Reynold [Ruffins] had a job he didn't want to leave because he had a family at that time, so he joined us a little later, when we were a bit more established, and was with us for a few years. Ed left after a year and a half. Milton and I carried on, and we started hiring people, especially those who would bring in work. Then we started doing *The Push Pin Monthly Graphic*, as it was called at the time. We sent that out as sort of a newsprint tabloid paper. We had people joining us, like John Alcorn and Isadore Seltzer. And a few others contributed work.

Push Pin is frequently credited for bringing the worlds of illustration and design together. Were you conscious of that at the time?

Yes, we were. Most designers couldn't draw, and most illustrators didn't care about typography. We knew the people who were working in illustration were separate from design. We knew some of the designers; Paul Rand was the most famous. And we knew about the illustrators, too; Norman Rockwell, but he was considered our enemy at the time, mostly because he represented an America that didn't really exist. The kind of illustration I was interested in became much more expressive than the work that was going on, though that was also changing. We were riding the crest of that.

What was the studio environment at Push Pin like in those early days, when you were charting new territory in the 1950s?

When we started, we worked in a cold-water flat—a loft building—on Thirteenth Street, which we shared with a dancer. We had a heater in the middle of the room to warm up the place. We were poor artists. In the beginning we took home $25 a week, and it sounded like we were making a salary. When work arrived, we hired a guy to represent us, and before that we hired a mechanical man and a bookkeeper. Very slowly we expanded when we found ourselves busy. And then we moved a few times: to Seventeenth Street, to Fifty-Seventh Street, and back to Thirty-First Street. We did a lot of moving. Then we took on Paul Davis, one of our first illustrators. He was doing sort of funny painting at the time. He started creating his mock folk art on wood and doing very well with it. Jim McMullan had a reputation already. He did record covers, Paul did posters, and they were all working on *Push Pin Graphic* in the 1970s.

What was your collective process? Did everyone collaborate on *Push Pin Graphic* while also working on their own projects?

When Milton came back from his Fulbright, he started doing drawings. There were a couple of other old classmates who contributed work as well. Sometimes we collaborated, sometimes one of us would produce a whole issue. Paul got famous because people saw his work in *Push Pin Graphic*. He became busier than me, and then he left. Ed left to work for CBS.

When did *Push Pin Graphic* end, and when did you start *The Nose*?

Around 1975, about the time Milton left, we started representing illustrators and made a standard nine-by-twelve-inch *Push Pin Graphic*. We continued that way—I assigned illustrations to people we were repping and hired an editor for the first time—and we sent out about eight thousand copies. We tried to get paid subscribers, but since they were getting it for free, why would they pay? We did that until 1980.

The Nose started in 1997. I was sort of missing *Push Pin Graphic* and wanted to try something new. I started with James Victore and Steven Brower. Steve did one issue and gave up; he just didn't have time. And Victore just didn't bother. So I continued by myself for about twenty issues.

I'd love to do something online that has continuity to it, not as issues, but as something like the comic strip *Gasoline Alley*. When it started out, Skeezix, the main character, was a little kid, and as the paper went on, from year to year, the

Push Pin Studios, current and former members, c. 1970. Back row, left to right: Jerry Smokler, Vincent Ceci, Edward Sorel, Cosmos Sarchiapone, Tim Lewis, Milton Glaser, George Leavitt, Sam Antupit, Norman Green, Jerry Joyner, Paul Davis. Front row, left to right: Jason McWhorter, Herb Levitt, James McMullan, Reynold Ruffins, John Alcorn, Barry Zaid, Loring Eutemey, Isadore Seltzer, Seymour Chwast.

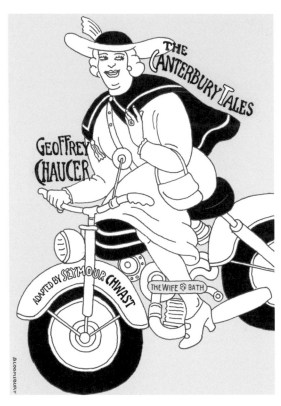

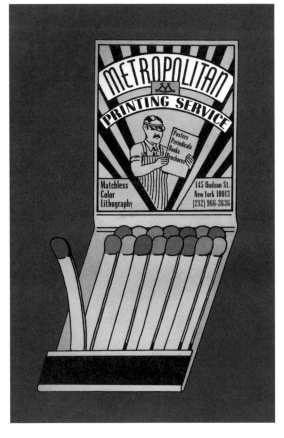

Top left: Cover of *The Canterbury Tales* (Bloomsbury), a graphic novel adapted by Chwast in 2011.

Left: Cover of *The Left-Handed Designer* (Harry N. Abrams, 1985).

Above: Advertisement from *Push Pin Graphic* issue 81, 1979. In exchange for production services, Chwast often created ads for printers, typographers, and color separators.

Opposite: Collages from *Brylcreem Man*, 1998, a series of fifty-three works inspired by vintage ads for a men's hair product.

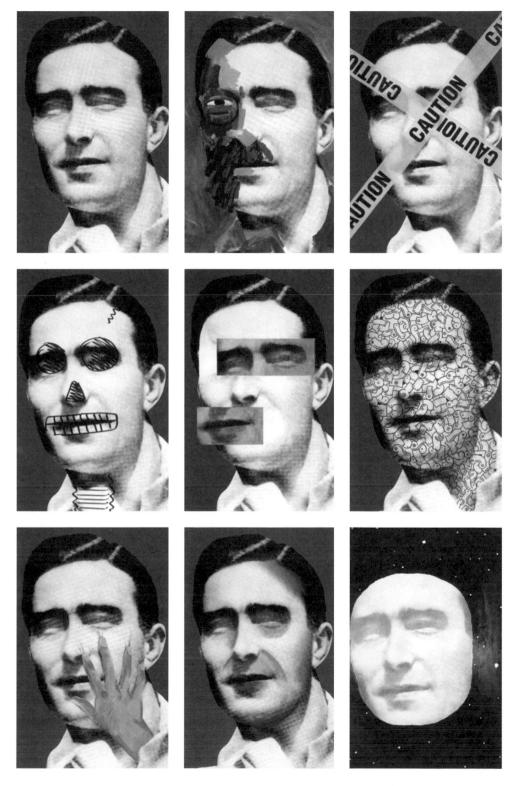

characters got older, which was unusual—that never happens. Superman never got any older. That kind of continuity is interesting to me. But also, like *The Nose*, when it creates its own identity, it has a name to it, it's much more than doing single things that have no equity. *Push Pin Graphic* did, and therefore Push Pin became a thing.

Do you believe design can have a significant impact on society?

Not as much as it should. A bunch of us make posters for peace, but there's still a lot of war. Design can help educate and promote and sell stuff. And be for good: Milton's "I ♥ NY" really helped to promote New York State for business and tourism. It's a terrific design.

When you were younger, did you hope that making posters with a political message would have a greater impact?

We didn't have any worldview of what we were doing. We were either trying to have fun, satisfy what the teacher was looking for, or make money—or be a designer and have a career. And then it sort of crept into us, the idea that social purpose could be in what we're doing. Whether our work has any real impact on society, we don't know, but we're compelled to try.

Are you interested in fame?

[*Laughs*] Well, I have an ego, but no, I don't understand fame at all. At some events, people come up and want my signature, and I don't understand it. Why do they want a signature? A book, a poster, sometimes it's a pillow or a piece of paper. What good is my signature here? Am I that famous, that they're going to show their grandchildren something I did with my signature on it? Some people are very nice to me, and I have fans, that's nice. But I just want my next job to be interesting, and to do it well. That's all I really care about.

Everyday objects often appear in your work—shoes, hats, cars. What draws you to these obsessions?

Because they can be used as vehicles for graphic ideas or messages. That's why I had a show of just heads. I've had two shows where heads were the main object because they can be very expressive; they say a lot. Cars, shoes—I do them the way Magritte or Dalí did, with surrealistic ideas. Incongruity comes into play; what's not expected. Go against what you think should be right. When I draw, something has to happen, something has to strike a chord—either for me or for the people looking at it.

How do you know that moment has happened—when something strikes a chord?

You *feel* it. Otherwise, it could be a terrible mistake. The things I've done that have been hits, I can't understand at all why it happened, why there's any value in it. There are other things that I've really liked and people have ignored. Then it's sort of sad, because you feel like you're working for nothing. If it's for me, it's okay, but I also want other people to see it. Because I have an ego. I want people to love me.

There's a strong sense of humor to a lot of your work. Where do you think that comes from?

I have no idea. Reading the comics when I was a kid, you start to see—if I want to make something funny, I know how to do it because of the conventions of drawing. A guy slipping on a banana peel, for instance. It may come out of my parents coming from Eastern Europe, I don't know. Mel Brooks and I both came from the Bronx. So did Milton and Ed.

You've also worked a lot with woodcut, linocut, and pen and ink. How have those techniques changed with technology?

What you use to reproduce a print has changed. I sometimes use the computer as a technique, to emulate those processes. When it's reprinted, you don't have any of the quality of the ink on the paper, but whatever a woodcut, a linocut, or an etching brings, some quality of the original print will come though. Silkscreen has some of that quality, but it's not the same as the print from a woodcut. In relief printmaking—woodcuts and linocuts—you can get a change in the color by

Push Pin Graphic

Number 64   December 1976

♥ *Mothers.* ♥

Above: Cover of *Push Pin Graphic* issue 64, on the theme of mothers, 1976.

Above right: A more modest version of *Push Pin Graphic*, *The Nose* was dedicated to relevant and sometimes trivial social issues. Cover of the "Crime Today" issue, 2009.

Bottom right: *Mucho Gusto*, acrylic and colored pencil on chipboard, 2008.

End Bad Breath.

End Bad Breath, 1968.

Cover of *Happy Birthday, Bach* by Seymour Chwast and Peter Schickele (Doubleday, 1985).

Woodcut portrait of Christopher George Latore Wallace, aka The Notorious B.I.G., for *Fader*, 2011.

rolling one color here, another color there, and in the middle it comes together and looks very nice.

On the computer, you can make changes in a second. It takes absolutely no time. Now, the difference in the way I do illustrations using color is that it's all on the computer. It takes a fraction of the time to do it and make revisions—it's so easy. It's a good thing—I can spend my time doing something else. But I still have to have somebody help me with the computer, because I can't do any of that stuff. Still too technical for me.

Do you dislike those technical processes?
Not as long as they don't get too fancy. I mean, when animation got very three-dimensional and realistic, it became less interesting and lost a lot of quality for me. The flat stuff is much more interesting.

You're a prolific designer and continue to produce so much work. Where do you get your ideas from?
Sometimes from unusual places. Often I look through books of old posters. It's usually concrete stuff, tangible rather than mystical. Solving a problem means taking two different things and

putting them together to make a wonderful image, although I guess there are symbolic things— like clouds—that mean something more. That's been the ideal: combining two ideas into one image. It's a job to try and find things that are less expected, places to represent what you are trying to say.

I get my ideas very early in the morning. Waking up, my head is clear. Something may pop in. But it's getting tougher. I don't know why, maybe it's because everything has been done before, but it's work.

What motivates you to do that?
It's my job.

Who would you say has been your most important mentor?
I learned a lot from Milton. But Saul Steinberg is the man, because he did everything. That was what was so discouraging about him: when I looked at his work, I'd think, There's nothing left to be done. I had to stop looking. I couldn't see his shows, couldn't look at his book for a long time. He sort of entered my brain. He's the master.

Chwast and Milton Glaser, 1960s.

Entrance to the exhibition *The Masters Series: Seymour Chwast*, at the School of Visual Arts, New York, 1997.

Did you ever meet him?

Yes, I had to go up to his studio in Union Square [in Manhattan] to get permission to reproduce one of his works for a book I was working on with Steve Heller, on the art of New York. I just said, "Hi, can we use this?" "All right." That was the kind of meeting we had.

What's your favorite designed object, and why?

There's something devious about that question. I've been following the design of cars through the years, but not in any regular way, and it's not an obsession. But it fascinates me, the subtle changes every year to cars, how they are becoming more like small tanks. Before they were like jellybeans, and then they became sculptural while the insides never changed—they still hold four to six people. And also quirky cars that come along, and why they succeed or fail.

Married to designer Paula Scher, you're one half of a very famous couple. How has that partnership affected your work?

I've learned things from her, but often I can't wrap my head around things that she's done. We can't work together, but sometimes I do show her my paintings. Watching Paula work on *her* paintings always amazes me, because of how focused she is. How few things she has to change. She seems to already have the whole thing worked out in her head beforehand, which is quite amazing. I'm much more tentative. I do things in stages in order to work them out.

You've become synonymous with the work of Push Pin. How has that association shaped or affected you?

I wanted to exploit it as much as I could, maybe because I was second banana to Milton. Another reason that makes good sense is that Push Pin has its reputation and I can glean from it whatever I can get, in order to do terrific work. I still had to do the work, of course. But it allowed me to get some jobs I wouldn't have gotten otherwise. It's my corporate name, it's where the checks come to, but people do know my name.

What advice would you give yourself at the beginning of your career?

If I could go back to the beginning of my career? Save your money. I didn't make any money until the middle of my career. Good advice for the middle of the career? I keep thinking about the jobs I got fired from—I guess I learned something from those, too. Really, I wouldn't change a thing.

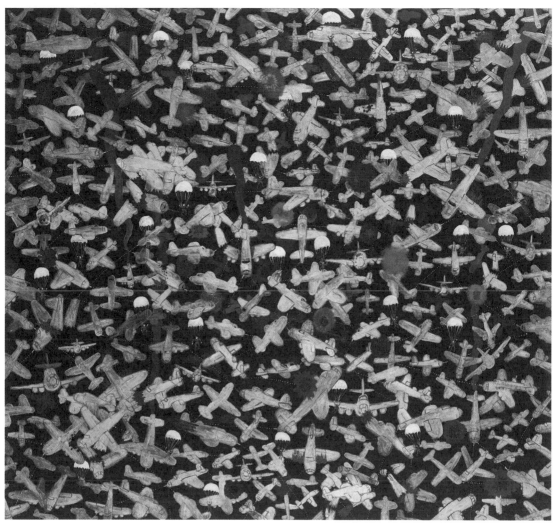

Overcast 7, acrylic on canvas, 2008.

Bob Gill

—

Graphic Designer, Illustrator, Educator
b. 1931

As the author of more than twenty books on graphic design and illustration, it's no wonder Bob Gill has an entire wall devoted to their storage in his light-filled Manhattan studio. He'll gladly pluck any one of his well-known tomes—nestled among hundreds of other volumes on art and visual culture—to explain, with great care and passion, his preference for ideas over concepts, and true originality over empty creativity. His eclectic career, which has spanned six decades and two continents, is a testament to individuality and an example for any young designer who feels burdened by the constant pull of trends and popular styles.

After studying design and drawing in Philadelphia, Gill made his start in New York City by launching a freelance career—his dream since age six—with assignments for *Interiors*, *Esquire*, *The Nation*, and *Seventeen*. He began teaching at the School of Visual Arts, and quickly built a reputation as a graphic designer and illustrator in high demand. In 1960 what he planned as a holiday to London turned into a fifteen-year sojourn. Gill's arrival coincided with Britain's burgeoning advertising industry and the explosion of youth culture, which drew a steady influx of American expats, mostly photographers as well as like-minded creatives such as Robert Brownjohn and Bob Brooks. Two years after landing in London, with Alan Fletcher and Colin Forbes as partners, he formed Fletcher/Forbes/Gill, the wildly successful studio that would later become the design consultancy Pentagram. The fashionable trio produced work for Pirelli, Penguin Books, and others, and published *Graphic Design: Visual Comparisons*, a visual treatise on graphics that sold over one hundred thousand copies worldwide—at the time, an unprecedented success for a book on the topic. A freelancer at heart, Gill left the studio in 1967 to teach, and to design independently.

Returning to his native New York in 1975, the unflappable designer directed a porn film, took on multimedia projects, and then cowrote and produced the Broadway musical *Beatlemania*. His books on design, published consistently over the last half century, implore readers to ignore the rules and abandon the formulaic trappings of supposed "good design," focusing instead on each problem as the way to an original solution. Gill's own work is deceptively simple, combining type and image in playful compositions that feel inevitable, yet incredibly articulate.

A recipient of the Lifetime Achievement Award from D&AD, and a member of the New York Art Directors Club Hall of Fame, the eighty-four-year-old recently retired from teaching but frequently lectures around the country. His unique mode of practice continues to inspire. For Gill, graphic design is a means, not an end.

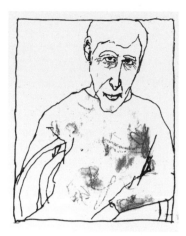

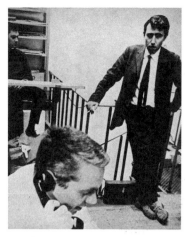

Left: Serigraph self-portrait, 2012.

Right: Alan Fletcher, Colin Forbes, and Bob Gill, London, 1962.

When did you first become interested in graphic design?

I have no idea! I only know that at a very early age, I drew. I don't know where I got the idea because I never met a designer and there wasn't anyone in my family that had any connection with design. I decided I wanted to be a designer, not only a designer, but a freelance designer. I never looked back.

You knew you wanted to draw?

I started like every child, but I was better than the average. But God knows how. When I was in the eighth grade, my teacher said, "You're very talented, you must go to the High School of Music and Art." The irony was I was there for four years and I learned very little about art. I hung out with the music students because they were sources of work. Every weekend, I got a job as a pianist, but the music and art teachers weren't very knowledgeable. Still, it was an interesting school because the kids were brighter than the average.

What are your thoughts on the differences between being a freelancer and a full-time designer?

Again, I had no choice. The idea of working nine to five, subject to the rules and idiosyncrasies of a company, was just impossible—I couldn't even imagine. So the only alternative was to knock on

doors and try to survive as a freelancer. It was very difficult in the beginning.

And yet, you were part of a very successful partnership—Fletcher/Forbes/Gill—for several years. Did you miss the collaboration after you left?

We started about 1961 and I stayed until 1967. I had less to do with Forbes because he handled the business, though he was quite a good designer himself. I missed Fletcher because I loved him like a brother; he's just wonderful. I can't describe all his wonderful qualities.

That was in London—what drew you to the city?

I was packing to go on a holiday, and I picked London just out of the blue, thinking it would be an interesting place to visit. A friend told me about an ad in the *New York Times* for some owner of an advertising agency who was at the Algonquin Hotel, interviewing possible art directors to join his agency in London. He thought Americans were the kings of advertising. So I went to the hotel with my portfolio. I had never been an art director, and I said, "I'll be honest with you. I would love to work for the summer, but I'm having a wonderful time in New York freelancing." And he hired me. The minute I got off the boat, I thought I'd spend the rest of my life there. There was just something about the atmosphere. I didn't end up spending the rest of my life there, but I did spend fifteen years.

What was London like when you arrived, in 1960?

It was amazing, and as Fletcher used to say, "It was like shooting fish in a barrel." I don't have much of an overview because I was in the middle of it. We wrote a book called *Graphic Design: Visual Comparisons*. It sold one hundred thousand copies. I happen to love juxtaposition; it's one of the things that I really get off on. It's impossible for me to put one thing next to another unless there's an amazing connection. We collected the work of other people, including our own, and it became a new work. Anyway, it was very successful. At the same time, the Tories came in and things started to change in the 1970s. Margaret Thatcher was *not* the Swinging Sixties. When I left, it made the newspapers.

What was it like to be living and working in a completely different city and culture?

Your perception of a city as a foreigner is very different from reality. So when I got to London, I just couldn't get over it, because everything was like the moon.

The first week that I was at the agency—incidentally it was a hack agency—I couldn't stand it. But I loved London, so I stayed there until I found something else. When I met Fletcher and Forbes we fell in love, and it was obvious that we would start our partnership. But my first week in London I did an ad for Nestlé chocolate. I made a sketch, and I went into the boardroom and everybody looked at it and loved it. I said, "Okay, now we have to get a photographer to photograph the package. The Nestlé chocolate." And they looked at me, and said, You can't get a photographer. The reproduction in London newspapers in 1960 was impossible. And Nestlé would never tolerate a rotten reproduction. They suggested a scraperboard artist—they described it as a fake etching. You cover a board with black, and scrape out white lines as if it was engraved. But it's very old-fashioned. New York

did that in the 1920s. They showed me, and I said I can't do that, that's impossible! That's the dopiest thing I ever heard of, I said. Always the showman, I pulled out a banknote from my wallet, which had a beautiful engraving. And I said to somebody who was in the room, "Get me the Bank of England!" I asked to speak to the engraver. Well, the chief engraver who was ninety was on holiday, but the assistant engraver, who was eighty, was there. So I spoke to him and I asked if he'd like to do an etching of a Nestlé chocolate bar. It was the first commercial job he'd ever had. He said, "I'm thrilled, I'd love to." And he did a nice job.

Is it true that you left London to direct a porno film in New York?

Someone asked me if I wanted to direct a porno. I said I'd love to, although I'd never seen one. It was horrible—almost took me off sex forever. But there was some very nice compensation. First of all, I made a feature, so that was interesting. But it was very low budget, and it was summertime. We were shooting in the Warwick Hotel on Sixth Avenue, and you couldn't turn on the air conditioner because we were shooting sound. Just horrible!

What did you learn from the experience?

There are two things that I took away from that porno. The first was when someone would ask me, what are you doing? I'd say, "I'm directing a porno." And suddenly people looked at me as if I'd just been elected President of the United States. I mean, it was everybody's fantasy to direct a porno. It was unbelievable; suddenly I was a different person in people's eyes. Of course they don't know what directing one means. The second was when we started casting and talking about crews and so forth, the producers said I had to meet this cameraman, like, "He's a sweetheart, he's wonderful." I said I didn't want to meet him unless he'd done nine pornos! I didn't want to be the only amateur on the set. I wanted everyone else to be a hardened veteran. They said he'd never done a porno, but that we must meet. Reluctantly, I did, and now he's one of my dearest friends. We formed a relationship that was terrific. So again, you never know.

Graphic design: visual comparisons
by Alan Fletcher Colin Forbes Bob Gill

What was your cultural education like as a young boy?

I had never been to a museum in my life. My mother was a single parent, very poor. She had no cultural life whatsoever. She was trying to make a living as a piano teacher, but she was a terrible pianist. I was her first student at five years old. She practiced on me, and then after about a year, she started to make a living. She charged a dollar. I remember when she had one student, and the student's mother would call up and say, "I'm sorry, but Mary is sick." And it was the most awful thing that could happen—we needed that dollar. So I had no cultural life. But then I went to art school.

The Philadelphia Museum School of Art?

In Philadelphia, my life changed. I wasn't interested in music, although I supported myself as a pianist because we had no money for tuition. I worked every weekend, and I was able to pay my rent and food. My eyes started to open up to a cultural world that I had never known. If I had come across Magritte earlier, my life would be different. We would not be sitting here now. I don't know what would have happened to me, but I would have been an artist, not a graphic designer. I felt closer to Magritte than any creative person that I have ever come across. What was so unbelievable—which also endeared me to him—was that he lived in a suburban house outside of Brussels. He didn't hang around with artists very much. He painted in a suit and tie in his living room. And he had these visions. All these books spend pages trying to understand his imagery, but there is no understanding. It doesn't mean anything! He felt like doing it. A railroad, a locomotive coming out of a jet, out of a fireplace—there is no meaning.

When did you discover Magritte?
Too late to change my life.

How would you define art versus design? Are they distinct in your mind?
Of course they are. Imagine this juxtaposition: clip art and Matisse. Why is the clip art crap? And why is a Matisse a masterpiece? Let's talk about the Matisse first. This is a real work of art because it's not about any one moment in time; it's universal. Also, it renews itself. You look at the clip art and you'll just see the same thing over and over again, however many times. Then there's the ends and means. The end of the artist has nothing in common with the end of the graphic designer. But the *means* of the artist and the graphic designer are exactly the same.

You've expressed a distaste for "good design," and a preference for "ideas" rather than "concepts." Why?
As I often say, a "concept" is something in the order of the Big Bang. That's a concept. That's a very big idea. Evolution is a concept. Global warming is a concept. You and I will never have *concepts*; we will have little ideas. That doesn't make us terrible people or anything, but in order for something to be a concept, it really has to be very big. And I'm offended by anybody who ever tells me they have a concept, because it never is.

I went to design school from 1948 to 1950, and like every other design student, I realized it all has to do with regurgitating what the culture at any particular moment tells you is good, as opposed to bad: a certain arrangement of things, the right typeface, the current typeface.

So design is the product of culture, and not the other way around?
Absolutely not. I've been teaching it for fifty-five years, so I know what I'm talking about. These people in my class haven't originated anything, they've been told what to do. So the first thing I tell them—and it's a heartfelt comment—I say, "I will hate everything you do. But I love you, so that'll make it easier." And I really do like them, and I really do hate everything they ever do.

Does that change by the end of the course?
No. Have I changed them? A little. It's much harder than I think. It's pretty easy to listen to me, and to learn not to ape the culture, but it's still very difficult.

For your own work, how are you able to separate yourself and have original ideas?
The process that I teach is that I don't know the answer to anything! I don't know what a good typeface is, what a good color is, what a good layout is, that it should have a lot of space, or that it should be crowded. I don't know anything. Now of course the culture keeps telling me what I should know, but I'm very good at telling myself not to believe it.

So when there's a job, let's say a logo for a dry cleaner, 99 percent of designers will sit at their computer, and they will try to think of an exciting logo for a dry cleaner. They can't. It's not possible, because there's nothing in their heads that's original. So I don't. Instead, I go to a dry cleaner. Simple. And I sit there. I have no idea what's going to happen; I have no formula; I have no trick. I stay there until I have something to say about dry cleaning that's interesting. And then I listen to the statement, that's the key to it. And whatever the statement tells me, if I'm honest with myself and I say that's an interesting thing to say about dry cleaning, automatically it'll be an interesting logo. Without even knowing what it's going to look like.

Have computers changed your practice, and design in general?
Not at all. They've made my life easier. I guess it's made the work more mechanical. The images are

Right: *Record Sleeve for an Eccentric Pianist,*
Troubadour Records, 1973.

Below: Party invitation, 1975.

Dear Friend,

**John Cole invites you to
a party on Sat. Sept 9
at 8:30pm at 122 Regents
Park Rd.NW1 Flat D.
RSVP Gro2291**

Please bring a bottle.

Dear Freeloader,

**John Cole invites you to
a party on Sat. Sept 9
at 8:30pm at 122 Regents
Park Rd.NW1 Flat D.
RSVP Gro2291**

Bob Gill
Sara Fishko

1200 Broadway, New York, NY 10001 Tel: 212 460 0950
1200 Broadway, New...

Top left: *Creativity*, Designers and Art
Directors Association, 2014.

Top right: *Smoking a Pipe Improves One's
Image*, The Learning Annex, 1995.

Bottom right: *Die-cut Letterhead for Two*, for
Gill and his wife, Sara Fishko, 1985.

more mechanical. And of course designers are hypnotized by the magic that the computer can do. That doesn't give them better ideas; it's the same crap. But I think it has changed design.

In 1977, you and Robert Rabinowitz were asked to write and design a multimedia history of the 1960s, which became *Beatlemania*. A Broadway musical seems like such a massive shift in scale and media. Did you approach that project differently?

Nothing is a massive shift; it's a problem. Everything is a problem. Everything is the same! That's what makes it so interesting. Having thought about the Beatles and their career, I came to a wonderful conclusion: their songs mirror the history of the time. In 1960, when they did "I Want to Hold Your Hand," it was a dopey, simplistic pop thing, and it was the beginning of the Swinging Sixties. Then by the middle, psychedelia started to take over, so it was a terrific juxtaposition. That gave us the order of music. What an excuse it was to do five thousand slides, two half-hour films, one on a scrim, and one on the back—it was the whole history of the time. Starting with the assassination of Kennedy, and going all the way to the modern day. It was incredible. Incredible! I had a wonderful time. So you see what I mean? It's exactly like doing a book jacket. It's the same thing.

What would you describe as your greatest professional triumph?

There's no such thing as an interesting job. To me it's just another job—whether it's a poster for aspirin, or for Obama. Jobs are not interesting. The problems are not interesting. The *solutions* should be interesting. People ask me, what kind of a job do you really want? I say it doesn't make any difference. The more unexpected it is—the poster for aspirin for example—I'd never thought about aspirin in my life. So it becomes something to think about.

Does that mean there are no setbacks then, either? Is there no problem that's more interesting than another?

Of course distinctions are useful. An anti-smoking campaign, for example. If one can prevent lung disease, that would be a wonderful thing for a graphic designer to try to solve. So there are important functions to be served by a graphic designer. But someone has to ask me. I can't go to the government and say, I think I should design an anti-smoking poster. I'm limited in that I usually get small jobs. The biggest mistake I ever made was leaving Pentagram. They're all rich; I'm not. But I have to do what I have to do. In retrospect, I could have been the crazy partner who was working in a corner.

But perhaps you wouldn't have been as happy.

I don't know. You can't be too smart about these things.

You've said teaching is "part of the designer's craft." What's your view on the current state of design education?

Teachers can only teach what they know. And again, the same proportion exists: many teachers are not capable of doing a first-class job. And there are a only a handful—probably twenty-five—designers who are brilliant. I have no monopoly on this. Maybe half of them don't even know how they do it, they can't even describe their process; they do it instinctively.

Why teach? What do you get out of it?

It clarifies things. I love talking and clarifying; it's one of my passions. I love being invited to design conferences because I light a fire under people's asses. Everyone always comes up to me afterwards and says, "Oh my God, you changed my life." Well, I didn't, because look at the work they do after that—it's exactly the same. But they get a terrific kick out of it, and I get a kick out of moving people. I really enjoy it. Now, I have no idea what I sounded like thirty or forty years ago. I wish there was some record so I could see if I learned anything. Also, I like the idea that I may be able to change somebody's life. It's a very exciting thing, to change somebody's life.

Has anyone changed your life?

I certainly had people that I admired very much. When I got out of school in 1950, the first person I had to see was Paul Rand—"the president." At that time, you would leave your portfolio (he was at an agency). I left my portfolio and two days later, I got a call: "He's seen it, and there's a note on it that Mr. Rand would like to meet you." When I picked up my portfolio, they called inside and he walked out and held out his hand. So I shook it. And he didn't let go, he just held on. It must have been thirty seconds; that's a long time for him to say nothing, to hold my hand and not release it. And then he said, "Stay in this business." I wouldn't let his hand go. I made him wait the same amount of time and I said, "Okay." And because I never had a father, I was always trying to make him love me. Every time he came to London, somebody would throw him a party because it was the president coming. I would sit next to him and try to make him love me, but he was such a curmudgeon. This went on for twenty, thirty, forty years. Finally, I had lunch with him and he said to me, "You're a schmuck. You've angered everybody in this business, and you're so unsuccessful, but you're my favorite designer." Also, Lou Dorfsman at CBS. Brilliant, wonderful, modest. I was very fond of him. At one point, I was doing a number of posters for Silas Rhodes at the School of Visual Arts. I did a poster, and Rhodes, who was usually a great fan of mine and accepted everything I did, said, "I'm sorry I hate it." I was devastated. I went home to my studio, it was about 7:30, and I couldn't get it out of my mind—this masterpiece that I had done, that Rhodes wouldn't print it. So in desperation, and even though it was after 7, I called Dorfsman at CBS, and he happened to be working. He said, "Come over, kid." And he loved it, he loved it.

It's been quite a ride, I must say. And I'm still doing the same thing.

What are you working on now?

The book that I'm working on now is called *Stealing Is Good*.

What's it about? Appropriation?

Stealing. In the beginning, I say if you can find an image that does exactly what you want it to do, but it's not what the original creator intended, steal it. That's different from taking someone's job.

If you could go back, what advice would you give yourself at the beginning of your career?

Double it. Let me explain: I did an ad or a poster for Barbra Streisand once, and her live-in boyfriend came to New York to brief the advertising agency and me. He kept saying, "And Barbra will record the title song, and that'll bring in $80 million." Everything was heady figures, I just couldn't believe it. And then I thought of my mother, who used to say to me all the time, "Why don't you get a haircut?" But when she'd ask me, "What does a haircut cost these days?" I knew that if I told her the truth, she might drop dead because it seemed so extravagant. So I cut it in half. She *still* almost had a heart attack, and I realized these things are generational.

To you, a dollar is nothing. When I was your age, a dollar was a meal. It was a different thing. So it's very hard for me; I can't charge what you would charge, because it just seems astronomical. So, I'm always charging less because of the generational thing. On the one hand, I'm a terrific salesman. But I'm a bad negotiator. I just don't get what I could have gotten. I don't know what the answer is, except once in a while my wife says, "You haven't given a price yet. Double it." So that's the advice. It's practical, but it's not very profound.

Bob Gill, so far.

Cover of *Bob Gill, So Far* (Laurence King Publishing, 2011).

Milton Glaser

—

Graphic Designer, Illustrator, Educator
b. 1929

There are many graphic designers whose careers have been defined by New York City, but far fewer for whom the inverse is equally true. Milton Glaser, father of the ubiquitous and enduring "I ♥ NY" logo, cofounder of *New York* magazine, and auteur of countless projects that have shaped culture for over six decades, is one of them—though his work has extended far beyond the city's limits.

Born and raised in the Bronx, Glaser, eighty-six, has lived, studied, and practiced in New York City his entire life, residing elsewhere only briefly, during a Fulbright fellowship in Bologna, Italy, where he trained with painter Giorgio Morandi. As a student at Cooper Union, Glaser cofounded the legendary Push Pin Studios with friends and classmates Seymour Chwast, Reynold Ruffins, and Edward Sorel in 1954, producing colorful pop-driven illustrations and figurative work during a period still dominated by modernist minimalism and geometric abstraction. Among Glaser's earliest independent works is an illustration of Bob Dylan, inserted as a foldout poster in first-edition printings of the musician's 1967 *Greatest Hits* album. Picturing a profile silhouette of Dylan with a coiffure of technicolor plumes blooming from his head, the bold, art nouveau–infused graphic remains a collectible today. Glaser's output during this time so defined the era that, decades later, he was asked to recreate a pastiche of his own work for the television series *Mad Men*, set in a 1960s Manhattan advertising agency. Glaser obliged, though he's always preferred to look forward.

In 1974 he established his own studio, Milton Glaser, Inc.—which he still operates today,

working across the disciplines of print, branding, and architectural design—and for a number of years partnered with Walter Bernard to form WBMG, a publication design firm. That Glaser's most iconic design was created free of charge speaks to his generosity. First launched as part of a tourism campaign in 1977, the "I ♥ NY" logo was contributed pro bono as an act of goodwill for his hometown. Owned by the Empire State Development Corporation, today the trademark is estimated to generate more than $30 million a year through licensed goods.

Glaser has been the subject of solo exhibitions at the Centre Pompidou in Paris and the Museum of Modern Art in New York, and his work resides in the permanent collections of several museums. In 2004 he received the National Design Award for Lifetime Achievement from the Cooper Hewitt, Smithsonian Design Museum in New York, and in 2009 he became the first graphic designer to receive the National Medal of Arts.

Engraved on a windowpane above the entry to his studio of over forty years—a landmarked, Beaux-Arts row house that was once the headquarters of a Tammany Hall association—are the words "Art is Work," one of many aphorisms for which Glaser, a longtime educator, lecturer, and public advocate for ethical and socially conscious design, has come to be known. From his desk, Glaser reflected on his ongoing role as a history-making designer, illustrator, and public figure.

I ♥ NY.

The ubiquitous "I ♥ NY" logo, created pro bono for ad agency Wells Rich Greene, commissioned by the New York State Department for Economic Development, 1977.

The "I ♥ NY" logo and the 1967 poster of Bob Dylan remain some of your most well-known designs. How does it feel to be known for those selected projects that are part of a much larger body of work?

That's the nature of the way things work in life. You become known for certain things, and you can't live them down. Then people know an aspect of your life, the same way that people know an aspect of your personality. That's what they get, that's what they see. That's the inevitable consequence of life itself.

What's your relationship to those works? Has it changed over the years?

My work has changed significantly since those early works, but as you know, there is nothing you can do about that sort of thing when you become visible.

Recently I've had to revive that work by imitating it for the *Mad Men* ad series. They asked me and I said, "I don't know if I can still do that." That attitude, that vernacular, that sense of the moment. I'll do a counterfeit version of it. But my path in life was modeled after Picasso's, which was: Once you learn something, you can forget about it. I tried to move away from what I had mastered.

When I started Push Pin with Seymour Chwast in 1954, a large part of what we did was a particular combination of design and illustration. Because design was a kind of drawing, we said, You can still draw and be a designer. We had the idea that design, typography, layouts, and drawing were all one thing. They're one manifestation of how to convey information. We had a certain stylistic reference that picked up on a lot of different threads; we reintroduced historical ideas because we had all been dominated by the idea of modernism. Modernism was what the school was teaching, and that's what we learned. We were all in that world.

Intellectually, abstraction had dominated naturalism, and drawing from observation seemed a little corny. I always felt how stupid that was, this parochialization of activity in terms of status. But that's enough of that. I did plenty of it, and we did plenty of illustration, and so on. For the last thirty years I have been doing very different things. But those pieces—the Dylan poster—will come up every time anybody talks about my work.

"I ♥ NY"—which was done at this table in 1977—will never go away. I'm stuck with it. But one shouldn't complain. It's hard enough to get any idea into the culture without it being discarded after six weeks.

You mention modernism as being the dominant school of thought while you were a student. Elaine Sorel, Edward Sorel's wife and artists' agent, once said that Push Pin "heralded the end of modernist rule." Was that something that was consciously in your mind as you were working on those projects?

No, I don't think so. Well, it may have been unconsciously in our minds. I had a Fulbright scholarship, and I had just come back from Europe. I realized how stupid I was, and how little I knew about art history, architecture, food, behavior, and everything else. I felt there was a wider compass than the one I had learned in school. An attitude that there were extraordinary things in human history, and we had the extraordinary privilege of being able to use anything as a reference point for our work. Modernism had been so dominant in creating an ideological way of looking at the world, that it also became an enormous limitation to your understanding. But, I don't think we went about it in a philosophical way. We liked to draw, we liked to design, and we knew about typography and layouts; we had been well trained. So we just did everything.

Fold-out record-sleeve poster illustrated for Bob Dylan's 1967 *Greatest Hits* LP.

What we were conscious of was a different point of view, and it was not popular. The world was divided between illustrators who were sort of second-line, and designers who were first-line. One of the reasons I was always attracted to design was that you didn't have to follow somebody's orders like you did if you were an illustrator. People were always telling you what to do. If you were a designer or an art director, only your boss would tell you what to do. Structurally, the power seemed to reside in the hands of those who could invent things early in the process of creating something, rather than those who had to execute it. And that was an important understanding on my part. I think everyone else, like Seymour Chwast, Ed Sorel, and Jim McMullan, found their own path. I wanted to see how much I could learn and how much I could discard.

It sounds like you identify more as a designer, but you could also be called an illustrator, or an artist. Has that changed over the course of your career?

I decided that those words are irrelevant. I'm a person who deals with visual material whatever it is—architecture, an object, a set of plates, wallpaper—right now I'm doing T-shirts. I know a lot about the way things look, and as a consequence, I try to see how much of that world I can embrace. I hate the parochialism of these divisions. It's one of the reasons, sadly, that so much of the design work you now see is typographical. It's because many of them can't draw. What they do is use available materials that you can fiddle around with on the computer. But they have limited control over the surface. That's an enormous limitation. Not that you can't be a terrific designer without drawing skills; you can. But it does establish a boundary that you can't go beyond. If you can't create form by the brain understanding what it wants to make, then you have to find it somewhere. We are now in the era of the collage. Collage is the sensibility of our time, and if you go to an art show, you see stuff that's been generated by the computer, collaged through the computer, and assembled through the computer. Most of what you see now is found, rather than made.

What kind of tools do you use, and how have the changes in technology influenced the practice of design? Do you use the computer often, or do you try to avoid it?

Well, I use the computer every day, but I don't touch the computer—I always have somebody by my side. But I also know more about how to use a computer than most people, because I am not dominated by the computer's sensibility. One of the problems with the computer is that it is such a powerful tool that people become susceptible to its will. The computer forces people, as all tools do, to work in a way that it likes to work—you begin thinking in a way that the computer prefers, and everything comes out looking the same.

How does this contrast with drawing?

It takes a long time to learn how to draw. It's funny; you learn how to draw naturally and realistically through observation. The secret of drawing is attentiveness. You have to pay attention to what you're doing, and that's very hard to do. And so you do that, and then you finally reach a point where you can draw accurately. Drawing may be the most complex act the brain is capable of. Maybe the most complex act that the brain is capable of. And it takes a long time. If you don't want to commit to it, it doesn't happen. You have to pursue it, day after day after day. You have to clear that path.

Is there a distinction between art and design, in your point of view?

Of course. But even in the best art schools, they don't have any idea what the difference is. I finally believe that art and design is like sex and love. They are fine independently—design is good, art is good, sex is good, love is good—and every once in awhile, you get both at once. But not often.

Within the realm of art, the objective is to transform the view of the spectator. Which is to say, in the presence of art your view has changed, your life is enlarged, and your perception of the world is different. In the presence of a great work of art, we become different. Design is moving from an existing condition to a preferred condition. It has an objective, and that's what we expect of it. We don't expect it to be art, and we don't expect

Above, left and right: Glaser at work
in New York in the 1950s; a recent portrait,
taken in 2012.

Right and below: Images of Glaser's
workspace in his Manhattan studio.

the user to be transformed. On that level, they have nothing to do with each other. But every once in awhile, you find something that was thought of as a useful object or designed object. A fifteenth-century Chinese vase enters into the realm of art, because it has managed to change your perception. So they have nothing to do with each other, but occasionally overlap.

I don't understand why, in art school, there's all this lumping together of art and design. I don't know what the consequences of clarification might be on this issue. Being an artist is self-anointed. Nobody tells you you're an artist. "I'm an artist." There it is and nobody can take it away from you. Isn't it remarkable? You couldn't do that if you were a brain surgeon. Being an artist is a declaration that only the individual makes. And I suppose you can't question that determination.

You've often been critical of advertising's role in society. But as a designer, you have to participate in that system to some extent. How do you negotiate the balance?
It's called life. There are no pure forms, everything is an accommodation. Life is full of these contradictions. What does being selfish mean, as opposed to being generous? There's no one who doesn't have to face that. I say this all the time, my essential mantra in professional life is: do no harm. Which is very complicated, because you never fully know whether you're doing harm or not. And the principle of unintended consequence is a dominant factor in life.

Are there times when you've really had to wrestle with that question, or is it always very clear for you?
Sometimes it is, and sometimes it's not. Smoking cigarettes, for example—there's no argument about that. You know you're not doing any good when you're participating in that. But with social issues, it's tougher. We have a sense, certainly, of conscience when we're doing things that we shouldn't be doing. And I try to be responsible for that, but I'm not always successful.

As acting chairman of the board of the School of Visual Arts (SVA), how has your view on design education changed from when you were a student, to a professional, to a teacher?
I don't know. I don't know what the state of design is, or who's teaching what kind of design. I have been teaching forever, but I don't know what everybody else is doing, what the students are admiring, or what they're influenced by now. I see the beginning of a certain consciousness toward a social benefit in design, but my apprehension is that it's largely positioning, rather than a real idea. It seems isolated from the actual world. You have a show of protest posters in a gallery and two hundred students go see it. And that's the end of it. It's an indication of your concern about doing good, but as far as actual engagement, the daily life of the city or something, there's less of that.

What drew you to teaching? And how important is teaching to your design practice?
It's been very important in my life. I always liked the idea of being a teacher. I feel that if you've learned something significant, you want to share it beyond your own life and your own activity. Teaching has certainly helped me understand what I've thought. It makes you come to terms with ideas that are sort of amorphous, to be able to articulate and share them with others. I've been doing it for about fifty-seven years and I'm still teaching. It's obviously something that I derived important benefits from.

What kinds of things do you teach?
In the last three years, I've changed the way that I've been teaching. I teach here at this table with ten students. We do everything collectively. The idea of the heroic artist against the world— the entrepreneurial model—is no longer the model of what has to be done. Now it's collaboration. We identify projects that have a social utility or component, and then we do them together so that there's no clear distinction about who's leading and who's following. The heroic model doesn't work because you get out of school and discover that everybody's a hero, and nobody wants you to

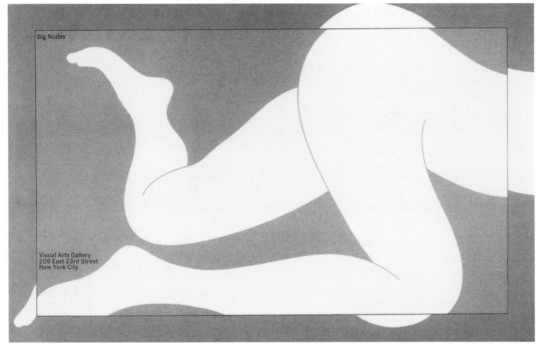

Big Nudes

Visual Arts Gallery
209 East 23rd Street
New York City

Clockwise from top left:
Logo created for Brooklyn Brewery, 1984.

Four-color lithograph promotional poster for
New York radio station WOR-FM 98.7, 1966.

Poster for the exhibition *Big Nudes* at the
School of Visual Arts, 1967.

Cover of the July 22, 1968, edition of
New York, featuring a cover story by Jerome
Snyder and Glaser, who cofounded the
magazine with Clay Felker and designed it
from 1968 to 1977.

Promotional poster for Olivetti's Valentine typewriter, 1968.

be elevated to that position. There's little opportunity for it, so it makes people crazy. But the legend persists. There are reasons for the mythology of the heroic artist seeking the unique against the ordinary. You have to encourage the possibility, but there's also a reality about where the world is at this time. I think because the economics of the world and capitalism are in crisis and sort of collapsing on each other, that form is no longer working for the good of the people who are on Earth now. We have to change both models, and engage the idea of collective work for all of us. We have to find a new economic form that goes beyond entrepreneurial activity where you have the infamous one percent controlling everything—that's over.

Did you have a mentor or a teacher who had a big influence on you?

I've had wonderful teachers. George Salter, who was a German book jacket designer and mentor, really cared for me at Cooper Union. I've had some singularly good teachers who shaped the vocabulary of my life, and my attitude toward teaching.

What sort of advice would you give yourself at the beginning of your career?

The only advice I would give anyone is, "Do good work." And that was the advice that a junior high school teacher once gave me. That's all there is. Good work. That's what I try to do.

What would you describe as your greatest professional triumph?

Staying alive and continuing to work. I think it's a great triumph when you can keep working, because the culture and the profession and everything else is structured so that you work your way out of it, curiously. Not necessarily for painters, but certainly for designers who need a community. At a certain point, everybody gets marginalized into a kind of post-central activity where they're doing little jobs for small publishers, and are fundamentally out of the profession. So my biggest triumph is at the age of eighty-four to still be in the profession. That requires patience and commitment.

Do you ever consider retiring?

No. That's like asking a painter if they would ever retire, because it's not a job. I imagine if I was working at work that I hated, I'd be happy to retire. But to work at things that are central to your life, and your perception of your self, why would you want to retire from that? I want to die at my desk. Retirement is an American concept. It's done so that another generation of workers can take over the jobs of the previous generation. There was an economic reason for that to happen, so they invented supporting activities like going fishing and endless vacation or something. The idea of retiring—even the word itself—it's terrible.

What about your largest career setback?

You have hundreds of setbacks. I view my life as first being extremely fortunate. Everything that happened in my life got me to where I am. I made a lot of mistakes, but none of them killed me. There were a lot of things that didn't work out the way I'd hoped, but in general the thrust of my life has been far beyond my expectations. The things that kill you in life are preconditions—what you expect it to be. You can only evaluate it in terms of how it ended up.

I've had a wonderful life, and I have to say that I've experienced it basically as being easy. I don't experience it as being a life of difficulty. Students are always talking about being "blocked." They can't do it, they need inspiration. Suppose there were no such thing, and there is no such thing. It's a contrivance, right? A contrivance that becomes institutionalized and attached to a romantic principal. But I've always simply done the work. People ask, "What's your process?" My process is to do the work. I'll come in here, I'll sit down at the desk, and it's done. The capacity of the brain goes beyond our understanding of it. And it's totally available to itself and the world. You know everything; you can use everything. There are no unrelated events.

The sign above the front door to your building reads, "Art is Work."

The only way to get anywhere in art is by work. You can't do it by simply thinking about what

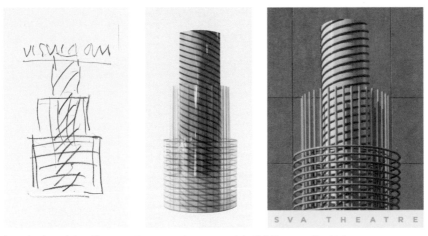

Logo sketch, model, and kinetic sculpture atop the marquee of the SVA Theater in New York, inspired by Vladimir Tatlin's *Monument to the Third International*.

you're going to do. So you begin. It's my entire secret: to begin.

What are some of your current interests or sources of inspiration?

There's nothing that I don't find inspirational. Vision and life and everything else are so remarkable. The way that light is reflecting off of those ice cubes [*refers to glass of ice water on the table*] is absolutely breathtaking. It's true that when I went up to see the Pieros at the Met, I was once again astonished by whatever Piero della Francesca had that nobody else had. But that is no more astonishing than that radiator [*points to radiator in room*] in some ways. The most important thing about professional life, in my point of view, is the connection you make between unrelated events and unrelated forms. The problem that people have in our profession is using the vernacular of design as their source. Forget it. As soon as you change your vantage point about what is useful to you, you discover that there isn't anything that's not useful to you. That gives you a very different breadth to designing.

You've lived in New York almost all your life and so many of your projects are visible and iconic to the public here. How do you think the city has shaped your outlook and your work?

I have said before that this city is not a place that yields to definition. It is so contradictory. When you're in Paris, no matter where you are in Paris, you know you're in Paris. In New York, you turn a corner and you're someplace else. The city is so full of anything that you want it to be. It's essentially a projection of one's imagination. So if you say that it's the worst place on Earth, that's absolutely true. Best place on Earth? Absolutely true. Worst people? Absolutely true. Best people? Absolutely true. It is totally mutable, it is no place except as you create it.

Have you ever considered moving somewhere else?

No. I couldn't do it, I wouldn't know where to go.

Michael Graves

—

Architect, Industrial Designer, Educator
1934 – 2015

"What's so great about design?" asks Michael Graves, in a 2007 television spot for Target. The answer, he explains by voiceover in the following fifteen seconds, is that design is reliable and surprising, accessible and affordable; that there is beauty in things that work well. A renowned American architect and the first designer to partner with the national retailer, Graves fully embodied that attitude. Over the course of his fifty-year career, he designed more than 350 buildings and 2,500 products. A household name with a signature blue hue, his effort to bring well-designed, everyday objects to the masses is widely recognized, as are his achievements in health care design. Though often labeled a postmodernist, full stop, Graves consciously pursued a distinct and varied creative path.

Born in Indiana, Graves was an undergraduate at the University of Cincinnati and received his master's in architecture from Harvard University in 1959. A love of classical forms took root during the two years he spent studying in Italy as a 1960 recipient of the Rome Prize. He returned to the States and, drawn by a teaching position at Princeton University, established his own practice in 1964 in New Jersey. His early work, specifically a trio of residences—the Hanselmann, Benacerraf, and Snyderman Houses—pushed the boundaries of the modernist white box by introducing symbolic elements and injecting playful dashes of color. Together with Peter Eisenman, Charles Gwathmey, John Hejduk, and Richard Meier— now known collectively as the New York Five—Graves further defined late modernism,

and reinvigorated the field through discussion and critique.

In the 1980s, he shifted away from abstract modernism. His commissions, including Humana's Louisville headquarters and the Portland Building in Oregon, which critic Charles Jencks once referred to as "the first major monument of postmodernism," reflected a deep interest in ornament and historicism, and his name quickly became synonymous with the developing movement. His controversial design for the expansion of the Whitney Museum of American Art in New York, proposed in 1985, made headlines but bruised his confidence when the commission ultimately fell through. By the late 1990s, he had changed course yet again, partnering with Target to create a signature line of products that delivered on the promise of design for all.

A spinal cord infection, which left him partially paralyzed at age sixty-nine, propelled Graves into his third act, redesigning the health care experience—including hospitals, wheelchairs, and interior environments—from the unique viewpoint of a patient.

What set Graves apart wasn't an adherence to a certain style but an unbending dedication to humanism. His ability to create accessible designs at any scale, to take ordinary objects and make them extraordinary, was truly unparalleled. And, to borrow a line from his Target commercial, "How great is that?"

Michael Graves died at his home in Princeton, New Jersey, on March 12, 2015. He was eighty.

**What first sparked your interest in design and
architecture?**

I remember being around eight years old, and
drawing all the time. My mother's friends would
come over, and I would draw Mickey Mouse
and Donald Duck for them. They would ask what
I wanted to be when I grew up, and I would say,
"An artist." My mother eventually took me aside
and said, "You don't want to be an artist unless
you're going to be as good as Picasso, because
you'll starve. Better to use drawing in a profession."
I asked, "What would that be?" She replied,
"Engineering or architecture." I said, "What do
engineers do?" She told me. I said, "Then I'm
going to be an architect." She said, "I haven't told
you what architects do." I said, "I don't care,
I'm not going to be an engineer."

The next day I was out on the street drawing
the neighbors' houses. And have never since
wavered. I have never doubted for a minute that
architecture is what I want to do.

**Have you always been interested in objects
and product design, as well?**

Yes. My heroes were Josef Hoffmann, Charles
Eames, Eero Saarinen, Mies van der Rohe, and
Le Corbusier, and they all made furniture and
objects. It wasn't until later that I realized a lot of
architects are not interested in that at all.

**Who or what has informed your approach
to design? Didn't you work for George Nelson
very early in your career?**

Yes, but I didn't learn anything from George, as he
wasn't in the office very much. He was always out
doing photography and other things. But I did learn
a little bit about how objects come to market: what
you have to do, the time it takes, and so on. Richard
Meier's girlfriend was the public relations woman
for George Nelson, so he would come to the office.
He introduced himself, and we became friends.
We worked on the Roosevelt Memorial competition
together in that office.

**In 1960, you won the Rome Prize and were
awarded a residency at the American
Academy in Rome. How did that experience
affect your practice?**

Rome was everything for me. It gets into your
blood. Rome is, for me, a second home. I love the
city, I love its architecture, I love its mistakes and its
successes. It's just a terrific place to be brought
up as an architect. At the University of Cincinnati
when I was an undergraduate, I learned how to
"do" Mies van der Rohe, but I didn't know who
Palladio was. At Harvard, I learned how to "do"
Le Corbusier, and I still didn't know who Palladio
was. It wasn't until I got to the American Academy
that I learned how really stupid I was. So I took
myself to the library every night after dinner and

worked until midnight, reading and drawing and planning trips. I needed to read all the classic texts on architecture, and I did while I was at the Academy.

Have you since returned for visits?
I went back every year because I was on the board of trustees until I was paralyzed eleven years ago. Then I didn't go back until last fall.

What was it like being back after all that time?
Glorious. It was just glorious. I remember sitting in the Porta Pia and just sucking it in. It was a beautiful day. Rome is where I learned how I build, why I make drawings of plans and facades in my perspectives. I see objects *in situ*—in their context.

Along with Peter Eisenman, Charles Gwathmey, John Hejduk, and Richard Meier, you were part of a group known as the New York Five. How did you all come together?
I knew Peter Eisenman from Cambridge, Massachusetts, and then we met again in Rome. I really got to know him when he came to Princeton. I had been teaching one year when Peter arrived. We worked together on competitions. And Peter and Richard are distant cousins, so they knew each other—I can't say that they were happy about that, but they learned to love each other. And then Peter and I got to know Charles Gwathmey because he was brought to Princeton

by Bob Geddes as a visiting critic, so we found a friend there. Everyone besides me knew John Hejduk already.

At the time, were you conscious of the impact that the group and your conversations would have?
We simply wanted to be able to discuss architecture like Team 10 did. CIAM was a discussion group that Le Corbusier organized, along with Sigfried Giedion and many other people. Then the Young Turks in CIAM broke away and formed Team 10 (there were ten of them) because they had different ideas about urbanism and architecture. CIAM would sometimes get on a boat to talk, just to avoid distractions. We wanted to do a similar sort of thing, so Peter and I sent letters to probably twenty-five people, and got responses from most of them.

What shape did your discussions take?
A lot of people came to our first meeting in Princeton. It was solely to discuss architecture. Some wanted a manifesto, in a European sense. I wasn't one of those people; I wanted to have a critical debate on the projects we'd done. But we never really had that until the group focused down to just five.

One weekend, with the permission of Arthur Drexler at the Museum of Modern Art in New York, we arranged a kind of critique in which each of us put two houses up on the wall of a conference

Right: Graves painting while at the American Academy in Rome, 1960.

Opposite, left to right: Peter Eisenman, Richard Meier, Charles Gwathmey, and John Hejduk (with three unidentified individuals) at the "Conference of Architects for the Study of the Environment (CASE)," Museum of Modern Art, New York, 1969.

Opposite, right: Four of the New York Five in costume, 1985. Left to right: Graves, Gwathmey, Meier, and Eisenman.

room and presented our schemes to invited critics such as Kenneth Frampton and Colin Rowe, who then discussed the work as if they were faculty members and we were students. That discussion was very interesting.

People now mistakenly think that we had an exhibition at the Museum of Modern Art. Not true. What we did do was a book about the event. Each of us showed two houses and either wrote or had someone else write about us. The book was published by George Wittenborn, who had a bookstore in New York with a lot of material on modern architecture from the 1920s and 1930s; all of us were interested in that, and we visited his store quite a lot while trying to build up our libraries. One day Peter was in Wittenborn's and George asked him, "What are you up to?" Peter said, "Well, we've got this group, and we talk about architecture," and one thing led to another and taking a chance, George said, "Why don't we publish it?" Just taking a chance.

How did the name of the group come about?
The book was going to be published, and we didn't want to be a group like the Beatles. The names the New York Five and the Whites came later after being used by other people. But at the beginning it was just Eisenman, Graves, Gwathmey, Hejduk, and Meier, alphabetically, on a white cover.

Since we were all doing work in the manner of Le Corbusier, we were coined the New York Five by Philip Johnson. The Whites, I don't know who started that. When the book took off, we started getting invited to do lectures all over the place. Nobody was talking about architecture yet, just as nobody talks about architecture today (except within the schools). When I first came to Princeton, for example, there was just one architecture lecture for the year.

When you say no one talks about architecture, what do you mean?
There is no real public forum for it. All the schools ask teenagers, really young kids, to talk about theory, but they don't know theory, for God's sake. They barely can draw a line. I'm talking like an old curmudgeon, but I think it's sad that we rarely hear from people who have something to say and have been doing it for a while. I give lectures all over the place, but they are to health care groups, people in museums, and so on.

Your architectural projects after 1970 marked a shift away from the modernist style. Would you say you defected from that sensibility?
I had built the Hanselmann House, the Benacerraf House, and the Snyderman House, and designed the Rockefeller House. They were all Le Corbusian. I was teaching a course at Princeton that had to do with the meaning of architecture, and I was bringing Rome into that study. What is a door? What is a threshold? Where do we get the name

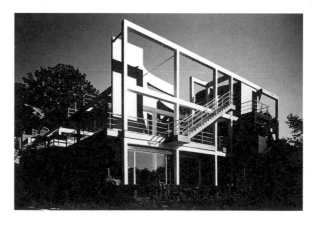

Top: Hanselmann House, Fort Wayne,
Indiana, 1967.

Middle: Benacerraf House, Princeton,
New Jersey, 1969.

Bottom: Snyderman House, Fort Wayne,
Indiana, 1972.

"threshold"? Is the threshold a myth or a ritual? It turns out that it comes from thrashers—holding a thrasher over a sacred plot of ground. I found that sort of thing terribly interesting and a part of architecture I never knew existed. So I read all of Ernst Gombrich's books from one end to the other. That's what he talks about, those kinds of myths and rituals of architecture and art.

I started analyzing art and architecture relative to Gombrich rather than the modern movement, because I found I had nothing to say. I did it very well, though. There are still people such as Thom Mayne who say, "Your Hanselmann House is so great." They wish I was still doing that kind of work. I did enjoy doing the Hanselmann House. But with Gombrich and Rome and coming to my senses around the same time, I started to break away, little by little. It was a long process; it didn't happen overnight. It involved a couple of years of trying things.

What drew you to join the Memphis collective?
Memphis is a relatively minor part of my history. Since I wasn't in Europe, I wasn't really a member. Ettore Sottsass was a good friend of mine, and he asked me to do a dressing table. I understood what Memphis was doing, so I turned up the volume on the dressing table. It was mildly successful. Barbra Streisand had one. I know that because after she decided to change her interior, she put it on auction.

How do you view the current state of architecture? You've expressed criticism of "the Zaha Hadids and the Rem Koolhaases." What do you mean by this?
My heroes are like Gunnar Asplund. The quiet people. The people who did brilliant work in the modern movement. Even early Alvar Aalto—not late Aalto, but early Aalto—when he and Asplund were influencing each other in the 1920s and 1930s.

I was criticizing Zaha's MAXXI Museum in Rome. It's anti-Rome. It is a building that couldn't be more distant from the context of Rome. I don't wish it were a palazzo, or something, I just wish it had a different sensibility.

And Rem does foolish things. He makes a building that goes up and comes back down, lays on its side and comes back up again—for a television station in China. It's not architecture, it's a trick. I love architecture so much that I just can't stand it when someone gets a commission like that and then makes a joke of it.

I also can't stand people like Santiago Calatrava who do too much—break the bank, and run the projects into bankruptcy.

I think there has to be consensus in architecture. What is the city? What is a building? When there's no consensus, it's just a free-for-all where everyone's a master. No discipline. Everybody for themselves, out to win.

Do you see a way toward that consensus in architectural education?
No. The schools aren't teaching consensus of architecture, consensus of cities. They're not even teaching the notion of the city.

You've taught for nearly forty years. How has teaching enriched your practice?
I taught because of discoveries such as Gombrich. From that point on, I found other people who I liked and studied. People who were part of an academic frame, not a professional one. A university is the best place to talk about these things. For a period of time, maybe ten or fifteen years, we had something extraordinary going at Princeton. We had, on occasion, Colin Rowe, Tony Vidler, Ken Frampton, Robert Maxwell, Peter Eisenman, and myself. And sometimes a visiting critic or two. Those were glorious years, where there wasn't *full* agreement but *enough* agreement that you could have a conversation.

How do you situate your own work within the field? What sets you apart as a firm?
I suppose what sets us apart is simply humanism. We try very much to make something—no matter what we're doing, whether it's a spatula or a new museum—humanistic in its foundation: the way it acts on its site or in your hand. It's not born out of technology or someone's writing. Students used to say, "I did this because of Deleuze." What are

they talking about? They don't know. Theorists—Chomsky, et cetera—become catchphrases for people. It's plenty difficult enough for Peter Eisenman to do Chomsky, let alone a beginning student.

Why do you think there's such a lack of humanism in health care design, specifically?
There's a lot of work to be done in health care design, and what I like to call "the three-letter firms" realize that. They have these companies of three or four hundred people, and they've got to feed the monster. One of the ways you do that is to get a lot of work. If the work is in health care, then they become "health care experts." But they've never been in a wheelchair. They don't know. So what they're doing is making interiors, like a hotel. *Interiors*. They're not conscious of it. They're not there physically, so they are not conscious of the trauma of the patient and what he or she is thinking and doing in that hospital room. Once you have endured it, you can never go back and create something simple for a situation that complex.

Does that understanding absolutely have to come from personal experience?
I'm listening to Steve Jobs's biography right now on tape, and I think his interest in making something perfect was outside the hospital, inside the hospital, on his way home, on his way to work—every fiber in his body was trying to make better products. He did what those three-letter firms don't: he made better products and let the money flow from being the best. Making money was never the primary goal. I smile when I listen to the book in my car, because he's saying the same things we say: make the object good. Make the building good. The rest will take care of itself.

Do you believe that design can have a significantly positive impact on society?
I don't think it can claim too much. It can give you a better sense of yourself and so on, but those who think it's going to save the world are probably mistaken.

How much has place influenced you and your approach? You grew up in the Midwest. Rome obviously had a very strong impact, then Harvard, and perhaps on a smaller scale, the hospital rooms you spent time in during your rehabilitation.
The answer is a very strong yes. I absorb every place that I'm in. Growing up in the Midwest, there are clichés: of course he's a nice guy, he grew up in Indiana. Well, it's true, you're not so bitter in the Midwest. You're a little more forgiving.

If you spend time in a hospital—and I've spent time in eight hospitals—you realize that if you are ever responsible for a hospital room or a hospital itself, you will make sure that the physical environment exudes empathy. And you do that through the furniture, the colors, the textures. But that can only go so far. A major part of it is the people. We're currently working on a hospital in Omaha, Nebraska, where the director is the most empathetic person you could ever meet. So it's a glorious affair to be involved in.

Your designs for Target and other large retailers popularized the concept that design is for everyone. What did you see in that opportunity?
The Bauhaus and the Wiener Werkstätte wanted to make objects that everybody could afford. But they made them by hand, so nobody could afford them. Not then, and certainly not now. Only collectors could.

I designed a toilet brush for Target. I get a call from my brother and he said, "Your toilet brush is in *TIME* magazine. Why do you do that?" I replied, "They sold six thousand toilet brushes this week." And he said, "Ah, OK. I understand." The numbers are tremendous, and when they're not, the work is taken off the shelf. We designed two thousand products for Target. For Alessi we designed about one hundred and fifty, and they're expensive. You buy a teakettle from Alessi for $185. You can buy a teakettle from Target for $39.

You were one of the first guest designers to collaborate with Target.
Yes, when we started at Target, we were the only

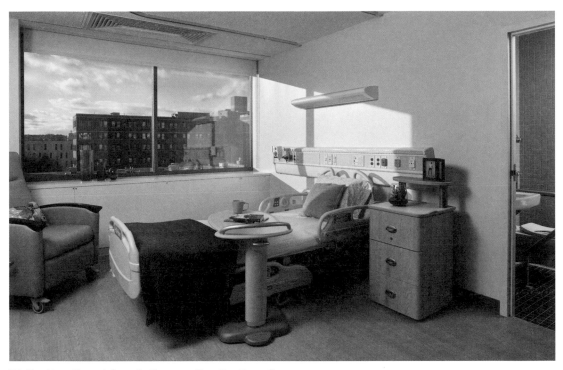

Yale New Haven Hospital, Center for Restorative Care, New Haven, Connecticut, 2014.

one. Then they added Isaac Mizrahi, and even Philippe Starck for about six months. At one point they had seventeen outside designers. We were the first, and the last. Our participation became less and less, and they asked us to do less and less, until there was nothing. Then they eventually decided, "We can do this ourselves." They started out with zero designers in house, and now they have five hundred. That's probably the biggest design studio in the world.

Do you still have products at Target?
Yes, but it's not the same now. One of the reasons I did so well at Target was because of the way Ron Johnson (then-vice president of merchandising at Target) introduced our collection. For a while I had a Michael Graves shop within every Target store, which was really terrific. Then when Ron was out, the shop was no more. Now I'm only there in the things they had to make molds for, like the toaster, teakettle, waffle maker, and some small

electronics. Our toasters are mixed up with all the other toasters, with which we now have to compete. They also don't advertise us at all. Target recently took out a little ad in the *New York Times* saying "Congratulations to Michael Graves on the fiftieth anniversary of his practice," but what we really wanted was a picture of the toaster in the ad!

Is there a moment or project that you would describe as your biggest professional triumph?
No. If you asked Richard Meier that same question, he might say when he got the Getty Center in Los Angeles. I don't know if he'd already won the Pritzker or not, but the Getty was such a feather in his cap. It's an enormous complex of buildings and a huge budget and great materials and a wonderful site. That certainly would have set anybody's career on a trajectory. He opened his Los Angeles office, and he's been busy out there ever since.

To get a commission like that is beyond rare. I've never had anything like that happen to me. When I

Top: Pop Art Toaster for Target, 1999.

Above left: Coffee and Tea Piazza, part of a limited-edition series commissioned by Alessi, 1980.

Above right: Kettle 9093, aka the Whistling Bird Tea Kettle, Alessi, 1985. The kettle's wide base makes water boil faster.

Left: Sketch of the Portland Building, 1981.

Right: Portland Building, Portland, Oregon, 1982.

did the Portland Public Service Building and then the Humana Building in Louisville, I thought I would get more office buildings to do. But instead Kohn Pedersen Fox got them.

What would you say has been the greatest setback?

One setback was the addition I proposed for the Whitney Museum in New York. To get the Whitney commission was terrific. The art critic—not the architecture critic—of the *New York Times* called me after I'd been named the architect, and said, "I don't know who you are." I replied, "Ask Mrs. Ada Louise Huxtable."

So I got the job, and then Thomas Armstrong, the museum's director, lost support of the museum's trustees. And Leonard Lauder, who then became chairman of the board, didn't like the design. So I was out. Then they hired Rem Koolhaas. Our budget was $37 million. Rem did a scheme that was estimated at $400 million. He cut it in half to $200 million, but then he was thrown out, too. We could have done something better if we'd known at the time that the budget could be larger.

How did you bounce back?

I don't know what one does to bounce back from something like that. It certainly cut into my future commissions, and I didn't get as much work after that. But we absolutely can do museums. We don't do them like Renzo Piano does them— I don't make a slab and spindly columns and call it a museum.

If you could go back, what advice would you give yourself at the beginning of your career?

I always wonder whether I should have stayed in Princeton or gone to New York, because being here made it so hard for me to get commissions. There was no local work except additions to houses and backyards. But I love this town. My kids went to school here, and ultimately we stayed. It's a rare place where you have a university that is so dominant, yet the town is manageable and walkable. It has this kind of convivial sense that I would never get on Eleventh Avenue in New York.

Is there something you wish people knew about you?

A lot has been written. People often come up to me and say, "I just love everything you've done. I love the San Juan Capistrano Library, I love the Clos Pegase Winery, I love all of it. You've made no mistakes," et cetera. It's rare that when you do a building someone says it's awful, but I do think we've done pretty well with the buildings we've designed. We designed a lot of buildings in Japan that people in the United States will never know about.

After the Whitney, I've been published less. Michael Graves hasn't gotten a building published in years! That's hard to fathom. I used to have the editors of the magazines come here, sit where you are, and ask to see my latest stuff, what I'm working on now. Those were the heady days, I guess. I didn't know how heady they were at the time.

Why do you think that is?

You tell me. I think I'm doing the wrong thing. I think I'm still seen as a post-fucking-modernist.

But you don't think you're doing the wrong thing, do you?

No. I'm making buildings, good buildings.

Why do you think everyone's so stuck on that postmodern label?

I don't know if it's that, or if they want controversy. My buildings are not controversial anymore. They're good, sound buildings.

How would you describe your dream project?

The next one. Always. I don't care what it is, I really don't. Make it a parking garage. Somebody just asked me to do a treehouse for their grandson, and I'll do that. I love making things. I love to work.

Proposed addition to the Whitney
Museum of American Art,
New York, third scheme sketch (top)
and model (bottom), 1985.

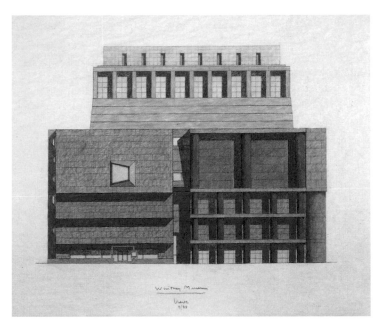

Charles Harrison

Industrial Designer
b. 1931

As a designer of over 750 consumer products, Charles Harrison has a body of work matched only by his enduring desire to improve the quality of everyday life. Taking the form of everything from toothbrushes, televisions, and sewing machines to radios, binoculars, and lawn mowers, his work has brought recognizable convenience and utility to the American household. He is responsible for designing the now-ubiquitous plastic garbage can, introduced in 1966 as a replacement for its heavy, loud, and rust-prone metal predecessor, and the iconic View-Master toy, a childhood staple since 1958.

A southerner by birth, Harrison grew up in Louisiana, Texas, and Arizona during the economic scarcity of the Great Depression. His rural upbringing, coupled with the steadying influence of his parents, instilled a sense of natural form and order. He graduated high school at the age of sixteen and moved to California to attend the City College of San Francisco. Initially a weak student, Harrison took a vocational test that revealed his aptitude for art and industrial design; shortly thereafter, he transferred to the School of the Art Institute of Chicago, where he excelled. In 1954, after being drafted into the US Army as a cartographer remapping postwar West Germany, his worldview expanded considerably. Harrison returned to the States determined to make his mark on humanity.

That goal was achieved largely through his thirty-year tenure at Sears, Roebuck & Company, where he was hired full-time in its design department after varied freelance assignments and a brief period working for his mentor, architect Henry Glass. The first African American executive to serve in the company's seventy-five-year history, Harrison led the design department to considerable success, navigating racism and corporate bureaucracy along the way. Initially a mail-order catalog retailer geared toward rural customers, during Harrison's tenure Sears expanded into the urban and suburban retail markets, pioneering the modern midcentury department store as a practical resource for durable home goods and hardware. The diversity of the company's offerings suited Harrison's talents, as he created a vast portfolio of attractive and user-friendly products for domestic and industrial use.

Since retiring from Sears in 1993, Harrison has devoted his practice to teaching, public speaking, and writing, publishing his memoir, *A Life's Design*, in 2006. He holds an honorary doctorate of fine arts from his alma mater, SAIC, and was awarded lifetime achievement awards by the Industrial Designers Society of America and the Cooper Hewitt, Smithsonian Design Museum, New York. He is dedicated to passing his hard-earned wisdom on, believing that a designer is never working solely for him or herself but always with someone else in mind—and always for the greater good.

Left: Charles Harrison in his office,
Sears Tower, Chicago, 1974.

Right: The Harrison family, Scotlandville,
Louisiana, 1934.

When did you first become interested in design?

I was probably interested in it long before I was aware that I was interested in it. In my second year at San Francisco City College, I was not doing well scholastically, so I took a course in vocational guidance to help me find my niche. Every Tuesday I'd take a test and then research a profession, and I began to suspect that design was where my interests lay. After completing the course, my instructor looked at my scores and told me I might do well in design and art.

Had you always been interested in objects?

Yes. My father was a teacher, so we lived a very modest lifestyle, but he was quite good with his hands, in particular woodworking. He made most of the things we had in the house, including the furniture and a lot of my toys. I took an interest in what he was doing, and I certainly appreciated it. My mother was a housewife—she managed our home and its appearance—and she had a strong inclination toward music and the visual arts. She worked to make the house and its interior beautiful. I would assist her with whatever she was working on, and that's how I learned to appreciate design, how things were arranged.

As a young kid in the South, I lived in a very rural environment and observed a lot of nature: animals, trees, plants. I think that experience also helped me to establish a vision of what is beautiful or compatible—what combination of forms, factors, and colors are pleasing to human beings.

Who was your most important mentor, particularly early on in your career?

There are two people who I can immediately say influenced my approach and interest in design. Henry Glass is one: he was an architect, primarily, who also taught industrial design to first-year students at the School of the Art Institute of Chicago, where I was a student. And Joseph Palmer, also a trained architect and an industrial designer. Palmer had a design firm in Chicago, and taught part-time at the School of the Art Institute of Chicago. I was very impressed and engrossed by him. He had what I thought—and still think— is important for a designer, namely, a very high level of skill in aesthetic modeling. They both had a knack for innovation and creativity.

Was it Henry Glass who first started giving you freelance work?

Carl Bjorncrantz gave me my first freelance assignments. He was a designer with a strong interest in furniture, and headed the Sears Roebuck design department when I applied for a job there. He took a look at my work, and I think because I also had a strong interest in furniture design, we found ourselves on the same wavelength. He recognized that and gave me some furniture design work to do. In those days, his department was divided into groups: one section was furniture, another section was automotive. The sporting goods section designed things like tricycles and fishing equipment. After I completed a couple of assignments, he attempted to hire me as the furniture design lead. As part of the process, I interviewed with people in several different parts of the company, and took a battery of tests that measured things like personality, interests, intelligence, and so on.

Did that ultimately lead to a job with Sears?
No, that came later. I went in to visit Carl after one of the interviews, and I could tell from his expression that he was uneasy. He said, "I don't know how to say this, but the fact is, I've just learned that Sears has an unwritten policy against hiring African Americans, and so I cannot hire you to be on staff. However, I do have a bunch of projects that I control, and I would like to use you as a freelance designer on them." And he did. So that's how I got my first jobs.

Carl would give me weeklong assignments. I would work on one at home, then come into the office and present what I'd done. This went on for six months. Then one day when I went in to deliver my design—usually sketches or mock-ups or drawings—he told me that he didn't have any more freelance budget and couldn't continue to keep me on. By some act of fate, I happened to get a call that very day from Henry Glass, who asked if I would come down and talk to him about working for his design firm. Of course I jumped on that right away. Henry really didn't have to interview me, as I'd studied under him as both an undergraduate and graduate student. He knew my work and me as a person, and put me right on his tab. I stayed there for at least a year, and I was just delighted to have the privilege of working in furniture design, and to work for my former professor. I learned a lot from the other employees on his staff, many of whom had more experience than me. At one point, I got a call from Bjorncrantz at Sears saying, "Charles, I can hire you now." I said, "Well, thank you, but I already have a good job."

What other firms did you freelance for?
After my time at Henry's office, I worked for a couple of other people, including Edward Klein—who was heavily into radios, stereos, television design, and other electronics—and Robert Podall Associates. My furniture design skills led directly to these jobs, as television sets were considered furniture pieces in those days. We worked long hours, with little pay. All night on many occasions, with maybe a hamburger around nine o'clock. I really wanted a job like the other guys I knew from school who were working from nine to five, with no late nights, and vacation and sick pay. I really was anxious for a proper full-time job with benefits.

When I was working for Podall, I got yet another call from Carl Bjorncrantz's office, offering me the opportunity to come back in and talk, which by then I was quite ready to do. Carl made me an offer. I was being asked to come work for Sears now—inside the company, inside the building.

What was that like, to go from being told that you couldn't work there, to later becoming the head of Sears's in-house design department? How did your relationship with the company evolve?
I just took it in stride. I see it as a parallel to Nelson Mandela's life under apartheid, for example, where he was put in prison and then one day became president of the country. That's how I feel about it; I don't know what they thought about it. They just looked the other way. I don't think the discrimination was willful. Ultimately I think they decided it was time to make some efforts to show that Sears was not so rigid, or mean-spirited.

What was this period like for you? How would you describe the social and political climate of the 1960s?
It's difficult for me to talk about even today. That was just life in America. A lot of that racism still exists. It was understood clearly that African American people were on the outside of American culture. I was in a hostile environment, and as a young boy I learned how to live with it. Or, at least, I accepted it as the way life was going to be, and that I'd have to learn how to negotiate. And I did.

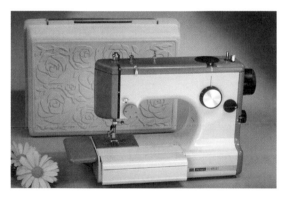
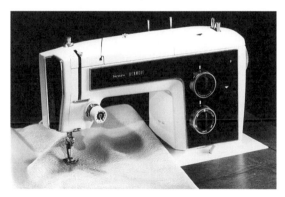

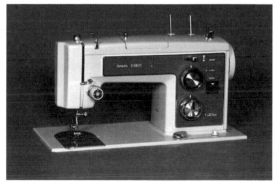

Sewing machine models designed for Sears, 1972–1980. During this period, Harrison designed eight to twelve sewing machines a year.

Dropped in mid-summer from a helicopter when loaded with 25 pounds of sand.. also dropped when frozen at 20° below zero..IT BOUNCED! But Sears new exclusive Trash Can simply wouldn't break!

(and because it's all heavy-weight plastic there was no noisy metallic clang).

Yes, Sears has everything
..and everything is so easy to buy when you have a Sears Credit Card

10 SEARS

Left: Advertisement for Sears, highlighting the plastic trash can's durability and ease of use, 1966.

Below: Blow-molded plastic garbage container, Sears, 1966.

My father did it, my brother did it, and my uncles and all my relatives. My mother, fortunately, did not have to work much outside of the home. My father was the one who had to go out and hustle, so to speak.

Did he face similar discrimination?
He faced it more than any of us, as did my older brother. We had very few employment opportunities, or options of other sorts. I recently attended a holiday gathering of young design people and someone came to me and said, "I read your book and would like to learn more about your life. I'd like to spend some time with you, if you'd be willing?" Of course, I offered to sit with him and discuss any questions he might have. He asked, for instance, why I never owned my own design

firm. I told him it was not possible for an African American man to own a design firm back then. And even if I had, I would not have been able to get any business. You could just as easily ask Jackie Robinson why he didn't ever own a baseball team. No, those kinds of things were not options. It was a given that we would not participate in that aspect of the American economy or American life.

How would you describe your design process?
Designing is a process of problem solving, so the first thing I try to do is understand the problem. I define the problem and the project, then see what all the negatives are. If the product is in the marketplace, I also look at what the competition is offering. I find that information either through shopping, going to stores, or looking through

periodicals, magazines, and newspapers. In terms of appearance and function, we must at least meet the competition, and, in most cases, improve upon what the competition offers.

You've designed hundreds of everyday items: sewing machines, hair dryers, toasters, and even the now-ubiquitous plastic trash can. When you're working on a design, are you ever able to foresee or predict its success?

Never. You know, so many good designs get stopped. Far too often, the designer is given the burden of responsibility for a product's success or failure. Having been in corporate America for as long as I have, I'm aware of all the ways in which management can affect the success of a product. It could be marketing or engineering; it could be financial or distribution-related. There are so many factors and influences that are beyond the designer's control. I just had to believe that if we could do a better job than anyone else, if we could produce a product— say, a garbage can—that was superior in function, durability, and ease of use to anything else out there, then the sky was the limit. I feel very good that I've made a contribution to humanity. That's as much as anyone could wish for.

What do you mean when you refer to a designer's burden of responsibility?

So often people will say, "What was the designer thinking when they made this thing?" But they don't understand the many levels of management that influence whether, how, and what a design turns out to be. It could be some powerful vice president, or the manufacturing company, or a marketing person. So much power playing goes on in these corporations; they input or delete what they do or don't want.

Given your years of experience in the field, what are your thoughts on the state of industrial design today?

It has played a crucial role in the economy. Industrial design got this country out of the Great Depression. Prior to that, everything was built on function alone, and not designed per se. If an engineer could put it together, that's what it was. Customers had very little to select from, and there was no need to give a product anything more than functionality.

Once industrial design picked up, America's heartbeat started accelerating. The economy got stronger and stronger, and more and more products became available. Those products became more user-friendly and more attractive. There began to be a popular understanding of the factors that must enter into any good design: ease of use, ease of understanding, compatibility with human beings.

You taught for twenty years after retiring from Sears. What did you try to instill in your students?

Always remember that you're not designing for yourself; you're designing for someone else. Thousands of people could be affected by what you do. Don't think of it as a piece of fine art; you don't wake up, grab a piece of paper, and start designing just to satisfy yourself.

In what ways do you think industrial design education has changed?

I wish there were more teachers out there who actually had experience in the practice of industrial design, in the real world. There's an excess of teachers who are shy on experience. Perhaps they were unable to find an entry-level position in the field, so they went back to graduate school to get some credentials, then fell into teaching because they couldn't do anything else and needed an income. But I think the situation is in transition, and will settle in a place where the students will demand instruction from teachers who have actually been there, who have "walked the walk" and are experienced. Design is not something that you can memorize from a lecture and then repeat. People who can recognize good design but can't execute it may find a place in academia, but I wouldn't want to be a student in their class any more than I'd want them as my manager or art director.

When the Cooper Hewitt, Smithsonian Design Museum awarded you the Lifetime Achievement Award in 2008, you were the first African American to receive the honor. Do you feel that's indicative of a lack of diversity within the profession, or rather a lack of recognition?

Both. There's also a dearth of women. It's a very white, male-dominated profession.

How can more diversity in the field be encouraged?

It'll happen, but I don't know when or how. I have to believe that it will; I want to stay positive on that score. Perhaps when white American males relax and are no longer fearful of losing whatever privileges they have—when they don't mind sharing some of the goodies in the economy, and in American life.

What does receiving awards and honors mean for you?

That I've slipped through the cracks yet again. There's a big wall up, and somehow I got through. That's how I think about how I got my first job as a practicing designer, and every job since. All those cracks I slipped through and "they" didn't catch me.

Do you consider yourself an icon?

Only in the sense that I'm an African American designer. There have not been many before me. I'm glad that I was able to change the field with my presence, and maybe I've created opportunities for those who come after me. I hope so.

What moment in your career would you select as the high point?

The ten years when I was manager of the design group at Sears Roebuck & Company. I was not actually doing a lot of design myself, but I was directing and conducting much of the design activity that Sears produced and sent out into the world. That was as high as I could go professionally. There was no better position from which to direct and affect the design of American products. I couldn't have had nearly as much

influence, for instance, from a position of owning and running my own firm.

And what about a low point?

The sweatshop days, when I was really struggling. I was extremely low paid and overworked. Those were rough times. But it was also a time when I was developing my professional skills—drawing skills, and learning how to transform ideas into real products.

What advice would you give yourself at the beginning of your career?

To learn how to be a professional as quickly as possible. And then, to break away from the dominance of other people and environments where I was forced to compromise my ideas.

What are some of your personal interests?

I have a soft spot for sailing. It's very similar to design in that you have to identify the steps that are necessary to accomplish a goal, and carefully execute them. On a sailboat, you have to take into consideration uncontrollable elements—the wind, the water, and the sails—then arrange them in a compatible fashion to move the boat, so that you'll move in the direction you want to, at the speed you hope to achieve.

Is there something that you wish people knew about you?

What I'd like most in life is to be known as a person who is trying to help. I have offered what I can to help people, to help society and culture all over the world. That's what I want: to give something, to help people.

You have a diverse portfolio of more than 750 different products. What has driven or motivated you to create so many things?

The challenge of improving something, and making people smile. Making life better for people—for humanity.

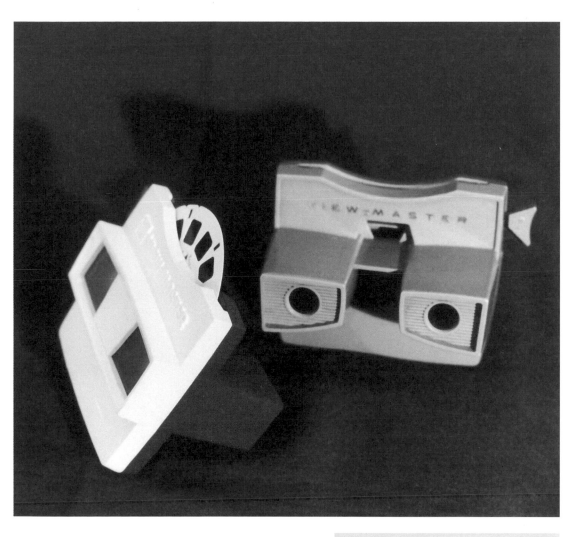

Above: View-Master, Robert Podall
Associates, 1958.

Right: Portable television for
Silvertone, Sears's private label, 1963.
Made in Japan.

Richard Hollis

Graphic Designer, Educator
b. 1934

For over fifty years, British graphic designer Richard Hollis has accentuated the nuances of the print medium to communicate complex issues with clarity and singular vision. In 1972 he collaborated on the design and production of *Ways of Seeing*, the groundbreaking paperback adaptation of John Berger's four-part BBC television series. With a sense of immediacy, the book design eschews convention, proclaiming the authorial role of the graphic designer. Its text begins abruptly on the front cover, continuing throughout the interior pages, woven into highly contextual compositions of image and text. So progressive was the design, Hollis recalls, that upon receiving the first galley, the publisher threw it out the door, saying, "I don't want that book anywhere near me." Despite its initial shock value, the book was released to great praise, and Hollis would continue his collaboration with Berger for many years.

As a young adult, Hollis began his career in the early 1960s with a brief stint as a designer for the Parisian department store Galeries Lafayette, and found himself in the city's hotbed of intellectual debate, youth protest, and avant-garde art cinema. He also traveled to Zurich and Cuba, immersing himself in Swiss modernist design, Concrete art, and left-wing politics. The influence of that era's revolutionary zeitgeist is evidenced in Hollis's longtime commitment to an independent practice, through which he has focused on long-term collaborations with writers, artists, architects, and cultural organizations whose interests mirror his own. Among these have been London's Whitechapel Art Gallery, independent book publisher Pluto Press, the Royal Institute of British Architects, and the Society for Nuclear Disarmament, as well the quarterly journal *Modern Poetry in Translation* and the weekly magazine *New Society*, both of which he art directed. Recognizing graphic design as a means of communication and as a service, Hollis has steered away from projects that contradict his own creative passions and political values.

His rigorous approach to graphic design has extended into a host of multidisciplinary roles: editor, writer, publisher, and production manager. A longtime instructor and lecturer, he is also the author of influential books on design history and theory, including *Graphic Design: A Concise History*; *Swiss Graphic Design: The Origins and Growth of an International Style, 1920–1965*; and *About Graphic Design*, a compilation of his writings and lecture notes. In 2012, a survey of his work was exhibited in London and traveled to Lausanne, Paris, and New York.

From the basement studio of his London home, Hollis continues to work independently on projects for which he can manage the production, concept, and execution of his designs with intention and integrity.

Richard Hollis in his studio, 2010.

You've practiced across many disciplines. Do you consider yourself a graphic designer first and foremost? If so, how would you define the role?

I have to accept "graphic designer." We used to call ourselves, not entirely seriously, "visual engineers." "Graphic designer" has been used so much as a term in the popular press, and unfortunately it's not always understood as a serious and responsible occupation because it's associated with marketing and branding and mass media, which includes aspects that are not in the interest of society as a whole—such as being environmentally and socially irresponsible, for example.

Is there a different term you'd prefer?

Just "designer."

When did you first become interested in design?

I always drew, and was making posters by the age of seven. I won an award for a bicycle safety poster when I was sixteen. The competition was organized by the local authority and advertised in the local paper.

What was your first job or commission, and how did you land it?

I've only had full-time jobs twice in my career. I was almost always freelance, or teaching. So I had eight years of experience before I took my first job in

Paris, at the publicity studio of Galeries Lafayette, where two celebrated designers, Peter Knapp and Jean Widmer, had been art directors. A friend worked there and suggested I apply.

My first project was too long ago to remember. But one of the first came directly from my typography teacher, who passed me on to one of his clients. He got me a job as a photo engraver's messenger, and I delivered blocks all over London via public transport. Other jobs came by chance, and sometimes through friends.

You traveled extensively to Zurich, Paris, and Cuba as a young adult in the 1950s and 1960s. How have your visits to each place influenced your interests and creative direction?

I first went to Zurich in 1958 because the Swiss Concrete artists interested me. I visited Richard Paul Lohse, an artist and graphic designer, who passed me on to Josef Müller-Brockmann at the Kunstgewerbeschule. In the same building I also saw an exhibition of the work of Henry van de Velde, an artist, designer, and architect, who had died two years earlier. His school in Weimar was the precursor to the Bauhaus.

I made several trips to Switzerland at the end of the 1950s and in the early 1960s and met many well-known designers. They were always friendly, very willing to talk about their work and give visitors samples. In those days my German was quite good. It was important to put translations in my book on Swiss graphic design. Most designers only see the formal aspect of the work, forgetting that graphic design is about words and images, which together make an idea. Without understanding the words, often the imaginative, conceptual aspect of the work is missed.

I went to Cuba in 1962 as the social revolution seemed to offer a new way, especially in relation to money. There was an idea that most day-to-day transactions would be through barter—an exchange of goods. My introduction was via a poet, Pablo Armando Fernández. Through him I became friends with the designer Tony Évora, who designed the famous poster of Che Guevara seeming to emerge from a map of Latin America. (The poster is usually captioned with another designer's name, perhaps as a feminist gesture, probably because Évora left Cuba in 1967.) He designed a marvelous weekly cultural supplement, "Lunes," to the newspaper *Revolución*. Picasso even sent a drawing for one cover. Évora sat with Castro pasting up the proofs of Che's memoirs, and the government sent him to Czechoslovakia for more studies. After the Soviet invasion he stayed in Europe. In 1963 I stayed in the same international student lodgings he'd stayed at in Prague.

And you mentioned your first job was in Paris.
I went to work in Paris in 1963–64. The publicity studio of the department store Galeries Lafayette was staffed by designers from Switzerland and Germany. The work was very fast—full-page ads done overnight—and there was a chance to attend photo shoots and work in darkrooms, making experiments. The French treated young designers as though they were artists, and if they wanted unusual materials, they would find them. I learned to paste up photo-prints of headlines letter by letter. Some aspects of French culture were significant, apart from films. Claude Lévi-Strauss's *Tristes Tropiques*, for example, explained a lot about visual communication. But Paris was just as important for its changing attitudes with respect to food and clothes and everything around us. An architect friend said that my motto at the time was, For furniture and objects, paint them; for clothes, dye them. That's about true.

Upon returning to the UK, you collaborated with John Berger on the design of *Ways of Seeing* (1972), which continues to be widely influential. How do you recall the process of putting that book together?
This is a very long story. The book *Ways of Seeing* was put together in a rented BBC office in central London by a team of five people. John Berger was deferred to as author and Mike Dibb was the producer-editor. The layout was intended to reproduce something of the television series, where you can look and listen at the same time. A heavy typeface, Univers 65, stands in for the energetic delivery. It signals, "Read me; don't just look at the pictures." And the reader finds that

the black-and-white, uncaptioned images are part of the text. It doesn't look like an art book.

Our influence was the book *Commentaires* by the documentary film director Chris Marker, which followed German avant-garde book layouts of the 1930s by the artists John Heartfield and Werner Graeff. In fact, this was when I lost my one, irreplaceable copy of *Commentaires*. After an early meeting, I seem to recall Berger going off with it.

Sven Blomberg, a collage artist, contributed large sheets of paper on which three or four reproductions were stuck. These provided separate pages in the book without commentary. My wife, the graphic novelist Posy Simmonds, provided pages from *Glamour* magazine from her archive. The book arrived on the desk of a Penguin Books director, and he threw it down the office corridor, saying, "I don't want that book anywhere near me."

How did you first meet Berger? What was your shared creative process like?
John Berger was a regular contributor to the weekly journal *New Society*, where I was the art editor. He had also occasionally taught me drawing at the Chelsea School of Art in the 1950s. He asked me to design his novel *G.* (Weidenfeld & Nicolson, 1972). Although this was printed letterpress, I pasted up all the pages of the book, sitting next to him. I would occasionally ask him if he could cut paragraphs or write new ones, which he often agreed to.

Ways of Seeing was different. Based on the television series, Berger rewrote the text for the book, and two others were involved in helping select the images. So it was a five-man "team." In fact, the final book was put together by me with the television producer Mike Dibb. Subsequently, I worked on *A Seventh Man* with Berger. The text was film set, and we worked as with *G.*, side by side, choosing the images and fitting them in with the text. This was done in France, in the summer, in the open air. Of course, there was a good deal of back-and-forth with the proofs later. Berger recently said it was the book he felt most proud of.

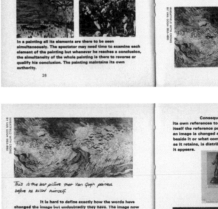
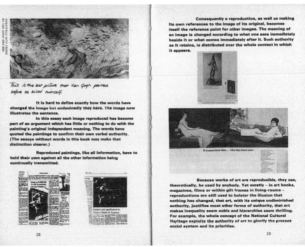

Hollis's design for the paperback adaptation of John Berger's BBC series *Ways of Seeing* (Pelican Books, 1972) offered a televisual experience, with a radically modern layout. Its text, interspersed with bold imagery, began on the cover itself.

A self-published lithograph poster based on Hollis's travels in post-revolutionary Cuba, printed in an edition of one hundred and sold for a penny each, 1962.

The influence of film on these print projects is fascinating. If you were to add a chapter to *Ways of Seeing* about the last twenty years of graphic design, what might it include?

I would have to talk about moving graphics. But I wouldn't write it myself, because I haven't the technical understanding or expertise (which is more concerned with print).

What strengths and limitations do you think the medium of print affords?

The print medium's only advantage is that it can be more permanent. The process is slower and can be considered over a longer period in the design process. But digital has so many more possibilities: it can move, it can have sound.

How would you describe your day-to-day working method?

I work in a room with tables, a printer, a computer, a scanner, and a great many books. Before 1990, it would have also had a darkroom with a process camera, a photographic enlarger, a chemical developing and fixing machine, and a waxer. The primary tools back then were pencils, colored crayons, felt, technical drawing pens, geometrical instruments, scissors, scalpels, rulers, a calculator, and a type scale. For typography, I would use

Graphic Design Department
Central School of Art and Design

Two illustrated lectures
on the most influential
design schools
of the last 50 years

G9
Wednesday 4 November
6pm

George Adams
who was a student at the

bΛuhΛus
Ulm

Anthony Froshaug
who was a teacher at the
Hochschule für Gestaltung

G9
Wednesday 11 November
6pm

18 January - 2 March
The Whitechapel Art Gallery

Whitechapel High Street
London E1
Admission free

Mario Merz

Admission free. 1-31 August 1980.

Open Sunday-Friday 11-6. Closed Saturday.

THE WHITECHAPEL ART GALLERY
Whitechapel High Street, London E1.
Aldgate East. Buses 10, 25, 253 pass the Gallery;
5, 15, 25, 40, 67, 78 pass nearby.

OPEN.

THE WHITECHAPEL OPEN EXHIBITION 1980

Top: Poster for two lectures (by one-time
Bauhaus student Georg Adams and
former Ulm teacher Anthony Froshaug)
at the Central School of Art and Design,
London, 1974.

Left and above: Exhibition posters designed
by Hollis over the course of his longtime
collaboration with London's Whitechapel Art
Gallery from 1970 to 1989.

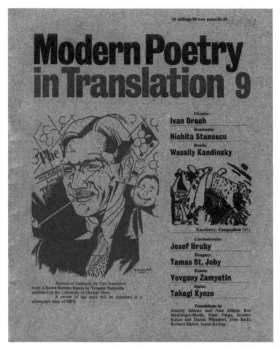

Cover designs, 1970s, for *Modern Poetry in Translation*, produced over the course of Hollis's forty-year collaboration with the quarterly journal.

type-tracing sheets, typesetting tables (for calculating the amount of space the text would take up), and typesetters' specimen sheets to trace layouts. Materials were paper (tracing and colored), a technical art board, color and plastic drafting film, and rub-down lettering sheets. And then ink (black and color), gouache, oxgall (to mix with gouache for painting on acetate), and process white paint for retouching and artwork.

I still cut and paste-up sometimes, using scissors and paper and wax adhesive. But digital working has made most of these tools and materials redundant. I use a camera more now. Computers changed everything, but made designing much less fun because of the speed. Before, you worked very slowly and deliberately.

How would you compare design culture and discourse in the UK to that of the United States (or elsewhere)?

It seems to me that there is generally a low standard in the UK. I haven't come across any serious books,

although there are some intelligent contributions to magazines such as *Eye*. It is much stronger elsewhere, certainly in France. Though *Back Cover*, out of Paris, is the only one I'm aware of. And of course there is *Typographische Monatsblätter*, from Switzerland, but I'm told it's about to close.

What sort of publications or serious books would you like to see?

Books based on real research, so that the full context of individual works—the aesthetic, technical, economic, and social aspects—would be clear. Readers should be able to understand why any work reproduced looks the way it does; more like case studies. Not easy for the writer.

Where do you think design criticism is headed? Does it have an audience, or the potential for one?

I suspect it will become more academic, and not practiced much by designers themselves.

Which is not necessarily a bad thing. Design criticism by designers can be good for explaining technical matters: how a design came about in a physical sense. Academics—social historians, for example—can better see how work fits into a general pattern of visual communication.

And how do you think design education has changed?

I no longer teach, but I am shocked by what I have seen. Often there is no syllabus, and far too many students in relation to the number of staff. Many courses are now reduced to "branding." It is a very depressing picture. Most students leave with little understanding of the principles of communication, and no knowledge of the history of the subject. They may have computer skills, but no education.

As I say, I don't teach now, and haven't for about twenty years. I give lectures, about three or four a year, more in continental Europe than in Britain, and mainly on the history of graphic design.

Your 1994 book *Graphic Design: A Concise History* remains a seminal text in the field. What motivated you to start that project, and how did you begin to tackle the topic, from a pedagogical standpoint?

A friend of mine, Philip Thompson, had already begun to write a book on the history of graphic design. He was dismayed by the pressure put on him by the publishers, and gave it up. I had promised to read it when he finished, so the publisher then invited me to take it on. It took about three years to research and produce. The sources were mainly the professional magazines of the day, from all over the world. Anything to be reproduced had to be photographed from these sources; it was before the days of electronic scanning. The more recent, post–World War II work was often shot from the original.

My approach was quite different from that of Thompson. He saw graphic design as a branch of fine art, whereas I thought of it as distinct from art.

What distinguishes design from art, in your opinion?

Art is usually instigated by the artist. The designer works to a brief in order to bring about a determined effect.

What are your thoughts on the growing number of designers producing personal, non–client based projects, which some might consider closer to art than graphic design?

It's a welcome development. Words and images combined are a powerful, flexible medium. The growth of the graphic novel is one example of graphics used in a noncommercial context. But there are many possibilities for designers to express their own ideas.

What are some of your own independent projects (past or present), and how has your approach to these projects varied from those commissioned by clients?

Apart from the *I, Eye* broadsheet in 1962, I've done nothing of this sort, other than the books I've published on my own initiative.

How do your personal interests guide your client-based work? Over the years, you have worked with a specialized group of arts and nonprofit organizations, publications, and galleries, for example.

It's mostly through friends and friends of friends, who naturally share the same interests. They tend to be "arty"—writers and artists—or we share the same political attitudes.

You've specified that you prefer to work with "never more than one assistant." Why?

Because I've never earned enough to pay for more than one assistant. I have always worked from home, except for a very short period when I worked in a studio.

Do you have a method for teaching or mentoring those you employ at your studio?

My only method is to ask, "What are you trying to do?" Also to say, "Please, please, please, print it out."

Clockwise from top right:
Cover design for Colin MacCabe's
Godard: Images, Sounds, Politics (Indiana
University Press, 1980).

Book and cover design for Patrick
Kinnersly's *The Hazards of Work: How to
Fight Them* (Pluto Press, 1973).

One of six posters designed for the African
National Congress's International Year
of the Child, 1979.

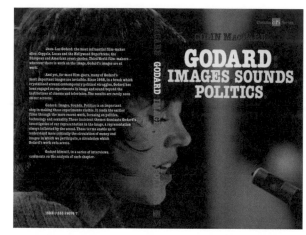

Are there people you consider important mentors or peers?

Many. Different people at different times. A teacher at the Central School, George Daulby. László Moholy-Nagy. Jan Tschichold. Anthony Froshaug. Paul Faucheux. Jean Widmer. Paul Schuitema. Among the Swiss, Karl Gerstner has been perhaps my greatest influence. And he was a historian and theorist, which, apart from his design work, makes him especially significant. I can think of a clutch of Americans, too— George Lois, Helmut Krone, Gene Federico, William Golden—whose brilliance I celebrated in my graphic history book. To us in the UK, they depended on a particular New York climate, and so were exotic compared with Europeans.

And there are very many others I'm not mentioning, who are, with the exception of Widmer, dead. Young people emulate those they admire, even imitate them. I did. As you become more mature, you simply admire. Sometimes those you admire you get to know. They can become friends. In a sense, even if you don't meet them, they're friends in that you understand— even share—their values and enjoy their work with no feeling of envy. But influences grow and diminish. Only a few remain heroes.

Can you recall any particularly memorable anecdotes from over the years?

I once absentmindedly put some work in a greengrocer's deep freeze and later rescued it unharmed. Another time, I left my portfolio on top of a parked car. It was still there when I went back—on top of another car.

What projects are you currently working on?

I'm researching and writing a book on Henry van de Velde, which I will also design myself. It is a combination of biography and critical study of the development of his work—the story of a Belgian painter who became a designer for social and political reasons. I will integrate the text with the illustrations, and the book will be published, with any luck, in 2019.

What was your last job?

An editor recently sent me 180 emails to comment on a layout. Yes, 180. That's why it was my last job. The job before that was a small-format book reproducing drawings by George Grosz. All black-and-white line drawings, already reproduced as lithographs in the 1920s. The publisher employed a photographer to shoot them, in color, at a resolution suitable for large posters. So they all had off-gray backgrounds. It would have been easier for me to scan them in black and white to a sensible size, but now they had to be Photo-shopped. I asked who was printing it. I was told, "China." Yet there is a first-class printer with his own bindery only a few miles away. The book was to accompany a traveling exhibition, and it finally caught up with the show at the third venue. A job that could have been done in a fortnight instead took four months.

You've developed identity systems for numerous cultural clients over the years, most notably Whitechapel Gallery in London. How would you advise designers to resist "branding"?

Beware of trying to do everything at the same time. If possible, change an identity only gradually. Often it's not necessary; it may need only refining. If you're starting with a new enterprise, then it means looking at all the possible uses. Such a job is far more difficult now, with things also on-screen.

More generally, what advice would you give to emerging graphic designers, educators, editors, and historians?

To students: don't go to design school, or if you do, go to work for a designer you respect. For educators: help the students to think, and organize your course on what you think the students need to understand. For editors: think always of the reader and not the designer. And to historians: just keep going.

Phyllis Lambert

—

Architect, Preservationist, Philanthropist
b. 1927

For Phyllis Lambert, architecture is and always has been a public concern. As client, custodian, and foremost steward of the Seagram Building, her passionate conviction led to the construction and preservation of a modernist masterpiece.

Designed by Mies van der Rohe and erected along Manhattan's Park Avenue in 1959, the elegant thirty-eight-story glass and bronze-plated-steel skyscraper expressed a remarkable purity of design. The building's generous setback and half-acre open plaza ushered the city into a new era of architectural awareness during a time of explosive postwar growth. It swiftly became an icon of corporate modernism, and Lambert, who became the director of planning for the project at age twenty-seven, would advocate for the building's landmark status and oversee its preservation for decades.

Born in Montreal, Lambert spent her childhood immersed in sculpture lessons and art. After attending Vassar College, she moved to Paris in 1954, continuing her education by studying examples of European architecture in France, Italy, and England. Lambert came to believe that great buildings make great cities just as her father, liquor magnate and Seagram founder Samuel Bronfman, was planning the company's New York headquarters. Seeing the unremarkable proposal he had already selected, Lambert wrote him an eight-page single-spaced screed—itself now an object of architectural lore—in which she implored her father to reconsider. With his assent, Lambert returned to New York and began six weeks of intensive research and rumination. Studio visits with some of the leading minds in modern architecture ensued, a formative trial that concluded when Mies was chosen to lead the design, with Philip Johnson as a key partner in charge of interiors. From 1954 to 1959, Lambert worked alongside as colleague, client, and devout champion to ensure that the project reached completion without compromising Mies's vision.

The experience solidified Lambert's desire to become an architect, and in 1963, while still consulting for Seagram and directing acquisitions for its art collection, she graduated from the Illinois Institute of Technology with a master's degree in architecture. In the early 1970s, Lambert launched an initiative to photograph and document historical buildings in Montreal, and founded the Canadian Centre for Architecture in 1979. Under her leadership, the CCA has emerged as a premiere research collection focused on the built environment and architecture's role in society, amassing related prints, drawings, photographs, periodicals, and archival works, that number in the hundreds of thousands.

A tireless advocate for the revitalization of affordable housing and sustainable development in her native Montreal, Lambert continues to influence architectural discourse and urban planning in Canada and abroad. A formidable architect, scholar, and activist, Lambert's concern for the ethics of building and the collective wealth of architecture defines her legacy.

Left: Phyllis Lambert sculpting a bust of her mother, Saidye Bronfman, c. 1943.

Below: A recent portrait of Lambert.

You've had many diverse roles in your career: architect, curator, scholar, preservationist. Is there one that you prefer over the others?

All of those things are related to being an architect. That's my answer.

When did you first become curious about art and architecture?

As a child. Children are pretty smart; they don't go around with nothing in their heads. By the age of nine, I was taking sculpture lessons, and by eleven I was exhibiting in juried shows at the art galleries of Montreal. I had a teacher who introduced me to the great sculptors of the past. And I was always very much attracted to the buildings of Montreal.

Was there a particular moment that sparked your interest in sculpture?

Getting the mumps. There were four children in my family, and we all got it. The nurse who took care of us had a brother-in-law who was a sculptor. She saw me making things out of Plasticine, and said to my mother, "This child takes to sculpture like a fish to water. May I speak to my brother-in-law about her?" I had been taking piano lessons, which gave me a terrible pain in the neck—quite literally. So I went to meet the man and began taking sculpture lessons instead.

You've long had a passion for architecture, and, in the case of the Seagram Building project, you found yourself working in the field before studying it formally at architecture school. How did that passion emerge and evolve?

Walking to school as a child in Montreal, I always saw the Greystone buildings, which were institutional, and liked them very much. In college, I didn't major in art history because I knew I would always be very interested in the subject; I wanted to learn other things. Sculpture always interested me more than painting, and, like sculpture, architecture is three-dimensional form. There isn't a great distance between them, is there?

After I graduated from college, I went to Europe and saw the architecture. I lived there on and off in the late 1940s to early 1950s, and became aware of the great quality. Montreal was a pretty sophisticated city, but it had very few marvelous monumental buildings, and I came to feel that was really essential.

That youthful passion is made apparent in the famous eight-page, single-spaced letter to your father, in which you criticized his plans for the new Seagram Building.

As I said, I was always looking at buildings; I was interested in them. My father, Samuel Bronfman, was planning a new Seagram headquarters for years.

Dearest Daddy,

Received your letter when in London and a day later found what you
call the building report and I, a plan of the building. To find a plan of
a building rather surprised me as I thought that you were going to have
a consultant first and then go about choosing an architect. Well now I will
set about writing the letter about which I have been thinking for a few days
and this letter starts with one word repeated very emphatically NO NO NO NO NO.
You will forgive me if sometimes I use rather strong terms and sound angry
but I am very disturbed and find nothing whatsoever commendable in this
preliminary-as-it-may-be-plan for a Seagram's building. Further I refuse
to use the term "Renaissance Modernized" and therin lies the crux of the
whole thing. When I talked to you of the Renaissance the point that I wanted
to emphasize above all is that to the man of the Renaissance the idea of
creating a beautiful building was the idea of creating a beautiful way of
life. It was a renaissance or a rebirth of ideas, a refinding rather a
rediscovery of a noble society which, to the man of the renaissance, represented
the very high ideals of a society and a way of life and culture. Through
the new scholarship of the 15th century (called in Italy the Quatrocento)
the high level of Greek culture in every field of endeavour was rediscovered
and the place of man in the universe was put into new relief. Man was now
the centre of the universe and God was to be apprehended no longer through
mystical ideas but through mathematical symbols, perfection in proportions
and harmony and man being a reflection of god perfect in his proportions
and able through his intellect to understand the mathematical basis of
the world and search for that harmony which was all important. Thus man
was conceived as a noble creature physically and morally and intellectually
as he had been considered according to the thinkers of the Quatrocento
in that admirable civilization of the Greeks. The Greek civilization is not
under discussion and as history is only the way one age looks at another,
what is important and tells us the thought of any given period, is how it
interprets other periods. There are, of course, documents to go by and
certain recorded facts, but then again it is always the interpretation of these
facts and documents that is important...what is emphasized and what is not.
Now then, the great document of the architect of the quatrocento was a book
on architecture written by a Greek, Vitruvius. In his third book on Temples
Vitruvius supplied the answer as to what sacred buildings should be like
and when the parts were properly harmonized and proportioned and that is
upon analyzing the proportions of the human figure, (and here again the manner
in which the proportions of the human figure are analyzed are indicative
of a way of thought, but I shall not go into that here) the harmonies and
perfections of the human figure should be applied to the harmony and proportions
of the temple. Thus the temple, or to extend it, any architectural unit
was to reflect the perfections of man, which meant the perfections of harmony
and thus pythagoras was carefully studied and the mathematical progressions
and relationships in musical harmony. It was Alberti, the advisor to patrons
and artists who set down verbally the tennents of architecture of the
Renaissance . It was a mathematical definition, based on Vitruvius stating
that beauty consists in a rational integration of the proportions of all the

[handwritten left margin, vertical:] You can't modernize the Renaissance — you can only learn from it understand what it meant a why their buildings were beautiful. By analyzing what is beautiful in the past one can analyze what is beautiful in the present but the present is different and a different vocabulary,

[handwritten bottom:] — modernizing the Renaissance is like modernizing Shakespeare — it would mean absolutely nothing

The first page of a letter from Lambert to her father, Samuel Bronfman, in response to his proposal for
Seagram's New York headquarters, June 28, 1954.

84

It motivated me that he had a proposal, so first I took graduate courses—things occurred rather slowly in those days, so of course time allowed—at the Institute of Fine Arts at New York University. I studied architectural history, which was wonderful. Then my father came to Rome to visit when I was staying there over Easter in 1954, and I tried to convey to him the importance of buildings. I took him to Palazzo Farnese, and discussed this with him. Two months later, he sent a drawing of a proposed building that was so appalling, I didn't know what to do. So I undertook to research who was out there making great work, then I wrote him the letter.

Through your articulate conviction, you were then tasked to research and identify the architect who would build the tower. How did you approach the project?

When you really care about something, you can go through a huge amount of material very quickly. I had a self-imposed deadline of six weeks. I'd ask to meet architects in their offices, of course, because it was the only way: the lion in its lair. If you ask an architect to meet you somewhere else, you don't see the environment they work in, you don't see what's on the tables, you don't get to know anything. Then the architects would give me further names to investigate. I met with architectural critic Lewis Mumford, Alfred Barr, Philip Johnson, and of course Eero Saarinen, who created a sort of methodology for deciding whom I should talk to.

How did you finally come to select Mies van der Rohe for the project?

I saw him at the end of the six weeks. I never asked the architects what they would do. Instead I asked them: "Who do you think would make a strong statement in New York City on Park Avenue?" People would always talk in terms of Mies. They'd say, "I'd do this differently from Mies," or, "I'd do that differently from Mies." He was always part of the conversation. I knew that Mies had not done very much in the United States—he had finished 860–880 Lake Shore Drive, and was just starting construction for the great S. R. Crown Hall in Chicago.

Le Corbusier's name also came up all the time. People would say Corbusier can't do this, he doesn't have a building in the United States, even though he'd already done the United Nations building in New York. But Mies said, "Of course Le Corbusier can do it. He's a wonderful artist." Here's one of the great architects, being asked about another great architect, and he says, "He's wonderful." Mies was very generous as a person. And his presence was formidable, too. With some people, you can just tell immediately how powerful and impressive they are. Mies had a kind of aura of assuredness. He was only twenty-one when he was chosen as the architect of the Riehl House.

After selecting Mies, you became director of planning for the Seagram Building at the age of twenty-seven, with little professional experience. When did you start to gain confidence in your work?

I never thought about confidence; I just did what had to be done. How ridiculous not to! It was impossible *not* to do the very best I could. It wasn't a job—I didn't consider it that way. It was just part of civilization, something that had to happen.

You worked on the project from 1954 to 1959. What stands out as a particular high point for you?

Working with Mies. My office was with the architects, not with Seagram. So I was involved and aware of everything that was happening throughout the process: how Mies worked, job meetings every Wednesday with the engineers, the associated architects, the appointments. It was absolutely fascinating. I remember walking down Park Avenue past the building while construction was underway, and I just knew this architect was doing something fantastic.

Mies worked very quickly; he started in December, and by March he had a bronze model of the building, about twenty-five or twenty-six inches tall. When we first showed it to my father, we expected him to fall over and say it was the best thing he'd ever seen. Instead, he said nothing. Later that day we had a celebration already scheduled, and we were all very downcast. But luckily that didn't last too long. It was such an elementary presentation, and once the details were worked through, the project was accepted.

Still widely regarded as a modernist masterpiece today, at the time of its construction, the Seagram Building presented a strong statement on how architecture should address public space. How do you see the building and its effect on New York? Did it live up to your vision?

I didn't have a vision. The thing for me is, I walk down the streets of New York and I look at the buildings, and I just wonder how it's possible that people can't do something that wonderful—or even approach it—more often. Buildings in the north and south and all along Park Avenue are not very distinguished, to say the least. So it's such a joy to look at it. To set it back from Park Avenue with the public plaza—that raised a lot of questions at the time. The fact is, it could have been twice as big as it is.

There's a beautiful line in your book, *Building Seagram*: "I learned what I thought as I wrote." Were there any surprises while you were writing and researching the book—things you rediscovered or remembered—that changed how you view the project and the many players involved?

I formed an idea of what the book's structure would be: I would talk about the preparations for the project, building the building, Philip Johnson's approach and where that came from, Mies's approach and where that came from, and then what happened to the building afterward. Before I started writing, I gave lectures at universities and museums for a couple of years, and I had just finished the exhibition *Mies in America,* so I really had a grasp of what Mies was doing.

In writing, I realized that even though I'd loved Philip a lot, and he was fun to be with, I never took him seriously as an architect. When I started to work on the book I had to reassess his role and came to appreciate him much more. His Four Seasons was a very important aspect of the building—it's crucial to have life on the ground floor—and Philip made that restaurant really wonderful. It's a great contribution. And the lighting was his. Mies wanted to have the building lit at night, but it was Philip who worked that out in a contemporary way.

Writing about the urban changes and regulations, city code changes and code itself—all of that was interesting as well, especially in the context of Park Avenue. For example, why, after the war, did all those buildings get built there? I don't think anyone ever pays attention to that. It's a real phenomenon of postwar architecture in New York—those glass and curtain wall buildings.

Why did you decide to go back to studying architecture after such success in the field?

I wasn't going to go back, I was going to go. I realized when I was doing Seagram that I wanted to be an architect. In the office, we had these little square partitions between Mies, Philip, and myself. I sat at my desk with a drafting board, a T-square, and a triangle, and learned to draft. I wanted to be an architect, that was clear.

I went to Yale because I thought IIT was very far away and that it was very much an undergraduate place. I was hungry, very hungry, but I didn't like how people were thinking about architecture at Yale. So, one summer after my second year, I went to work in Mies's office in Chicago. I saw what they were doing and I thought, this is what I want. I want to know what an I-beam is, how it works, how you construct these things." So I transferred to IIT.

In 1979 you founded the Canadian Centre for Architecture with the conviction that "architecture is a public concern." Can you elaborate on this?

As I wrote to my father, when a company decides to build a building, it has a responsibility. If you're going to put up something new, why put up something that isn't the very best you can do? It's for the people who work there, the people who will buy it, the area it's in, the city itself, and eventually the whole world. Why do something less?

Buildings make the city. They define the streets. They define the squares. They define

where the parks are. They define how you live in a city, how you walk in a city, what you do in a city; they can make it very pleasant or very unpleasant. Nobody really addresses architecture except architectural schools, but the people who live in a city must learn to recognize this.

It is a public concern; it's about wanting the public to act. Although whether you get good architecture or not actually depends on the rulers. The rulers are no longer princes, but bureaucrats and elected officials. If you tell the officials that you don't like what they're doing, you can effect real change. That was my sense of it: to have the public demand more than what they saw around them, to demand a marvelous city in terms of the greenery, trees, sidewalks, all of these things, and of course the quality of the buildings.

Stewardship comes up very frequently in all your work. Where do you think that sense of responsibility to document and protect things for future generations comes from?

As a young person, I wasn't interested in history. I didn't want to think about planting a tree that

eventually would grow tall in fifty or a hundred years. I didn't like thinking about that idea of continuity. That changed, obviously. I suppose the change was subliminal. I traveled a lot. When you see the wonderful buildings that exist in Europe, you start to see. In Greece and Turkey, you see things from thousands of years ago.

Contrast that with the offensive, wanton demolition of buildings in the 1960s and 1970s. It was like having family friends executed. It was socially abominable. You lose the texture, the quality, the history, the memory. We can't always be beginning, beginning, beginning. That's just impossible. So, those are the things that really made me. And this happens particularly in the poorer areas. We push people out and say, Oh well, you don't matter.

In 2014 you were awarded the Golden Lion for Lifetime Achievement at the Venice Architecture Biennale. What does that award mean to you?

I was thrilled. To me, it's so important. I get recognition in New York, in the places I work,

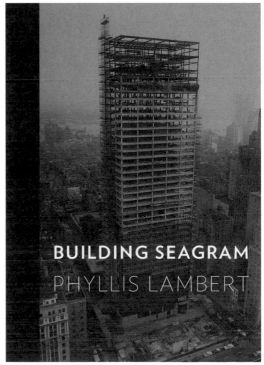

Opposite. The Seagram Building,
375 Park Avenue, New York. Mies van
der Rohe and Philip Johnson, architects,
with Kahn and Jacobs, associate
architects, 1954–1958. View from the
northwest at dusk.

Above: Johnson, Mies, and Lambert,
New York, 1955.

Right: Cover of *Building Seagram*
(Yale University Press), 2013.

Lambert receiving the Golden Lion for Lifetime Achievement, at the 2014 Venice Architecture Biennale from Rem Koolhaas and Paolo Baratta.

View of the visitors' courtyard, Canadian Centre for Architecture, Montreal, 2007.

very much so in Montreal. But these are my peers, and the Lion is worldwide. It's many people saying to you that you count in our world. And that's a pretty great thing, isn't it?

How do you view the current state of architecture?

I think it's fascinating because it's very much changed. There's a stronger sense of realization that cities are made up of buildings, and that buildings are much more than structures just sitting on a site. Environmental issues are forcing us to think differently. It's quite exciting.

Architects are doing a lot of planning for repurposing buildings or areas of cities. To me, the most fascinating thing is to work in existing cities. The kind of work Diller Scofidio + Renfro have been doing in New York, for example: everywhere the next stages are more and more reflective of a consciousness of the environment, the social environment, the mental environment. It's a major shift, much as the Industrial Revolution was. This is a renaissance in the sense that it's a new awareness of where we are in the world.

What about architectural education? Is that as fascinating to you now?

It's terrible. Appalling. It really needs to be changed. There are courses here and there run

by people who are doing good things. But most of it—at McGill University, for example, the department of architecture is still under engineering. We can do great things in engineering, and it's important, but the fact is that architecture is an art. With the new kinds of materials that are being developed, it's wide open, and architects have a broader view of things. How do we protect our cities against flooding? How do we deal with severe issues of poverty? At one point, we were struggling with how to keep glass buildings from being either too cold or too hot. Now we've achieved that. We're on to something much more important: quality of life.

Is there someone who stands out as your most important mentor?

I should say Mies. I learned methodology, how to think, and how to approach issues, from him. And my father also, because of his commitment. He loved what he was doing so much, and he was passionate about it; he called it "the romance of business." Children are very influenced by their families. If the parents are in the arts, the children tend to be in the arts. If the parents are doing nothing, the children tend to do nothing. So this great passion of my father, while it made him difficult to live with at times, made him care so much, and he passed that on to me.

The library reading room at the Canadian Centre for Architecture, Montreal, 2007.

If you could go back and speak to your younger self, just starting out, what advice would you give?

I hesitate to give advice to anybody. I would say to work hard because you're fascinated. Well, maybe not so much work hard, as be committed and passionate about what you are doing. When I was starting out, I just followed what I thought was absolutely important. I didn't want to live in a world without great cities and great buildings. And you can't just be passionate, you have to be really hard-headed, too.

Do you consider yourself a visionary?

Not really. I think Le Corbusier was a visionary. He had a dream of a new kind of city. Mies was a kind of visionary. I guess great artists are visionaries. I don't think of myself as an everyday Joe, but I do think I'm lucky to never have been bound, never held by convention.

Lora Lamm

—

Graphic Designer, Illustrator
b. 1928

In 1953 Lora Lamm, a freshly minted art school graduate and Swiss-born graphic designer, moved to Milan to jump-start her career. The decade that followed established her as a pioneering force within Italy's progressive design scene. Her work for clients such as Pirelli, La Rinascente, and Olivetti, incorporating brilliantly lively illustration and photography, embodied the innovative modern spirit of post-war Milan. Her use of playful shapes, a bright yet delicate palette, and refined typography—a style that was neither resolutely Swiss nor Italian—set her work apart.

In Switzerland, Lamm grew up amid an endless supply of natural beauty, with snow-capped mountains and lush forests just outside her front door. She attended the Kunstgewerbeschule (School of Arts and Crafts) in Zurich, studying under Johannes Itten and Ernst Keller, who taught lettering. Her first professional post in Milan was at the storied Studio Boggeri, where Xanti Schawinsky, Max Huber, Carlo Vivarelli, Aldo Calabresi, and Bruno Monguzzi also worked over the years.

Huber, a classmate from Zurich, brought Lamm into the advertising department of La Rinascente, a forward-thinking Italian department store that originated the Compasso d'Oro, Italy's premier award for industrial design. Here she flourished, designing everything from catalogs and packaging to posters, advertisements, invitations, and in-store exhibitions. She led the department from 1954 to 1958, nurturing a fondness for experimentation and an uncanny ability to bring warmth and good design to corporate advertising. The tight-knit office was recognized internationally—Andy Warhol once sent a fan letter—but the rare combination of youthful talent, enthusiasm, and culture did not last long, and the group dissolved sometime in the late 1960s (Lamm left in 1963). By night she moonlighted for Elizabeth Arden, Latte Milano, and others; her freelance client base grew quickly. Lamm was soon hired by Pirelli, an Italian tire manufacturer, to invigorate the company's image. Her designs—colorful illustrations combined with product photography—often featured women biking and motoring, but avoided routine depictions of femininity.

Returning to Switzerland in 1963, Lamm continued freelancing, and later became a partner in a small advertising agency, where she worked until 2000. Upon leaving Milan, she made a conscious effort to break from the illustrative style she had become known for, focusing instead on photography and typographic projects. Her work was the subject of a major exhibition at the m.a.x. museo in Chiasso, Switzerland, in 2013, and is in the collection of the Museum für Gestaltung (Museum of Design) in Zurich. Though officially retired, Lamm is mum on the subject of her ongoing work; as a freelancer, she admits, you never truly stop.

Left: Lora Lamm at home in Arosa, Switzerland, 1938.

Right: Lamm at her studio in Zurich, 1964.

What are you working on now?
I stopped working as a graphic designer in 2000. My actual work involves being interested, participating, living in the present.

What led you to stop working?
Clients are getting older, as graphic designers do. A new generation of clients and graphic designers has arrived with new ideas based in the digitized world of the computer and the Internet. As a freelancer, I will never be "retired," even if I no longer participate in creative projects.

You grew up in Switzerland. What was your childhood like?
A happy one. Living in the mountains with a sister, two brothers, and wonderful, strong parents. We had six months of snow every year, which meant a lot of skiing. My family was open to every kind of creativity, supporting my siblings and me in our choices and our future professions.

My father was a master craftsman, painter, and hotel proprietor. His hobbies were making films and taking solo voyages. Our wonderful mother was a perfect housewife and indispensable "assistant" for my father.

Do you remember when you first became curious about design?
In my school days, everybody wanted a drawing from me on their slate: a Shirley Temple portrait, an Easter bunny, or Santa Claus. My five years

of instruction also sparked my interest in design, and then logically, by doing.

What led you to pursue a career as a graphic designer?
Enthusiasm. Participation. Joy of living.

How did you learn about graphic design as a career?
A teacher at my secondary school noted my talents in designing, writing, and dancing, and proposed that I attend *Kunstgewerbeschule* for design. Plus a friend of our family, who lived in our village, was an illustrator of all kinds of things: mushrooms, mountain flowers, birds. So I realized at a young age that this could be a profession.

Tell us more about *Kunstgewerbeschule*.
Kunstgewerbeschule (school of arts and crafts) is a federal institution with a final federal exam. I passed the examination for admission, then completed one year of preparatory work and testing to enter the four-year course for graphic design. When I attended, the school was led by Johannes Itten, the great Bauhaus master, and the lecturers included Ernst Keller and Ernst Gubler.

Do you identify more as a graphic designer, illustrator, or artist? And has this changed during the course of your career?
It depends; sometimes my work is more illustrative, but its always graphic design.

How do you define graphic design?

Graphic design has to have a clear, immediate message. If the message is not easy to keep in mind, the producer will not sell it.

In your view, what is the responsibility of the designer?

To inform without confusion.

The Milanese design scene of the 1950s and 1960s is now legendary. What was it like to be an integral part of this group?

All involved felt we were members of a *rinascimento*, though we were ignorant of the importance it would later hold. Only in the last few years has it become clear, as archives and exhibitions devoted to that time have appeared. And because history takes a few generations. I am equally surprised that the 2013 exhibition *Lora Lamm, Grafica a Milano 1953–1963* at m.a.x. museo in Chiasso, Switzerland, made a legend of me.

Was it unusual to be a woman working in design at this time?

Oh, yes! Though I never had any problems. I was considered first of all a feminine being—young and blond-haired—which I thought was acceptable. Italian colleagues saw me first as a woman, and then as a woman doing well professionally. That did not bother me at all; I felt proud and accepted.

As a young designer, how did you get your start in Milan?

My start in Milan was with Studio Boggeri, coordinated by Frank C. Thiessing, a copywriter at the famous Graphis Press Zurich. It was a prefixed, two-month stay because Aldo Calabresi, a Swiss graphic designer, was expected later on. I did some good work, but Boggeri's accounts were strictly in chemical and industrial fields—not my area of expertise!

You also worked at La Rinascente, another Italian cultural icon of the 1950s. What was it like to work there?

Everybody took part and worked hard. We were a perfect, enthusiastic team comprised of an architect, a stylist, a copywriter, a displayer, a photographer, a graphic designer, and of course the boss, Gianni Bordoli. But as time passed, our wonderful group began to dissolve.

In 1958 you became head of La Rinascente's creative department after Max Huber's departure. How would you characterize this time in your career?

The method of work did not change, but the salary did! And I was allowed to sign my work. From then on all my posters were signed, and my published works included "graphic design by Lora Lamm." I'm rather modest by nature, so I, and all concerned, never saw myself as a boss!

TUTTI
IN
ACQUA

*la*Rinascente

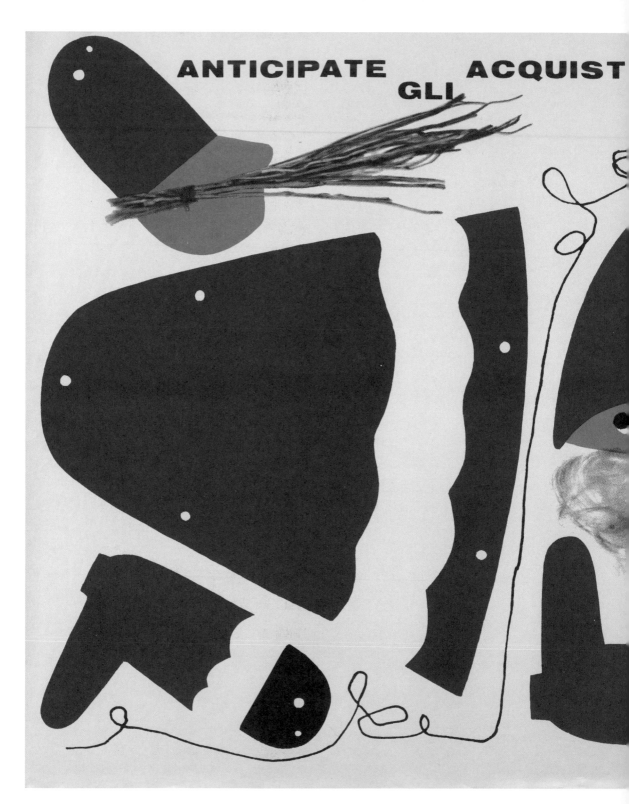

ANTICIPATE ACQUIST
GLI

A holiday-themed poster for La Rinascente, 1957.

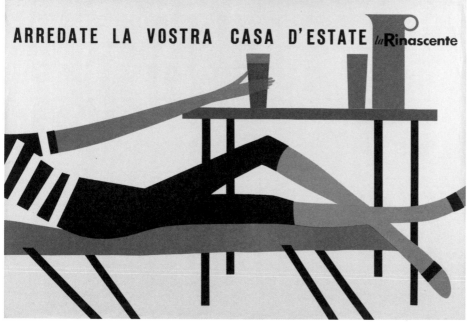

Posters for La Rinascente. Top: *Fashion Starts at La Rinascente*, 1960. Bottom: *Furnish Your Summer Home*, 1956.

Was it unusual to freelance for large clients like Pirelli when you did?

Pirelli at this time had only freelance graphic designers. I may have been the only woman. Entrepreneurs had public relations agencies, and graphic designers worked freelance. My clients were Elizabeth Arden (wrapping paper, illustrations, scarfs, advertising), Niggi Cosmetica (packaging, corporate identity), and Consorzio Latte Milano.

What other sorts of freelance jobs did you take on?

After Milan, I continued working in Italy and planned to leave for the United States. I did not get a permit to work as a resident in Italy, so I had to return to Switzerland again. Meanwhile, I continued working as a freelancer with the small and smart publicity agency belonging to Frank C. Thiessing. Our client list grew internationally, and I enjoyed the direct contact with each producer or owner. It was fascinating to observe how products such as Hennessy Cognac, Fitted Carpet, Fight Jet, or swiss cheese became successful because of publicity. I felt happy and considered in that world. Time passed quickly, and my plans for moving to the United States turned into plans for visiting.

Your work—and by extension, you—have become synonymous with Milanese design of the 1950s and 1960s. How, in turn, did Milan shape you?

Milan was an important time, but I've since been conscious to avoid the "Lora Lamm style." I strictly concluded this epoch and began a new and long career as a graphic designer, with rich and various projects in typography, lithography, and photography in collaboration with printers, editors, and clients. A new period arrived, and I was ready for it.

Your illustration style—playful, colorful, vibrant—still feels extremely fresh and modern today. What influenced your approach to design and illustration?

I think it has been my aptitude for observing, along with my facility for drawing, describing, writing, dancing, and loving nature.

Who has been your most important mentor?

Frank Thiessing and Amneris Latis. Frank was involved with my professional life from the beginning. We immediately understood each other from the very first moment. Importantly, he convinced me to bring originals and copies of my work to Zurich, where he carefully conserved them. I worked with Frank as a freelancer for his agency, and then as his partner. The partnership went on until Frank's death six years ago at the age of ninety-two.

Amneris Latis, a Swiss native living in Milan, was a freelance copywriter and stylist at La Rinascente. We both felt the same way about communication. I remember a week one summer at the Latis house in Liguria, Genova, planning the whole fall and winter publicity for La Rinascente: drawing, noting, laughing a lot, swimming, drinking aperitifs in Portofino, enjoying the passing by of [Aristotle] Onassis and his guests. We maintained a close friendship until Amneris died four years ago.

What was your biggest career setback?

Surviving the years 1970 to 1980. Crises all over: the economy, accounts getting smaller, agencies closing.

What was your greatest career success?

The present! Living the effect that my ten years in Milan has caused.

What advice would you give yourself at the beginning of your career?

Keep your eyes open. Observe. Translate. My teachers taught me to always be ready; to absorb what you observe. Translate means learning to render ideas into a visual context. Always know the difference and make it apparent between an illustrative or a photographic solution.

Jack Lenor Larsen

—

Textile Designer
b. 1927

For master weaver and wanderer Jack Lenor Larsen, every object in his vast collection evokes a place and a memory. The same might be said of his lustrous textiles: Aubusson, Glacia, Nocturne, Orpheus, Happiness, and Swazi Stripe, to name a very small few. Each fiber tells a story—of a far-flung adventure, an inspirational figure, a moment collected, or a commission gained. And there are many stories to tell.

Larsen, who at eighty-eight has been a member of design's inner circle for sixty years, simply followed his heart. Trained as an architect, he found his true calling in textiles and translated his love for handwork into a lifelong commitment to craft. His New York studio, founded in 1951, grew quickly, and his richly informed global perspective—shaped in part while working as a consultant for the US State Department—changed the landscape of cloth in the 1950s. Introducing texture and color to a hungry American market, Larsen's work caught the eye of architects such as Marcel Breuer, Louis Kahn, Gordon Bunshaft, and Frank Lloyd Wright, who became his collaborators and friends. Bringing warmth to many of the most famous midcentury interiors, his gilded draperies hung in the Lever House lobby, and his vibrant upholstery adorned Pan Am jet airliners, Wright's rustic Fallingwater, and the conversation pit at Eero Saarinen's Miller House in bursts of deep blue, ochre, and burnt orange.

As a writer and curator, Larsen continues to shape our understanding of interior design, dyeing techniques, and the role of objects in everyday life. As a cultural ambassador, he has immeasurably nurtured wider knowledge of textile traditions the world over. His passionate love of design is contagious. A collector since the age of eighteen—he began with woven baskets from thrift shops in Seattle, his hometown—Larsen continues to surround himself with objects and people that inspire.

Today, Larsen splits his time between an understated apartment on Park Avenue in New York and LongHouse Reserve, the sixteen-acre East Hampton estate that doubles as his country home and a publicly accessible case study of his thoughtfully considered lifestyle. Modeled after a beloved shrine in Ise, Japan, it houses thousands of objects. Larsen frequently leads tours of the grounds and sculpture garden when he is not otherwise engaged in a project. He has no patience for idleness; a maker, not a dreamer, his next idea is never far away.

Jack Lenor Larsen, 1960s.

When did you first become curious about design?

I suppose when I went to college at eighteen and studied architecture. I was interested before that, but I wasn't involved. I had a friend who was wild about Frank Lloyd Wright and had all of his books, and the work was exciting to me. My father was a contractor, so I knew something about buildings, and I couldn't imagine anything better than architecture.

How do you describe what you do? You trained as an architect, but you're also known as a textile designer, a collector, and an entrepreneur.

I'm a maker. I left architecture because I didn't draw well. I only wanted to build models of everything, but that wasn't enough of a reason to stay. So I became a weaver, working with my hands, which I did better and more happily. There was less competition, as well. On the West Coast in the 1940s, Dorothy Wright Liebes and other weavers were renowned—they were all women, of course—and their work seemed like a profession. When I was in college, I started to get weaving commissions, which was encouraging, and to work with architects was delightful. It was a vote of confidence that someone was willing to pay money for what I was doing.

Has that "maker" designation changed over the course of your career?

No. Though I've become more aware of it. My chief project now is related to our foundation, LongHouse Reserve. I'm the curator and landscape architect and many kinds of things for projects that all have to do with making—not building. I enjoy making connections. I see Cs that I like to make Os—to make things happen that should be happening.

How did your studies in architecture inform your practice—as a textile designer and a maker?

Planning: of imagining a finished project as a structure, what it will be made of, how it will be put together, and who will be using it.

Who or what influenced your relationship to color?

There were so many influences. Mark Tobey was a friend in Seattle, and he taught me the importance of value: "You don't see it until you put it against a gray wall." Value to him was most important. When Clyfford Still had a show in Seattle, I was so excited about his colors that I stayed up all night trying to weave what he had painted. I was very involved in pre-Columbian fabrics. In Morocco, Mexico, and other places where I worked, there was local color, and local color limitations.

In the late 1950s, you were a consultant for the US Department of State. What did this job entail?

The object was to create jobs and exports, though most of those projects failed, partly because there was no value there placed on time or money. I eventually worked in sixty countries. Working in a different country was a lot better than visiting as a tourist.

Everything was first-class, with privilege and introductions. I was in Japan for a while, and then Hong Kong for a while, then I finally got to Taiwan. It turned out the United States was supporting and sending money to two of the worst dictators in the world. It just couldn't have been worse. But it was fascinating.

What was something surprising you learned in your travels?

I was in Port-au-Prince helping Haitian weavers, and I learned that hand-spinning was what gave the quality to the fabric. If you had handspun yarn, you didn't need much else, because texture was the watchword at that time. We didn't want pattern, we wanted texture. And color, sometimes.

Were local weavers willing to teach you their techniques? What about their processes did you learn?

It is better to learn things from others than on your own. In Vietnam I was trying out several techniques that I didn't know, and with no one to learn from, I didn't succeed.

One of the things I learned was that it's very difficult to change behavior that's culturally ingrained. I worked with the Peace Corps in Peru—proud graduates who wanted to change

the world and become famous designers with successful production lines. I knew Peru very well already. Women who traditionally wove two ponchos every year didn't want to do it every day, or do it wider, or do it faster—all changes that were being asked of them. In contrast, if you can find people who have never woven before and ask them to come every day and to weave it wide, they say "okay.".

How did you find a balance between adopting practices learned abroad and preserving heritage?

I don't think I tried to do foreign handcraft in America or Europe, but I wrote books on the subject. I wrote a book called *The Dyer's Art: Ikat, Batik, Plangi* about resist techniques worldwide and historically, and a couple on basketry and such. I also did resists in Korea with silkweavers, and taught them old technology anew.

Your client list includes many icons of mid-century design: Frank Lloyd Wright, Marcel Breuer, Louis Kahn, Gordon Bunshaft. What was it like navigating all those personalities?

My first collection was for Jim Thompson's branch in America. Wright saw it and bought two hundred yards for Taliesin's music room, so I met him very early. He was both easy and difficult. He liked to pull people's legs, but I realized he wasn't making fun of me—he was just making fun. Later he was living at the Plaza and my first showroom was on Fifty-Eighth and Park, so he dropped by. One day he announced he was doing fabrics for Schumacher, so he wouldn't need me anymore. That was his kind of humor. I did an important commission for his last residence.

There were two good things that I did in my career. I owned my company—or the majority of the stock—so I could call all the shots and make mistakes until I learned not to. And I worked with clients I very much respected. I would try to figure out what they wanted *me* for, so I could give them what they wanted, and this would pull me out of ruts. I would do new things I hadn't done before, like designing and producing fabrics for Pan Am. And that was invaluable. It led me further

Seasonal upholstery and pillows for the conversation pit at the Miller House featured deep reds in winter (top) and neutrals in summer (bottom), Columbus, Indiana, 1957.

and further astray, into different techniques and materials. I could avoid sales managers saying "make last year's collection."

How do you see yourself and your role in the arc of modernism?

Young people are constantly inventing the mid-century—imagining how things were. They're creative and you tell it the way *they* imagined it to be, which is often wrong. I try to prevent that when possible. I once made a fabric called Baghdad and then someone wrote a whole story about "Jack in Baghdad," but I've never been there. History is created!

Do you feel like that time is romanticized?

"Modern" had already started in people's minds before the war was over. It was quite different later in the 1960s, when contracts and big projects came in and retailers were changing to bigger production, not small makers, but large industries that thought differently than anyone did in the 1950s. It changed. And we also became more international. Knoll and Larsen opened in Europe.

We all thought we'd bought off the Establishment, that we had enlightened them or won them over, but they simply bought us off. Fifty million dollars or fifty stories, our heads were turned very quickly! Homeowners were small potatoes; we didn't have time for them. Salesmen didn't want to bother selling six chairs when they might get an order for two hundred.

It wasn't all bad. The Europeans were often more discerning than Americans; modern was not new to them. But it was very important, intellectually. People established their families on expensive furnishings, often gifts from their in-laws. A chair was forever, whereas for us, the feeling was, "that'll do until we get something better." In the United States, we were much more influenced by advertising, the market, and the people next door.

How do you distinguish art from design or craft? Or do you prefer to not make such distinctions?

I'm often called an artist, and I refuse to accept that. I'm a maker. What I make is useful. I am

trying to teach that craft is not necessarily handcraft. It's a quality of identifying the materials and the process of how things are made. A feeling that must persist in what's manufactured, because we're not going to have hand craftsmen very much longer.

Who are you trying to teach?

Consumers. To perceive what craftsmanship is, to enjoy it, and seek it out. Machine-made goods can be beautiful. They can have a sense of materials, function, and process. But one has to look for them. It's the same as with food. There's food that seems to be handcrafted and have flavor and texture. And it's probably the same with music, but it's difficult.

Government and industry want to persuade us to be sheep, to buy what they're selling. And not to think twice that there might be another way of doing things. Those of us who are perceptive must battle that. Tastelessness is a challenge. If you don't understand physical things like touch—understanding it in the unknown, the unseen, the maneuvers of politics—you're not going to understand that either, or care! There's a very strong minority trying to upset all that, but so far it hasn't worked very well. There are certainly those of us who are trying to buck the tide.

From your vantage point, how do you see the current state of textile design?

The most exciting country for textile design in the last forty years has been Japan. The designers for Issey Miyake and Junichi Arai and various leaders of the craft movements are doing the best work and they are successful with a worldwide audience. Here in the United States, there are exceptions. Some good things are happening, but generally it's so much more commercial than when I started.

And now it's hard to do what I did. No one had warehouses of modern fabric back then; you had to find a weaver and order it. It was easier to start, because you didn't need all that inventory and investment. In Britain, postgraduates aren't getting jobs in industry, but they're making things and learning how to sell them. They know their clients, and who's buying their products, and it's helping.

Textiles and upholstery for Frank Lloyd Wright's Fallingwater, commissioned by Edgar Kaufmann, Jr., Mill Run, Pennsylvania, 1980s.

How did you first become interested in collecting?

My teacher in interior architecture had taken long summer trips in Asia before the war. She had beautiful things everywhere. We envied her, and she said as long as you buy one beautiful thing every year, you'll soon have some nice things to live with. And I thought, if you did it every week or every month, it would go faster. So I started collecting Indian baskets from thrift shops in Seattle, among other things. I furnished my house from antique stores and thrift shops, and anything that my mother didn't have. And I haven't stopped since.

The mission of LongHouse Reserve "exemplifies living with art in all forms." What sort of impact do you hope to achieve?

Generally speaking, seeing something in a place is a better teaching tool than simply seeing a photograph of it. Partly because we're hardened to photographs, we're not impressed much by them. So both in terms of gardens and living space, I consider LongHouse a teaching tool, a case study. *Arts & Architecture* was very successful in the 1940s, producing Case Study Houses by promising architects. They were small houses, but they showed people simpler, better ways of thinking about things without spending a lot of money. For me, LongHouse is a similar case study. And we have lots of visitors and lots of tours.

Why split your time between a pied-à-terre in the city and your country home?

I think both are necessary. The only thing cities are good for is culture. Otherwise it's better in the country.

Top: Silk hangings for Sears Bank & Trust,
commissioned by Skidmore, Owings &
Merrill, Chicago, 1974.

Bottom right: Upholstery for Braniff
Airlines, 1969.

Bottom left: Wall hangings for First Unitarian
Church, commissioned by Louis Kahn,
Rochester, New York, 1968.

What inspires you?

I lie awake at night dreaming up projects. It's pretty much the same as when I was four years old, or when I was in school. During the week I would figure out what my friends and I were going to accomplish on weekends, and that hasn't changed. The idea of "hanging out" seems like a terrible waste of time! What does that accomplish? Just make something. I did it with my employees, and I do it with our volunteers and staff at LongHouse. I sleep a lot in the daytime because I don't at night—I'm dreaming up the next adventure.

Who's been your most important mentor?

Stanley Marcus, of Neiman Marcus. He was creative, and he demanded excellence and ingenuity. He also traveled, so that's how I got to know him—we'd suddenly be in Tel Aviv on the same day. I learned many things from Stanley, but not everything. On some levels, he was rather cautious. He'd usually buy the "next best," in terms of art or something he was purchasing personally. Otherwise, he was a pretty smart man. We were on several boards together, and he'd always speak last instead of wasting words during the argument. We'd all pick up our pencils and open our ears, because he usually had the right answer.

Edward Larrabee Barnes was such a gentleman. So likable, and attractive, and simple. He would go away for four days with the same suit and tie. And he was still the most popular person at any place.

Frank Lloyd Wright was magnetic. When he did his very commercial fabric and furniture line, we were all furious with him. We went to a benefit, and he asked if we'd ever tried swimming upstream. He said he had all of his life, and now he seems to have come down so far, so fast he could talk to us eye to eye. [*Laughs*] It was well said, we couldn't really argue with him. That takes some skill.

Is there a moment or a project that stands out as your biggest professional or personal triumph?

One of them was my retrospective show at Palais du Louvre. The first American to have a one-person show there was my friend Mark Tobey. I later convinced them to do a show with Dale Chihuly, who was my protégé, and also from Seattle.

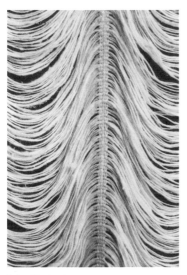

Bahia Blind, 1964.

Terry cloth towel from a collection designed for J. P. Stevens, 1965.

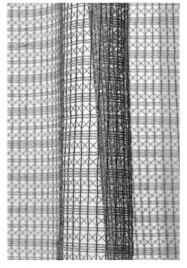

Interplay, a woven textile inspired by traditional African basketry, 1962.

Top: Inspired by a shrine at Ise, Japan, LongHouse Reserve sits on a 16-acre sculpture garden and reserve that has been open to the public since 1992, East Hampton, New York.

Bottom: Objects from Larsen's personal collection.

How did Dale Chihuly become your protégé?
He had also been in interior architecture. We had the same teacher, at different times. She said I had to help him because he worked as hard as I did, and he was trying to weave glass strips. I sent him to Harvey Littleton to learn to blow glass. We've been friends since, and he's never forgotten. Most people don't remember how it happened that they became famous, but not Dale.

Is there a moment that stands out as a setback, or something you had to bounce back from that was difficult or challenging?
I was once convinced by a vice president that since I'd done everything else, why not try fashion? I tried. And it was all wrong. One night I would do a ball gown, and the next night I would do bathing shorts. We had a few successes—actually Neiman Marcus tried out a hundred garments and came back with a big order. We either had to change everything to fulfill such an order or stop. We decided to stop.

Afterward, my staff said, "Jack, don't stop doing crazy things." That was terrific. They could so easily have said, "Now we see why you're so crazy." We lived through it.

You grew up in the Northwest, attended Cranbrook in eastern Michigan, and you lived in Los Angeles, New York, and now reside in Long Island. Which place do you consider home?
Any place I've lived, I've tried to make it my own. When I spent a winter in London, I took along some fabric to put on the walls. I've often had to hide a sofa or cover it up because it was so ugly. I once had a chauffeur's apartment in the Hamptons, and I used beach towels to cover the upholstery. That's an excellent way to learn: renting a beach house and figuring out how to hide things or cover them up, or get something to distract the eye. You have to be creative. You wouldn't do such experiments if it was going to be forever. But to practice creativity—it doesn't come without practice. I always practice it. Fortunately now I can usually find places that aren't so ugly to begin with.

What advice would you give yourself at the beginning of your career?
To do exactly what you want. Follow the heart! The head can play all kinds of games; you can rationalize anything! I was offered two great college jobs with good income, and then I came to New York with no reason except that I loved it here. I didn't know that this was the only place to be a designer because the press is here, the market is here. So following the heart was the right thing to do.

Getting a job—that sounds pretty dull—unless it's a footstep to something more interesting. The heart is a good reason. But we're taught to do the things we "should" and so it's hard. You can't get to the sun from the moon. You might as well try for the top, and if you don't get there, you'll probably have fun trying. I certainly have!

Ingo Maurer

—

Lighting Designer
b. 1932

Ingo Maurer, founder of the eponymous avant-garde lighting house, never intended to be a designer. The son of a fisherman, Maurer was born and raised on Reichenau Island in Germany's Lake Constance. Difficult postwar years and the loss of his parents at a young age led Maurer to pursue a skilled trade early on. His chance entry into the design world came through an apprenticeship in typography, a formative experience that attuned his eye to precision and the notion of visual poetry in the everyday. His studies took him abroad to San Francisco and New York City for brief stints, instilling within him a romanticism for the United States and a fondness for the bold, brash statements of American pop art.

Maurer's transition to industrial design emerged from a sudden desire to work with light. His big lightbulb moment, as it were, came with an epiphanic appreciation for Thomas Edison as he lay in his bed one night after a meal of pasta and wine, gazing up at a ceiling fixture. His very first lighting design—the 1966 Bulb table lamp—paid tribute to the everyday incandescent, one of many references to Edison that he would produce over the years. In the 1970s, Maurer also traveled frequently to Japan, seeking the tutelage of a master fan maker, Shigeki-san, and becoming acquainted with influential Japanese-American artist and designer Isamu Noguchi.

In spite of his reverence for these forebears, Maurer's own work has persistently forged ahead, incorporating emerging technologies to both commercial and artistic acclaim. He was among the first to experiment with the formal possibilities of halogen, for example, with his 1984 YaYaHo, a kit-of-parts lighting system with assorted pendants that could be strung across a span of wires, and then adjusted, reconfigured, and customized into varying compositions. In recent years, Maurer and his team, ever on the forefront, have extended their focus to working with LEDs and OLEDs, not to mention illuminated surfaces, metals, and furnishings.

Describing his process as beginning, always, with light first and form second, Maurer is known to achieve artistry from an immaterial medium, imbuing spatial environments—from interiors, public spaces, and art installations to products, and fashion runways—with drama, theatrical dimension, and a sense of ephemerality. The subject of numerous solo exhibitions, he has produced more than 120 product designs over the course of fifty years. Now bicontinental, Maurer divides his time between Munich and Manhattan, a cherished second home and continual source for inspiration he visits as often as possible.

When did you first realize you had an interest in design?

I have always had this urge to create, even when I was a very small boy. I always had some kind of toy and was playing with little twigs and things like that; you know, always creating.

But I was very uneducated because I came from a generation that fought in World War II. I was fortunately not in the war, but the schooling was terrible. So I became a typographer, which turned out to be very good because you have to look and see very precisely.

How did you become a typographer?

Our father died, our mother died. I couldn't finish school and was forced to learn a profession and make a living, because there were five kids in our family. We were really five kids trying to make it. When there was a little more cash flow through my work in typography, I attended the graphic academy here in Munich for three years. And that, of course, gave me a new perspective and outlook; training, joy, and pain, all of these things together. I was an apprentice for four years, which I didn't

enjoy much at the time, but later on felt and saw how important it had been. It taught me discipline, and a way of looking at things carefully.

And typography has a lot to do with light. I enjoy recognizing that in my work.

How do the two mediums relate, in your mind?

Lettering can be so beautiful, with all the spaces between the letters that create a kind of light—a rhythm—that you can observe in both lighting and typography; I enjoy this very much. In typography, you also have to be enormously precise in your perception. And perception, of course, is extremely important not only in work, but also in life.

How did you shift from typography to lighting design?

My first lamp was the Bulb in 1966, but I'll tell you how I really came to light: I was in Venice working with glass, and I had taken a siesta. After I drank a whole bottle of red wine by myself with spaghetti, I went back to my little room and lay on my back, looking up. Suddenly, this light bulb really presented a sort of magic to me. At that very

Left: Ingo Maurer alongside his 1970 design Light Structure, produced in collaboration with Peter Hamburger.

Above: Maurer with What We Do Counts, an LED-integrated lamp released in 2015.

Comic Explosion, designed in 2010 with limited production.

moment, I jumped up on the mattress and knew what I wanted to do. That's where my career started as a lighting designer—I had this vision, I started to produce the design and went around to show it to people, and they liked it. I wanted it to be commercially viable and successful. I had a family already, with two kids, and I had to pay for diapers.

In your twenties, you lived and worked in San Francisco and New York. What led you to America, and how did your time abroad influence you?

After the war, as a young man in Germany witnessing all these speeches about America and reading literature about America, I got very excited by what I heard about the country. I always wished to leave Germany and maybe even Europe, because I felt very fenced in. Being in America opened me up tremendously. I could have stayed longer, but my wife wanted to go back to Europe, and I was very stressed by that. To this day, I'm still saying, "I'm going back!" Afterwards, we wanted to live in London, but at the time didn't have a working permit and it was difficult, so we finally came back to Germany for the first time. I suffered for at least

three or four months after that. But I somehow made it so I could come back to America to stay. I swore I'd be coming back, and I did.

How did New York's emerging pop art scene affect your approach?

Well, I was mostly impressed by America. I was impressed with the architecture that I saw, but of course pop art gave me a big, big lift.

You also traveled frequently to Japan in the 1970s and met a traditional fan maker, Shigeki-san. How did his work influence your own?

I was interested in licensed production in Japan, went there, and really loved it. I was looking for something special, and in Japan there was a movement back to nature. I found Shigeki-san and I worked with him.

When and how we met is a long story. I was looking for him, without speaking a single word of Japanese, and I didn't have a translator. When I finally found him, we stood in front of each other and we looked into each other's eyes—that was the foundation, the basis of our interaction. He was

Above, left and right: Canned Light, designed by Christoph Matthias and Hagen Sczech for Ingo Maurer GmbH in 2003. The piece can be wall-mounted or hung as a pendant.

Left: Maurer's first lighting design, Bulb, designed in 1966, houses a bulb-within-a-bulb made from a polished chromium-plated metal base and hand-blown crystal glass from Murano.

a warm and very simple person, very dedicated
to his work.

Using the fragile fans in my work was a risk,
because of the heat generated by the light. Loving
risks on all levels, I took one with the paper fan
pieces. Shigeki-san was a wonderful master. I tried
to meet with him again, some years later, but
he had unfortunately passed. His son wanted to
continue the craft, but ended up going into
computers. Shigeki-san's art has definitely died.

Who do you consider a mentor in your exploration of light?

Shigeki-san is a very strong personality in my soul
to this day. I met Isamu Noguchi several times and
have been his guest. I've also worked with Issey
Miyaki, and architects like Jean Nouvel. Now I have
a new job, working with one of the later designs of
the late Oscar Niemeyer. People come to me
because they expect a deeply thoughtful solution
to a particular challenge. This makes my life so rich.
It also makes me, sometimes, sleepless with joy.

A mentor, for me, is a bit different. I'll tell you
about a few. When I started, I had no idea who
Achille Castiglioni or Vico Magistretti was. Then
I came to Italy and learned about it all. My biggest
support came from thinking about and appreciating
the work of artists like Brancusi; I still get excited
by his work. I also like Giacometti—his *Spoon
Woman* sculpture is unbelievable. I have a big

picture of it in my loft in New York, just blown
up because I love that piece so much. People who
convince me of humanity, and of its strength—
those are the ones I consider my mentors, living
or dead. It's not that I could ever achieve what
those masters have done; I absorb the energy of
their work, in a way, into myself.

You've worked with light for nearly fifty years, subverting conventional notions of the medium and continually pushing it into new directions. What drives your creativity?

I consider myself like a weed, the way I grew into
design. Sometimes it's better not to know where
the energy comes from—just let yourself give in to
what you feel. This is my philosophy: don't plan
too much. Take life as it comes. It's exciting that
you can have all these wonderful flowers in life,
and different possibilities to encounter. It has been
very, very exciting, and it still is. I work with sixty
or seventy people now, and I feel very responsible
toward those who work for me.

Do you approach commissioned or commercial works differently from artistic, limited-edition pieces?

I follow my instincts and I think commercially—
I never make the things in my collection as art. It's
about making functional lights that have a certain
expression. A lot of people have described it as

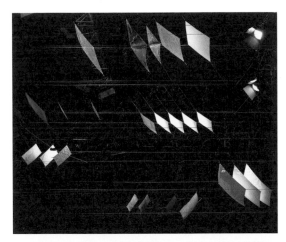

Above, left and right: Runway installation for Issey Miyake's A/W 2000 presentation in Paris, 1999.

Left: Maurer's Zettel'z, made from stainless steel, heat-resistant satin-frosted glass, and Japanese paper, 1998.

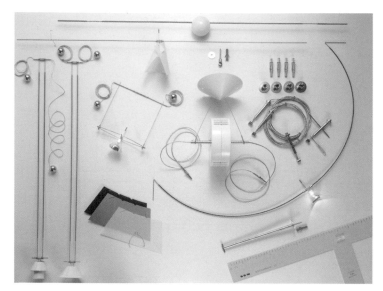

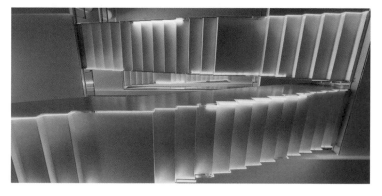

Top, left and right: Maurer's groundbreaking YaYaHo low-voltage halogen lighting system, a kit-of-parts set designed in 1984 that can be adjusted and installed in varying configurations.

Middle and bottom: Interior lighting for a staircase and entrance hall for KPMG's Munich office, 2001.

Opposite: Installation views of *Provoking Magic: Ingo Maurer* at the Cooper Hewitt, Smithsonian Design Museum, 2007.

poetry, but you cannot make poetry; you feel it and you just do it. I'd hate to be standing beside myself, watching myself work. I would become too conscious of everything going improperly. As I said before, risk has been a big element in my life on all levels. If you don't take risks, you'll never learn about yourself. It's more important, to me, that we don't complain of what we do, and instead have the passion for it.

Your works are so diverse, shown and used in a range of venues and environments. How does the eventual site of a lighting project or piece play into its design?
First, I have to feel the space. Maybe even before, I have to meet the soul of the client. I have to feel what they are. We don't just take on anything; we reject a lot of work. For me, it's important that we stay on a very harmonious level together—that we are at ease with each other. It's not just about money. It's about sharing in common the most wonderful gift that has been given to us: being human. Then, of course, of utmost importance is the space at hand, and how the dialogue goes with the architect, for instance.

As technology changes the formal possibilities of lighting, you've been quick to embrace new forms. You were one of the first to use halogen light, for example.

I was, I really was. The Ya Ya Ho halogen system was designed in the early 1980s. And I worked with LED to make Bellissima Brutta, which means, just as it sounds, "beautiful ugly." The first prototype of it is owned by Murray Moss. I also came up with the first OLED product. OLEDs are very expensive, though they've become a bit less expensive more recently. The light of an OLED is a kind of a monotonous light, though it carries a lot of possibility for the lighting market.

You've expressed a fascination with Thomas Edison, referring to the prototypical light bulb as manifesting "the perfect meeting of industry and poetry."
Yes, exactly—it's a fantastic symbiosis. We made a special show for Edison's hundredth birthday. My Edison lamp is a holograph that doesn't have an actual bulb, though it does make light in the image of one. It's a collector's item, made with a film that allows the object to appear. The fascination is that it's as if you have a light on the table, though there's no light bulb actually there.

How do you feel about digital light?
I find it without soul. My hope is that the industry will become more conscious, and hold a different perception toward light. I hope—and I will try to work on it for the rest of my life—to try to make very good, humane light that makes you feel well.

Opposite, left: A one-off prototype for Bellissima Brutta, 1997.

Opposite, right: Wo Bist du, Edison...?, an homage to Thomas Edison, featuring a holograph-projected image of a bulb within a plastic shade, 2005.

Left: Dew Drops table lamp, made from a hanging, transparent plastic sheet with 750 integrated LEDs, 2013.

Your work defies categorization, integrating a wide range of materials, and in some cases, introducing new typologies. How do you choose or decide which materials to work with? Is it a constant research process?

Of course, all the time. We're always keeping track, and we're lucky that many producers and manufacturers come to us and ask us to develop things together. Or, if we're able, to use the technology they bring to us. That's a very exciting moment. We have a recent project that has been really, really thrilling to work on: Dew Drops, as I call it. It's made of foil-like sheets with little LEDs, very minimal, and you can see the conductors that are synced up.

Through it all, what would you consider your biggest setback?

The biggest setback for me is that I haven't lived a private life. My work has been my life and my passion.

And your most significant professional triumph?

Of course, the second you asked me this question, I thought of the moment—which feels like not so long ago—when I looked back and realized what I've done over so many years. As I said earlier, I grew like a weed. I've been very lucky and there are weeds out there that are very huge [*laughs*]. I've had some moments working with really great

people—friends, colleagues, clients, and employees. That's always a big lift for me. Otherwise, I don't think much; I think consciously overthinking too much can be destructive. I often try to solve problems and visualize details at nighttime, when I can't sleep.

What advice would you give to emerging designers?

Above all, be ready to work hard and show discipline. Don't keep your head in the clouds with the first couple of things you've thought up. You have to remain down-to-earth, with your feet on the ground. This is very important. And, of course, never give up if you fail.

I like to work with young people very much. It's great to see what kind of possibility they might have within them. The young Ingo Maurer had to invent and discover something like light to feed his two kids, pay for diapers and food. I was pressured, but I was free to design things that people liked. It was a hard beginning, but it was good, and I am really content with how things are now. I feel very blessed. And I must say, the best light is the one that comes from someone's heart.

Alessandro Mendini

—

Architect, Industrial Designer, Editor
b. 1931

With a philosopher's mind and eye, Alessandro Mendini has worked seamlessly across multiple disciplines—architecture, product and furniture design, and publishing—but it was the expressive power of illustration that first attracted him to the creative world. As a young child, the Milan-born designer was drawn to the imagery conjured by Saul Steinberg and Walt Disney, masters of a playful whimsy that one might trace in Mendini's own critical, irreverent body of work.

A leading figure of Italian Radical design in the 1970s onward, Mendini was a founding member of several progressive design collectives devoted to challenging the status quo, including the Global Tools "anti-school" and Studio Alchimia, which sowed the seeds for the Memphis Group, the short-lived yet influential cohort of countercultural designers led by Ettore Sottsass in the 1980s.

As a journalist and publisher, Mendini also documented and disseminated the activities and proceedings of these groups from a string of chief editorial posts at leading Italian design magazines *Casabella*, *Modo*, and *Domus*. Among the visually striking avant-garde projects featured during his fifteen-year tenure in publishing was a 1974 demonstration in which he and his staff burned a Lassù chair—one of Mendini's own designs—for the cover of *Casabella*. Lending itself more to sculpture than function, the Lassù, a four-legged chair set atop a sharply sloped pyramidal base, was a symbol of what Mendini viewed as the establishment's problematic worship of the "high priests" of design. Set aflame as an effigy, it voiced a rebellious articulation of dissent that was—visually and metaphorically—emblazoned in the annals of design history.

Mendini's theoretical inclinations have manifested in buildings, products, and furniture designs with equal rigor, drawing upon a wide swath of historical, literary, and cultural references. His 1978 Poltrona di Proust, named for the French novelist, takes the form of a Neo-Baroque armchair covered entirely in a multicolored Pointillist pattern, down to its ornamental wooden frame. Cast as a modern-day "redesign" of styles popular during Proust's time, the chair melds contemporaneous aesthetic movements and modes of thinking, entailing intricate details and production processes that bely the chair's central function. Initially conceived as a one-off, the celebrated design continues to be made in limited-edition variations. Mendini has also designed tableware and furnishings for several Italian manufacturers, including Alessi and Zanotta. His built projects include the Groninger Museum in the Netherlands, the Alessi residence in Omegna, Italy, and Arosa Casino in Switzerland.

From his studio in Milan, a large loft located downstairs from his apartment, Mendini continues to run Atelier Mendini in collaboration with his brother, Francesco, creating provocative works and commissions at the intersection of art, design, and architecture.

When did you first become curious about design?

I always loved drawing as a child, and was particularly fond of Walt Disney and Saul Steinberg. I went to a German-language elementary school, a science- and math-oriented high school, and received my degree in architecture from the Milan Polytechnic. But my interest in design *really* began when I was the editor in chief of the magazine *Casabella* in 1973. It was around the time we founded the Global Tools collective as a school for crafts. It was when I designed the *oggetti ad uso spirituale* (objects for spiritual use) that were made for the covers of *Casabella*.

You've long been regarded a leading figure in radical design and postmodernism. How would you describe the cultural climate of the 1970s? What sorts of issues did those movements seek to address?

Radical design was a movement that related all design issues back to primordial origins, and it preceded postmodernism. It coincided with the student movements of 1968. *Casabella* documented these ideologies in Italy (Milan, Florence, Venice, Turin, and Naples), elsewhere in Europe (Vienna, Barcelona, and Berlin), and overseas (Los Angeles).

Radical design worked on the hypothesis of a Communist society. It was aimed at opposing the mechanisms of large-scale industry and consumerism—the hand prevails over the pencil. Radical design and postmodernism have no direct relationship, but both criticize functionalism.

In 1975 you famously designed the Lassù—a nonfunctional chair not quite made for sitting—and set it aflame for the cover of *Casabella*. What inspired this rebellious, ritualistic act?

The burning chair was a performance in order to make a cover for *Casabella*. Those were the dramatic days, when bronze sculptures in yoga positions were being burned on squares in Burma as acts of protest. I wanted to show that even objects have a life, and that it can be tragic. Their trajectory goes from conception, to birth, through their years of life, old age, and finally death—which can be ritual. It would be nice if every object, even the simplest and most utilitarian, were used in a ritual manner. This would mean that every action we perform purposefully would have its own dignity.

The Lassù chair has multiple meanings: One, it is an affirmation that in your house, you can possess a small throne where you feel important. Two, the burning expresses that even objects have a life, with a trajectory going from birth to living to dying. Three, it proves that an object can produce a performance. At the time, the Lassù was publicly received as an artistic installation.

You were also a core member of Memphis, and before that, Alchimia. As a public intellectual, what schools of thought were you influenced by, or reacting against, in your early work?

I have always been influenced by romantic and spiritual theories like those of Søren Kierkegaard, Friedrich Nietzsche, and Herman Hesse. In the beginning, I studied expressionist architects such as Gaudí, Erich Mendelsohn, and Rudolf Steiner. I am interested in all groups and their stories—the Omega Workshop, the Pre-Raphaelites with William Morris, the Deutscher Werkbund, the Wiener Werkstätte, the Bauhaus, Ulm, and even Droog Design. Design groups are incredible sources of energy and verve.

How does working in a group differ from working on an individual basis?

I have always felt the need to work in a group, but on a parallel, I also need fully isolated activities. I need to discuss things and enjoy the synergy created within a team, but I also need to have space to draw and think on my own. The Radicals, Alchimia, the editorial staffs of *Casabella*, *Modo*, and *Domus*, and my atelier continue to be sources of exceptional experiences that I certainly would not have had if I had remained isolated.

What were some of the core ideologies of Alchimia, and how did it contribute to your later work with Memphis?

Alchimia originated in contradiction with academic culture and against traditional design. The attitude was liberating, peripheral, and anticonformist. Its visual language was connected to pop art, and in my case, cosmic fantasies of the world of futurism. Alchimia was the launchpad of opposition that paradoxically generated the institutional force of Memphis; two opposite approaches to romantic design. It is certain that of all my different experiences, Alchimia is one of the most profound, and it continues to give me methods for working.

The hypothesis of futurism, beyond its political ideas, was to apply style to every single thing—

Opposite: Mendini's Lassù chair, set aflame for a cover shoot for *Casabella*, 1974 (left) and a 1983 iteration of the Lassù chair, made of bronze (right).

Below: Illustration of men's shoes for Robot Sentimentale, 1983.

Right: Arredo Vestitivo (furniture dress), a performative piece produced by Studio Alchimia for the Italian fashion label Fiorucci, 1982.

toys, furniture, architecture, et cetera. This was the same hypothesis that Alchimia had. The styles of futurism and Alchimia are intertwined, especially through [Fortunato] Depero (clothes, tapestries, and graphic design). Memphis, a movement parallel to Alchimia, played a social role that was more institutional. Personally, I use methods derived from the relationship between different cultures, meaning still futurism, but also cubism, pointillism, art deco, and Bauhaus.

What is your reaction to the current resurgence of the Memphis-influenced, postmodern aesthetic? It's made a big style comeback in recent years.

Yes, I see much interest in those old heroic movements. I think that the people studying them today are looking for something that does not exist anymore, especially in terms of design ethics, utopian vision, and certain methods tied to art. It must be said that radical design in Italy was parallel to arte povera, and postmodernism was

parallel to the Transavanguardia. Nowadays, designers are dispersed and isolated in the ocean of virtual reality, so perhaps they are looking for roots and protection.

For many different reasons, I feel the present-day is devoid of groups, and this is a terrible shortcoming, in that groups have traditionally written design's actual history. One of the reasons is indubitably the solitary conversation that a designer has with the Internet. This virtual community is made up of groups of people who are actually, physically alone.

In a way, postmodernity is about collaging a diverse set of references, histories, and symbols. What were some of your major sources of inspiration or reference, whether formally, historically, intellectually, or otherwise?

Forming the base of my visual alphabets and language are the Vienna secession, Czechoslovakian cubism, and futurism. The Vienna secession,

et cetera, influenced me through the elevated expressivity of their shapes, their symbolism, their eclectic use of materials, and their romanticism. I also owe much to the histories of the magazines I directed, especially *Casabella* and its early director Ernesto Nathan Rogers, as well as *Domus* and its founder, Giò Ponti. Rogers, Ponti, and Pierre Restany were *maestri* with whom I had wonderful exchanges, affectionate and interesting, and each of these men opened my horizons in a different way.

Across your work, you often combine different mediums at once: art, fashion, furniture, performance, and so on. Do you feel there is a distinction between art and design? If so, how would you describe it?

I think of myself as a person putting on a show of *commedia dell'arte* (and tragedies, too), where objects, furniture, action, and architecture are composed and dismantled in a dynamic patchwork. These things interact with the audience and myself. It is an exciting centrifugal game, but very laborious. It ranges from craftsmanship to industrial design, from words to silence, and from optimism to pessimism. It is a kind of backstage assembly.

Do you think the role of the designer has changed over time as people have become more educated about design? In other words, does today's designer still work backstage?

I can't say if people today understand design better than before. In developing my work, I concentrate more on the project itself than on the audience.

You've had a long editing and writing career. How did you get involved in publishing, and balance your design practice in tandem?

In the fifteen years I spent directing magazines (five years each, in order: *Casabella*, *Modo*, *Domus*), most of my time was dedicated to the magazines as the editor in chief, as a critic, and as a journalist. From this activity of "orchestration" came my literary way of designing, and my habit of working with many groups. Anyway, I would have also loved to be a writer, and I have written very much. I still write methodically and continually, almost every Sunday. Perhaps my most structured writings were the editorials for *Casabella*, *Modo*, and *Domus*.

What was your involvement in the founding of Domus Academy? How did its curriculum differ from other schools?

The relationship of *Domus* magazine with many schools, universities, and groups led almost naturally to the invention of Domus Academy. At a certain point, it came naturally to conceive of an institute for research and collateral communications. The resulting setup was the fruit of many discussions, and the school has always had its own qualified originality. It was initially supposed to be a neo-crafts school, similar to Global Tools, but then it became a highly experimental school. I contributed to founding it, but I never taught there. I was interested in creating the structure, not working there.

I have almost never taught; only for two years at the Universität für angewandte Kunst in Vienna. I don't care for places of institutional teaching, and I don't like bureaucracy. I prefer communicating informally and on a personal level.

Who have been your most important mentors?
There was Fortunato Depero, and Balla, Marinetti, Sant'Elia, and many others. Depero was perhaps the most creative of all of them. He designed very important theater sets. He had a studio called Casa del Mago. He was a great artist. In his house in Rovereto (now a museum), I once held an exhibition called *Mendini versus Depero*. If Fortunato Depero had never existed, my work would be very different.

Who have been your most influential peers?
My way of designing is very autobiographical. I cannot be the maestro of anyone. Perhaps my existential testimony can be worthwhile.

What has been your greatest professional triumph?
I enjoy controlling my design game in its totality. Perhaps the object that best represents my fragile and fragmented way of working is the Poltrona di Proust, an entirely ambiguous piece of work that has continued to regenerate itself in my hands since 1978. The latest version is made in white statuary marble from Carrara.

I thought of the Poltrona di Proust as an object made only of "thought" and not of "design." The project is ambiguous because it is neither painting, nor design, nor sculpture. Then it contains the idea of obtaining the real from the fake. It is the idea of a literary object that would and could create a novel. The first Poltrona in 1978 was followed by an elevated variety of models and methods, meaning that the novel's story never ends.

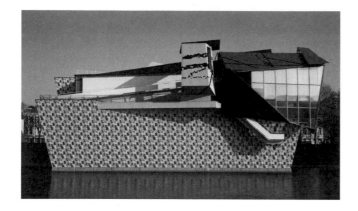

Tell us about some current interests or projects.
As happens to everyone, I am currently discovering the mysteries of China, its people, and their enormous history. Chinese vases are amazing.

You currently run an atelier with your brother. What is a typical workday like? What are you working on now?
I work with my brother Francesco, who is an architect. He's eight years younger than me. He is a fundamentally important person and a friend to me. He is the head of our atelier, and all of us place ourselves in his hands for his competence and his kindness. Like every office in Milan, we work from morning to night, but there are no fixed hours. There is no hierarchy. We spend much time talking and wasting time. I live above the atelier, and arrive directly from my house, connected by a small staircase. I have the privilege of being able to work on Saturdays and Sundays, too.

I work on many small objects with virtuosic artisans. I experiment with shapes and materials, and make things that are half prototype, half sculpture. With the atelier, with my brother Francesco, we work on a wide range of projects, from interiors to large buildings, art direction, industrial products, graphic design, and the design of exhibitions. In addition, I make wax pastel drawings on cardboard. I call them *Mostri*.

How have your ideas on design and making changed over the years? Do you have a different perspective on things?

I was born introverted and rather pessimistic. But over the years, I've found that I needed to be more optimistic and serene, and I want to communicate this positive message to others. In my mind and in my psyche, I have a number of permanent obsessions: death, love, violence, goodness, fragility, and solitude. Over time I have modified these *idées fixes* in ever different ways, updating their language to fit social changes. I think of all my objects as characters, for better or for worse, in a tragicomedy in which also I take part.

As a pioneer of the field, what is your opinion on the state of Italian design today?
The many invisible experiments being conducted by young Italian designers today are laboratory exercises of an enigmatic type, closed upon themselves. These designers are solitary, yet connected by unknown networks—these experiments are invisible because they are published little or not even made. I hope that their intelligence will give birth to a new radicalism.

Each era carries its own definition of radicalism—what do you think would be radical in the present day?
Radicalism today would need to oppose society's cold realistic pragmatism and aim for faraway objectives by raising its sights toward alternative horizons.

Jens Risom

Furniture Designer
b. 1916

Pictured alongside leading American designers George Nelson, Edward Wormley, Eero Saarinen, Harry Bertoia, and Charles Eames in a 1961 *Playboy* feature, Jens Risom stands out from the pack. The only figure not seated, he rests his hand gently on the back of a C140—an armchair he designed in 1955—its curved walnut frame and apricot upholstery an open invitation. The legendary centerfold captures midcentury furniture design at its peak, and casts Risom as one of its leading figures.

Meticulously crafted, with clean, pure lines, the C140 is typical of the Danish modern furniture Risom introduced to the American market, first through a partnership with Hans Knoll and later through his own ventures, Jens Risom Design and Design Control. The son of a renowned Danish architect, Risom was born and raised in Copenhagen. At the urging of his father, he studied business before turning to furniture design and attending Copenhagen's School of Arts and Crafts, where he was a student of modernist furniture designers Ole Wanscher and Kaare Klint. A few years after graduating, a chance encounter with an American ambassador, who advised him to move to the United States, sent Risom across the Atlantic and set his career in motion.

Upon his arrival to the States in 1939, Risom landed a job with interior designer Dan Cooper. In 1941 he left to partner with manufacturing entrepreneur and German émigré Hans Knoll. A four-month, cross-country research trip to study the needs of architects, designers, and the American market resulted in the Hans Knoll Furniture Company, which launched in 1942 with its signature 600 Series, the majority of which Risom had designed. The collection of Scandinavian-inspired chairs, stools, and tables incorporated surplus wartime materials such as parachute webbing paired with prefabricated and easy-to-assemble cherry wood parts. From this fledgling collection, Knoll built a foundation, becoming a leading design firm in the postwar period; several pieces of the original 600 Series are still manufactured today.

Risom was drafted into the army in 1943, and upon returning from service he founded his own company, with himself as the sole designer. Jens Risom Design expanded quickly during the 1950s, serving residential, and later commercial, markets with showrooms across the country and licensing agreements overseas. In order to spend more time on design, Risom sold the company in 1970, but mismanagement by the new owner ultimately led Jens Risom Design to fold. Three years later, Risom founded his freelance business, Design Control, its name referring both to his exacting standards and the conviction that he'd never again cede authority over his own practice.

At ninety-nine, Risom has yet to retire. In the last decade, he's collaborated with Ralph Pucci, reissued designs through Rocket Gallery and Benchmark in Europe, and launched new products for Design Within Reach. His family mantra—"If you're going to do a job, do it right"—remains at the heart of every decision.

Your father was an architect. Did his work influence your career?

No, in fact, the opposite. I didn't want to be an architect because I could see all the difficulties. In furniture design, you could design it, you could finish it—you could easily do it all.

How did your schooling in Copenhagen affect your approach to design?

I didn't start with furniture making, but with furniture design. It was a school for cabinetmakers, but I was allowed in partly because my father was an architect, and also because of sketches that I had done. After I graduated from that design school, I got a job with a very good furniture designer.

How would you compare your experience in Copenhagen to design education in the United States?

I don't know much about education in the States, to tell you the truth. When I came to the States in 1939, I didn't know how primitive design education was. There was no furniture education, period. There were technical schools, all very uncreative. There wasn't even modern furniture in America—people still put traditional furniture in their homes. A modern house would not necessarily get modern furniture.

After a chance meeting in 1938, you decided to move to the United States. Who did you meet that day?

I was walking from the train station one day, and a man pulled up in a large black car and asked if I was going to town. I said yes, and he offered to drive me. He was the American ambassador to Denmark. We drove to the embassy in Copenhagen and he introduced me to many people who had connections with architecture in the United States.

One of your first design jobs in New York was working with a young furniture and interior designer. What was the experience like?

I had a job in furniture and interiors with Dan Cooper, who had a decorating shop. He was beginning to think about contemporary pieces, and he only had one employee—a bookkeeper. When I came in, I was more of a known designer because I had made and shown some designs: little tables, things that would sell in the shop. He trained me and gave me what I needed and so on. I introduced modernism to the shop and the furniture I made, which he then sold. It was good, good design that sold for good money, but I got nothing.

When did you decide to move on?

It was obvious that I wasn't going to stay there all my life. And he knew that. I finally went to him and

129

said, "I've been here a long time and I think
I should earn more." At the time, I was getting
forty-six dollars a week. The shop was also where
I first met Hans Knoll. He came in and said
hello once or twice.

**What were your first impressions of Knoll,
and how did your collaboration come about?**
Nobody particularly liked him, and I didn't know
Hans Knoll from Adam. He was not a designer at
all, but he came from a German furniture family
and he had a small showroom in New York. When
he had a design problem, he would come to me
and ask for advice. Soon he and I decided that we
could move outside of the shop—we could design
furniture and see that it was made well.

How would you describe your design process?
The dimensions and construction are where
I begin. There are certain dimensions to consider—
especially with seating, and furniture. I have
always said a chair is not a sculpture. It should
be practical, so that you can sit in it comfortably.
All of that must be taken into consideration.

Why do you work with wood exclusively?
Early on I decided to work in wood, not metal.
Why wood? Because it's an attractive material.
If somebody makes something in metal or glass,
it becomes something else. Metal is a dead
material, but wood has life, and color. It is beautiful, strong, and it lasts. There are all kinds of
reasons why.

the answer is Risom

RICHARD AVEDON

Previous, left to right: George Nelson,
Edward Wormley, Eero Saarinen,
Harry Bertoia, Charles Eames, and
Jens Risom as photographed
by Marvin Koner for *Playboy*, 1961.

Below: Risom, 1960s.

Right: Chair sketches, 2005.

Below: Patent drawing, c. 1945.

Bottom right: Table detail, Jens Risom
Design catalog, 1951.

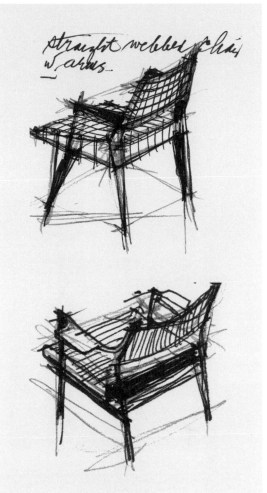

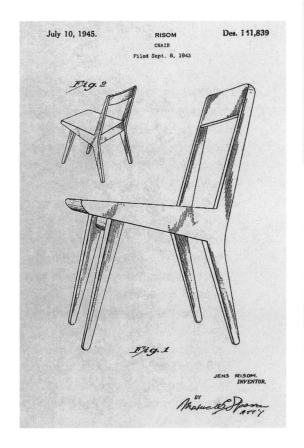

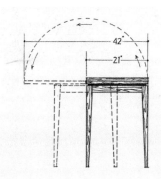

Furniture

Risom Design

C.120 Armchair

C.220 Sidechair

Parallel sides allow placing of chairs in closed straight rows.

6

U.420 Low Armchair

CHAIRS SOFAS

U. 112 Sofa, 85" long, with 3 loose cushions.

U. 312 Large Easychair, with loose cushion.

Left and middle: Cover and interior pages, Jens Risom Design catalog, 1949.

Bottom: Advertisement for Hans Knoll Furniture, 1940s.

HANS KNOLL FURNITURE

SHOWROOM · 601 MADISON AVENUE · NEW YORK · PLAZA 3-363d

"CHERRY WOOD" LINE BY JENS RISOM

SPECIAL DESIGNS MADE TO ORDER

SPECIALIZING IN FURNITURE CONTRACTS

CATALOGUE UPON REQUEST

INTERIORS

You have worked very closely with architects throughout your career. How did they influence your practice?

Yes, I got very close to them. Architects were always in need of furniture for their jobs—one hundred desks for IBM, for example; that was a big thing. When I first started out, especially, they were the ones who really got the market going. And they liked wood furniture in particular, because they agreed that wood was better than metal.

You have always maintained an independent position, working as the creative director of your own firm and freelancing quite often on a solo basis. How would you describe your approach?

From the very beginning, you are one man. You are designing, you are drawing, you are selecting. You are it. You create it, a piece of furniture.

What informed the name of Design Control, your later firm?

Design was a very convenient name. And control is rather obvious. Design Control was just to have a name under which we would design furniture but also desk accessories.

Do you have a favorite object?

I don't think of an object as such. Perhaps wood furniture as a whole, but there isn't much besides that.

Why has it been important for you to dedicate yourself to furniture design?

You have to pick your passion.

Do you believe that design can have a positive impact on people's lives?

Yes, very much so. Just like good architecture, like good art: if it gives pleasure, is well made and attractive, and fits together, it can improve lives. It's like anything artistic.

What's driven you to create pieces that might have that kind of influence?

It has to do with good quality. Not all furniture is good quality. If you want to sit in a chair without it collapsing, without it breaking down—you need good quality to create a good piece of furniture. It's got to be made in such a way that it stands up—that you can sit in it and be comfortable. I always told my children, "If you're going to do a job, do it right." And that's how I've tried to live my life.

What advice would you give yourself at the beginning of your career?

Only quality is worth doing.

Richard Sapper

Industrial Designer
b. 1932

Richard Sapper hasn't stopped designing since the age of twenty-four, when he began his first job, in the styling department of Mercedes-Benz—a position that was offered to him while researching the company as an undergraduate. Relocating to Milan in the late 1950s to work for Italian architect Giò Ponti, and shortly after as a designer for La Rinascente, the legendary department store rife with postwar talent, Sapper has lived in the city for more than sixty years. Running his own practice with alacrity and consistency, he has introduced dozens of design classics at the intersection of design, technology, and engineering.

Born in Munich, Germany, Sapper came of age during World War II and experienced a tumultuous childhood. While a pointed interest in design didn't arise until he was a young adult, his creative interests had been cultivated for some time: his father was a painter, and the influence of the Bauhaus was, Sapper says, unavoidable in those days. Industrial design remained a rarified course of study at university, however, so Sapper pursued a business degree, also taking classes in philosophy, anatomy, and engineering—the confluence of which can be seen in the wide range of his designs, which are marked by a technical complexity, visual precision, and ease of use.

Sapper has worked with numerous brands, including Brionvega, Lorenz, Artemide, Tag Heuer, Fiat, Pirelli, and IBM, and collaborated with architect and designer Marco Zanuso for nearly two decades. Ranging from lighting, product, and furniture designs to consumer electronics, automobiles, and bicycles, his prolific output has introduced more than a handful of new typologies and firsts.

Designed with Zanuso, his 1965 Grillo telephone for Siemens and Italtel, for example, was an early prototype for the now-common flip-phone; in 1964 the duo also produced the first all-plastic chair, the K1340 for Kartell, exposing the material's structural possibilities to the market. Sapper's best-selling 1972 Tizio desk lamp for Artemide, made with low-voltage current-conducting arms to reduce wiring, made early use of halogen bulbs. Years later, as chief design consultant to IBM, he helped launch the ThinkPad line of laptops in 1992 with the 700C, which both introduced the first non-external tracker mouse and signaled a shift to the sleek, minimalist clamshell machines that remain predominant today.

Sapper is the recipient of countless awards, including no fewer than fifteen Compasso d' Oro honors, Italy's highest achievement in industrial design. His designs are held in the permanent collections of twenty museums worldwide, including the Museum of Modern Art in New York and the Victoria & Albert Museum in London. Today, he continues to work in his Milan studio with the same unwavering ambition to explore the synthesis of cutting-edge technology and design.

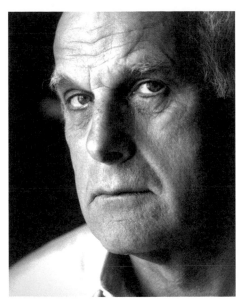

Richard Sapper, 1994.

When did you first become interested in design?

I studied philosophy. There were no design schools in Germany at that time. While I was at university, I discovered the profession of industrial design. There were still not many design schools in Germany, but I got very interested.

Do you think the Bauhaus, which closed the year after you were born, somehow influenced your thinking?

When I was a child, I was in the middle of World War II: bombs were falling almost every night, there was nothing to eat, we heard air-raid sirens. My father was on the front as a soldier, and then as a POW. We had other things to think about.

My father was also a painter, so I had a very close relationship with culture and the arts in my family. It would have been impossible not to know, or be impressed by, such a huge cultural fact as the Bauhaus. When I asked my father what you learned at an academy of arts he said, "Sharpening a pencil." If a teacher has a great personality, you can learn how he looks at life and how something is made. Design education depends on the teacher.

What drew you to teaching, and how does it inform your design practice?

For me it was an adventure, a type of human relations I had not experienced before. I enjoyed it very much.

How did you land your first job in the styling department at Mercedes-Benz in Stuttgart?

I was still studying and needed information about Mercedes-Benz for my thesis. I asked for a meeting with Karl Wilfert, who was then the world-famous design boss at the company. We had a long conversation, and at the end he asked me if I would like to come to work at Mercedes once I finished with my schooling.

You then moved to Italy, and worked in Giò Ponti's office. Did the job influence the move, or was it the other way around? Did you already speak Italian when you moved there?

Not a word. I just went. It was not a difficult time; it was fantastic. I met more interesting people than ever before in my life—all young and from all over the world. For design, you need no language, and after one year we all spoke Italian fluently.

Giò Ponti was an extremely gentle genius. What did I learn from him? How a really great artist is made, how he reacts to life, everything. I worked closely with him, and also with Alberto Roselli, his son-in-law.

How would you describe the zeitgeist of 1960s Milan?

The general attitude was, "We can do everything!" We were all friends. I knew all the important designers in Milan, including Lora Lamm. Later we had our "club," the ADI (Associazione per il Disegno Industriale).

How did Italian modernism compare to modernism elsewhere?

It was much more elegant. The design scene was, and is, really cosmopolitan, and this fact is probably the reason for the particular "style" of Italian design.

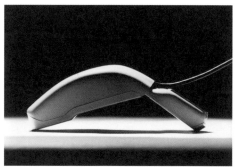

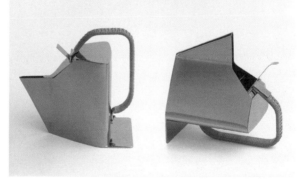

Opposite, top: The TS 502 transistor radio, designed with Marco Zanuso for Brionvega in 1962, remains in production today.

Opposite, middle, left and right: Grillo, designed with Zanuso for Siemens Italtel in 1965, introduced one of the first flip-phones to market.

Opposite, bottom: La Cintura di Orione cookware collection for Alessi, 1986.

Top: The counterbalanced Tizio desk lamp, produced in 1972 for Artemide.

Above left: Teakettle 9091 for Alessi, featuring a brass melodic whistle tuned to the notes "Mi" and "Ti," 1983.

Above right: Designed for Alessi in 1990, the dual-orientation Bandung teapot allows tea leaves to be steeped and separated.

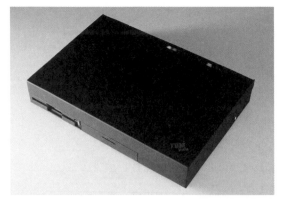
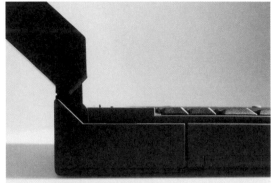

Above left and right: The ThinkPad 700C laptop computer, the first of the ThinkPad series, developed with Kaz Yamazaki for IBM, 1992.

Right: The X 126 Softnose, an experimental automobile prototype developed for FIAT in 1974.

There are so many firsts in your career—you designed the first flip-phone in 1965; the first stacking chair produced entirely in plastic; the Tizio, one of the first lamps to use halogen bulbs; and the iconic IBM ThinkPad 700C, with the special red tracking button.

Yes, I invented the use of the auto-headlights for a table lamp, and when I designed the ThinkPad for IBM, I used the color black for the first time. Over the years, IBM sold numerous units of the ThinkPad laptop, still with the same design brief as in 1992 when it was first presented for sale.

You've been compared to Dieter Rams. Did you encounter him frequently in your career?

We are very close friends. We met at the German Academy of Arts, of which we are both members. We have never worked together, but I think our work is pretty similar.

Steve Jobs once approached you about working for him at Apple. What was your interaction with him, and what made you pass on the opportunity?

I had an exclusivity agreement with IBM.

You recently launched an online portfolio of your work, with products you designed from 1956 to the present day. You're clearly still hard at work. What keeps you designing?

Clockwise from right:
A stackable children's chair, the K1340 was
the first chair entirely built of injection-molded
plastic. Produced in collaboration with
Zanuso for Kartell, 1964.

Sapperchair, a collection of office seating
designs for Knoll, 1979.

Tosca stacking chair for Magis, 2007.

I like to make the things that surround our lives interesting, I want to make the tools we use better.

What does a good or ideal design embody, in your opinion?

In my mind, design is one of the oldest professions of mankind. The caveman was already able to make extraordinarily beautiful tools, jewels, and other objects. He was prepared to employ much more time to make his objects beautiful, rather than just functional. The key characteristics of design have not changed in the last fifty thousand years, and any visit to a museum of human history can prove this. Mankind has always desired beauty because it is a sign of eternity.

What's your ideal project?

I do not have ideal projects. But my work consists of bringing projects to life; if they are ideal, there is nothing to do. It is like having ideal children. Can you imagine that?

What would your advice be to aspiring or emerging designers?

To be true to themselves and the objects they are working on.

Ricardo Scofidio

Architect, Educator
b. 1935

One of the most prominent architects in the field, Ricardo Scofidio almost abandoned the discipline in the 1970s. Disillusioned with what he perceived to be limitations of the practice, he toyed with leaving but instead returned anew, invigorated in part by his personal and professional union with Elizabeth Diller and the formation of their studio in 1979. In the thirty-seven years since, his work has explored the delicate and overlapping peripheries of art, design, performance, and public space, and has challenged and expanded the definition of architecture in the process.

The son of jazz musicians, Scofidio maintains a quiet, introspective rhythm and credits his New York upbringing with a resourcefulness that ranges from skilled car repair to playing the double bass. He attended Cooper Union, and earned a master's in architecture from Columbia University in 1960. He began teaching in 1965 and found the act so integral to his growth as a thinker that he continued for more than forty years.

His early work with Diller defies categorization, encompassing performance, site-specific installations, and the occasional stage set. In their design for Slow House, an experimental residence commissioned for a seaside site in North Haven, New York, in 1991, Scofidio and Diller proposed projecting a live feed of the ocean onto the home's only sea-facing window. Though never built, the project entered the Museum of Modern Art's permanent collection and led to a slew of new commissions, including *Soft Sell*, a video installation in Times Square that centered on a giant pair of talking lips

soliciting passersby from the window of an abandoned porn theater. In 1999 Diller + Scofidio became the first architects to receive a MacArthur Fellowship, and in 2003 Charles Renfro joined the firm as its third partner.

Scofidio has learned to channel his measured restlessness into work, spending nights and weekends in the office, with breaks for reading and music. Over the last fifteen years the scale and complexity of his projects has grown in step with the visibility of the firm. There's the update to the Brasserie restaurant, a windowless marvel in the Seagram tower; Blur, a structure of steel and fog erected on Lake Neuchâtel for the 2002 Swiss Expo; Boston's Institute of Contemporary Art, perched dramatically on the city's main channel; and the High Line, which transformed a decommissioned elevated railway in Manhattan's Meatpacking District into one of New York's most popular and unique public spaces. Even larger commissions have been quick to follow, including a striking overhaul of New York's Lincoln Center, completed in 2013.

Scofidio, whose energy belies his eighty years, is looking to the future—toward a controversial MoMA expansion, and the twenty-six-acre Culture Shed, a major performance and exhibition space set to open at Manhattan's developing Hudson Yards site in 2019.

When did you first become curious about design and architecture?

I originally wanted to be a musician, so I studied music throughout my childhood. My whole family was musical: my father, mother, brother, grandmother—everyone played an instrument. But when it came time to think about college, I started considering a different path. I remember my father telling me, "Music is a terrible profession. Don't do it."

Art was another passion, so I applied to Cooper Union and was accepted. At that time, during the first year of study, students learned a little bit about everything: calligraphy, painting, sculpture, and, of course, architecture. I enjoyed architecture a great deal—it touched a technical side of me that music and art never allowed me to express. So I switched disciplines.

Would you say you identify more as an architect or as an artist?

I don't believe in policing that border. I just do things that I enjoy doing.

Ricardo Scofidio, 2009.

How has your lifelong love of music influenced your practice?

I love music, but I have always found more inspiration in reading and observing—looking, listening, and absorbing the world and its many narratives. I don't doubt that the linear form of music helped construct the way I think, but I can't say simply, "I'm this because of that."

In the same way, I don't always try to relate everything back to architecture. There are so many things that go into the mix, and it is this bouillabaisse that makes me who I am.

You've taught for many years. How did you first get involved in teaching?

In 1961, after returning from a year-long travel fellowship in Europe, I called up the architect whom I had worked for before I left. He asked me to come in that same day—it was a Sunday—because there was an emergency. When I arrived, I saw that a beautiful rendering by John Hejduk, who was working with the architect on a project for IBM, had been defaced. John had drawn this beautiful ink rendering—every brick of the building was individually outlined—and someone had added heavy color to it, destroying its intricate elegance. They asked me if I could do anything to save it, and I surprised them by taking the drawing to a big sink and scrubbing it down with a wet brush. The rendering had been done in waterproof India ink on good Strathmore board, so all the ugly, added colors washed away and it became once again delicate and beautiful. John turned to me and said, "You've got to come teach at Cooper."

In the beginning, teaching was a source of income that gave me a certain freedom. Then after a year or two, I began to realize its influence on the way that I thought. Teaching is also learning; teachers are in constant dialogue with themselves. I enjoyed engaging with the students, of course, but for me, the job was about my growth as much as theirs. For me, the critical thing was questioning the pedagogical approach to teaching architecture. There was a continuous evolution between how I taught when I began, and how I was teaching when I finally decided to retire.

What are your thoughts on the current state of architectural education?

Many students choose an architecture school because of its name rather than a sincere understanding of its disciplinary philosophy. This always baffles me. Harvard, Yale, Cooper, Princeton, Berkeley, Michigan—ranking them makes no sense; each has its strengths and its weaknesses.

It is this same competitive drive that gives many students a misplaced set of priorities when they begin their education. Teaching undergraduates can be especially difficult. Primed from standardized testing and the vicious admissions process, they enter the classroom asking, "What do I have to learn to get an A?" It was challenging—and always rewarding— to convince them that they were there to develop themselves—to find their perspective, their approach, and to discover what they could offer the discipline.

I believe that everyone should spend at least two years studying architecture before selecting a major. The cross-disciplinary precision with which architecture analyzes and synthesizes ideas can't be found in any other field.

There was a period in the early 1970s when you left the architecture profession completely. What was that time like?

It was an in-between stage, like treading water. I wasn't sure whether I would go back into architecture. I started helping a photographer, and I was still teaching at Cooper. I decided that if I didn't go back into architecture within two years, I'd stop teaching and find something else to do. It was during that period that I realized I didn't have to practice architecture the way the profession practiced it.

My involvement with Elizabeth cemented that alternative form of practice. When we started working together, we focused exclusively on projects that we found challenging and interesting, across a wide range of artistic disciplines: theater, public performance, opera, objects. We were also investigating the gray areas of social conditions—issues such as domesticity and surveillance. Many of our investigations weren't projects that would be traditionally associated with professional architecture. Architects would say, "These are not architects," and artists would say, "These are not artists." Because we were exploring so much cross-disciplinary material, it was difficult to get grants. We couldn't squeeze ourselves into most application categories. So it was incredibly rewarding when the MacArthur Foundation recognized us for the work we had been doing. I had been trained as a musician and an artist, but I looked at the world through the eyes of an architect. Even in the period in which I decided that the profession was not particularly interesting, I still found the discipline rich and rewarding.

Your firm is known for fluidly operating between architecture and art. How do you navigate between these different worlds?

If there is a formula, I don't have it. I've been so fortunate to have Elizabeth as a partner. We continuously challenge each other. In the beginning, there was a long period in which we were living together, working together, and jointly teaching a class at Cooper. It was twenty-four-hours-a-day, nonstop collaboration. Those were like dog years, meaning, one year for us was the equivalent of five years for most couples.

Liz eventually reached a point where she needed to move on from Cooper. We were getting into a rut; life was too cohesive. Her move to Princeton was a refreshing change for us. It brought us back to arguing, discussing, and challenging each other rather than agreeing in complacency.

Over the past three decades, architecture has had to contend with rapidly changing technology. We have strived to adopt the newest tools, materials, and modes of production, while at the same time critiquing the widespread disciplinary changes engendered by these changes. The shifting role of technology is something that has always interested us. Each project—whether a theater production, art exhibition, museum installation, or high-rise building—offers its own set of challenges, and we're smart enough to know when to turn

Right: *Bad Press: Dissident Housework Series* (1993–1998) in *Scanning: The Aberrant Architectures of Diller + Scofidio* at the Whitney Museum of American Art, New York, 2003.

Bottom right: *Moving Target*, a multimedia dance work in collaboration with Charleroi Danses, Charleroi, Belgium, 1996.

Below: Scofidio and Elizabeth Diller, in their first studio, Cooper Square, New York, 1993.

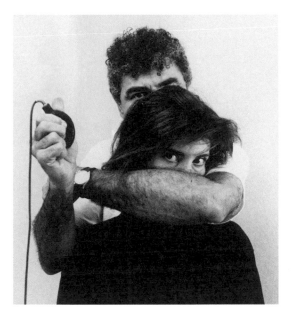

to an expert, while still remaining critical. It's about being supple and flexible so that we are willing to let go of fixed preconceptions and grow.

In the early years of your practice with Elizabeth, which began in 1979, you created performances, dance videos, and gallery installations, which seems quite a distance from making buildings. What inspired your move back into architecture?

We didn't start with some future destination in mind. We were open to exploring and looking. In the early years, we were fortunate to know Anita Contini at Creative Time, who encouraged us to

get involved in Art on the Beach. There was also Creation Production, a theater company founded by Matthew Maguire and Susan Mosakowski. Matthew invited us to work on a piece that he was doing at La MaMa. We were fortunate to be involved with those projects. We weren't just putting yellow trace up on the gallery wall; we were actually building and engaging with the public. And that was critical, because we were able to step back, look at the results, and ask: What did we accomplish? And what was the reaction to it?

There were strange connections that led us to bigger jobs. One of our early art projects, for example, led to a commission for a large social housing complex in Japan called Slither. Arata Isozaki had seen *Bad Press,* which was an exercise in dissident housework made with twenty-five generic men's white shirts, an iron, and spray starch. The piece scrutinized ironing as one among other household tasks that are still governed by motion-economy principles designed by efficiency engineers at the turn of the twentieth century. Isozaki was selecting architects for the housing development and was interested in searching for a new model for this type of building in Japan. He realized that we were exploring and questioning issues of domesticity, and invited us to participate.

How has your practice evolved over the years as the scale of the projects has increased?

When we were doing smaller works, it was easy to bring in four or five people to work on a project. The project would finish, we'd thank them, and then let them go on their way. There was a great deal of flexibility, which I enjoyed. Now that the scale and number of projects has increased, we have more than a hundred employees, many of whom have families and children. They've committed themselves to being here, and, therefore, we have an obligation and responsibility to them. It adds another dimension to how the office evolves, and how we work as a studio. I don't think my attitude toward work has changed at all, despite the fact that we now occupy two floors. If I had wanted to walk away before, I probably could have, but now I realize that it's no longer that easy. It's now critical that the work that we bring in is what we want to be doing.

How important is collaboration to your way of working?

It is essential. The more voices you can bring to a project, the better. We collaborate with people who offer ideas—people with whom you can argue at length, reaching for some unknown resolution that you can't quite grasp but will recognize when you get there. You might end up bloody and on the floor in the process, but everyone will be able to shake hands and feel great about the conclusion. I don't think that we could have achieved what we have without a somewhat combative process.

I know that I couldn't have achieved it as a sole practitioner.

I find traces of this process in my memories of being an architecture student. I would sit in class and absorb all I could, but usually I would arrive at the solution to the problem—the moment of creative synthesis—much later. A year afterward, I would see a passing image, or overhear some comment, or read a piece of text, and suddenly things would come together. But this only worked because I had been thinking about that problem for a long time. I don't believe in the sudden epiphany, the bolt of intellectual lightning, the divine inspiration. My brain works by continually reassembling ideas until it finally makes the last connection. It takes time and hard work. It's like a mathematical formula that you can't seem to get, but you keep studying, doggedly, until finally there's a moment when all is understood—when hard work finally makes those connections happen across the brain synapses.

How would you describe your process leading up to those points of clarity?

You have to chain yourself to the desk to keep working and remain focused. There's always a great urgency to distraction—to get a cup of coffee, read a book, browse the Internet—but that loss of focus is extremely detrimental. When I just sit in front of the project, and work on it long enough, there will be a moment when there is a breakthrough. It's not a bolt from the blue; it's just work that gets me to where I want to be with the project. That is, until Liz walks by, says a few words, and everything changes again.

Recurring themes in your work include display, travel, surveillance, reality versus virtual imagery, and domesticity. What draws you to these subjects?

Years ago, I read a short story about a murder. The police interviewed everyone in the neighborhood, but no one had seen anybody on the street. It turned out that the murderer was the neighborhood postman. He was invisible because he was so constant and familiar; people didn't notice him anymore.

Slow House model, Diller + Scofidio, 1989.

Tourisms: Suitcase Studies, an installation at the Walker Art Center in Minneapolis, explored the effect of tourism on American cities, 1991.

Do we accept constraints because they're so familiar that they're invisible? Should a design respond to that? Why is a traditional residential plan, for example, laid out the way it is? The important work, for me, has always been the investigation of things that we don't often think about—that have become unnoticed and yet control our behavior. In terms of the way we act and the way we build: What do we take for granted without ever questioning? This is fascinating to us: that domesticity, for example, or surveillance, can serve as central, organizing forces of society, essential to the way the world grows and is designed around us, and yet remain largely ignored in terms of their effects on human experience and behavior.

In *Suitcase Studies*, for example, we looked at tourist attractions in the fifty United States and realized how much tourism was changing and transforming cities. Fifty identical Samsonite suitcases transported the contents of the exhibition, and doubled as display cases for those contents. Each suitcase was a case study of a particular tourist attraction in a given state, offering a critical look at official and unofficial images and texts. We focused on two types of sites: famous beds and famous battlefields, sites in which the subtlety of tourism's construction of aura most strongly feeds the hunger for the real, no matter the degree

of artifice required to produce it. When we did that project, tourism wasn't yet discussed as a factor that was transforming cities or affecting the way they're designed. We were not trying to be prescriptive; we were not trying to find answers. We were trying to expose a condition.

Where do you think that impulse to question comes from?

I've always been curious about why do we do things a certain way, why rituals affect us, and why we hold onto certain repetitive conditions. I have never been one to live in the past. I can very easily walk away from things or forget about them if necessary. The most difficult thing for me has been to live in the present, and to resist thinking about what the future will look like. We're always wrong, regardless. A lot of reading has influenced my thinking, from Neal Stephenson's *Snow Crash* to Voltaire's *Candide*.

In a 2007 profile in the *New Yorker*, you said of the High Line, "My hope is that it doesn't become engulfed by developers." How has your view of that project and the site changed in the years since its realization?

One has hopes. You can wish for things that you know may never come true, but it doesn't hurt to at least wish for them. With the High Line, we were

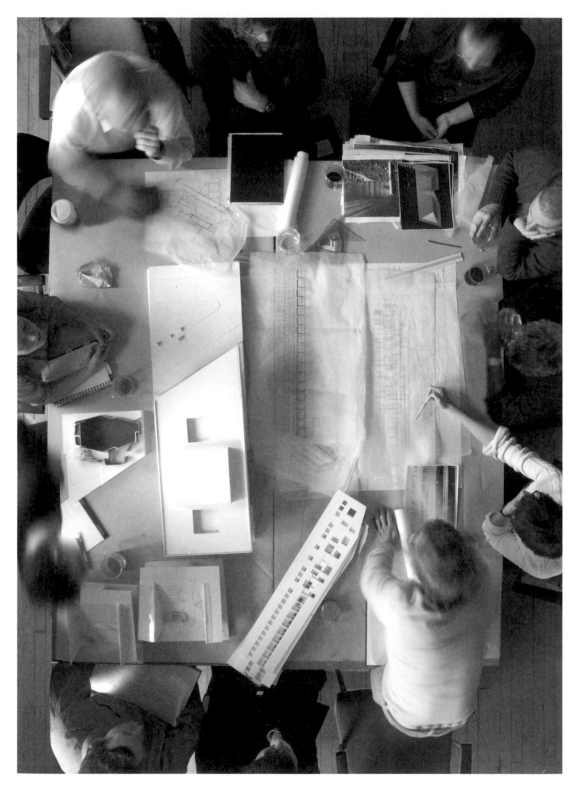

Opposite: Collaborative design session at DS+R for the redevelopment of Lincoln Center for the Performing Arts, 2005.

Right: Hypar Pavilion with lawn roof and Lincoln Ristorante, Lincoln Center for the Performing Arts, New York, 2011.

Below: Alice Tully Hall, Lincoln Center for the Performing Arts, New York, with renovations and expansion by Diller Scofidio + Renfro, 2010.

fortunate that the New York City Planning Department under Amanda Burden established new zoning for the area north of where the High Line crosses Tenth Avenue, so it won't be totally engulfed with wall-to-wall architecture. There will be open spaces that will allow the High Line to continue to breathe. But the city will inevitably transform. Eventually, it will be like Hong Kong on the Hudson. Maybe things will change—we might figure out how to avoid that—but with real estate prices and developers' needs, it's difficult to imagine an alternate outcome. New York is endlessly changing. The High Line will, at some point, be swallowed up, particularly by the Hudson Yards high rises. But this would have happened regardless. Even if the High Line had been torn down, Chelsea would still have been overcome by development, perhaps even more so.

Is there such a thing as a perfect project?
You have to be careful what you wish for. To define the perfect project would likely involve a fixed set of rigid beliefs. Our studio is not invested in doing solely commercial work; our main interest is in cultural and academic buildings. But if a potential client walks into our office with an interesting project that I never thought I'd do, then we might still say yes. One of our earliest projects—a restaurant in the Seagram Building— was commercial. We took it on because we were fascinated by the conditions of the site: the restaurant was in a windowless basement in a skyscraper that is otherwise all about glass. It was a wonderful challenge. Projects that have a weird or strange twist to them will always interest me.

As a lifelong New Yorker, how have you been creatively influenced by the city?
It's an incredible, complex playground to be involved with. From the intelligent, artistic, imaginative areas of the city—there to rub up against, to see and talk about, to be challenged by—to the simplest experiences. When we

first started practicing, it would have been impossible to create the things we did if we lived anywhere else but New York. We also built a lot of our projects in-house. From the very physical, pragmatic conditions that existed—small budgets, limited space—we were able to dip into the more ethereal, artful, creative energies of the city to inspire and collaborate with us on our work.

You're one of few people to have ever stayed overnight at Philip Johnson's Glass House. How would you describe the experience?

We were probably the first people to sleep in the Glass House since Philip Johnson. It was incredible. Johnson said once that the Glass House has the most expensive wallpaper. I always thought that was silly, but at night, when it's dim inside and the lights are on outside, I did feel entirely surrounded by the landscape, as if it was pressed up against the glass. It was such a privilege to be there. But I don't think I could live there. I think most people need to feel a buffer—to choose when they want

to interface with the exterior. In the Glass House, you have no choice. It's always there, pressing up against you. Even more interesting than sleeping over was the morning after: Elizabeth making tea, bringing domesticity into this hallowed space.

You've mentioned reading as a favorite pastime. What are some other personal interests?

These days, I'm usually working. When I'm not, I enjoy listening to music in all forms and reading novels ranging from highbrow to lowbrow, pulp fiction in particular.

I also have a not-so-secret love of automobiles and automobile racing that, at times, consumes me. My father never trusted automobile repair garages; if there was something wrong with the car, he would fix it. But he was terrible at repair work. After his supposedly well-done jobs, we'd be driving somewhere and the car would come to a sudden stop and have to be towed home. Finally,

for purposes of self-preservation, I decided to learn to fix a car. As a teenager, I could completely rebuild a motor and put it back in. Ever since, as a hobby, I'll find a sports car with problems, work on it, get it running, drive it, enjoy it, sell it, and buy another. Over the years, I've had an enormous number of very strange, unusual cars.

I've also raced automobiles in the past. It's good escapism because you can't be on the track with a car and have anything else on your mind. The concentration required drives everything else out of my brain; it's a complete flush of workplace anxieties. I also like race cars because they're beautiful objects with mechanical integrity, which is also the way I think about detailing and design.

Who's been your most important mentor?
A mentor is somebody who is looking at what you're doing, advising you, and pushing you. So it would be Elizabeth. That's easy.

What would you describe as your biggest professional triumph?
I don't really think about it. It's like asking, "Who's your favorite child?" I don't value projects that

way—there's no hierarchy for me. Every piece we've done has richness to it, with elements that I've loved and enjoyed. There's an involvement and pleasure that comes from doing something and doing it well. If I didn't feel good about it, I wouldn't still be working.

Does the same go for setbacks, too?
If something doesn't go right, or we don't get a project, we just move on.

What advice would you give yourself at the beginning of your career?
I'm happy where I am now, so I must have done something right. Why would I go back and tell myself to do something else? The beauty for me is that I ran into this career full-steam. I didn't go cautiously, wondering if I should be doing this or doing that. I jumped in. Liz and I have done so many crazy projects—sometimes, we say that our work is like jumping off a tall building without a parachute, hoping to figure out how to land safely on the way down.

Denise Scott Brown

—

Architect, Planner, Educator
b. 1931

Denise Scott Brown made headlines in 2013 when a digital petition filed on her behalf by members of Women in Design, a student organization at Harvard's Graduate School of Design, went viral. Addressing the committee behind the Pritzker Prize—the preeminent international honor bestowed annually upon a practicing architect—the petition demanded that Scott Brown, partner of architect Robert Venturi, retroactively receive recognition for the Pritzker he was awarded in 1991. Though the effort was unsuccessful, much to the dismay of its nearly twenty thousand signees and the wider design community, it was a testament to the legacy and example Scott Brown—a highly influential architect, theorist, educator, writer, and advocate for women's equality in the workplace— has continued to uphold in the field for more than fifty years.

Born in 1931 in Zambia, Scott Brown grew up in a starkly modernist home—a minimalist box recalling the work of Le Corbusier—and, with this early exposure to architecture, found her calling at a young age. She began her studies at the University of the Witwatersrand in South Africa but soon left to study in London and travel throughout Europe, eventually landing in Philadelphia. Upon earning a master's degree in planning at the University of Pennsylvania in 1958, Scott Brown took up a faculty post in the department and met Robert Venturi, who would soon become her lifelong partner as well as her collaborator. Leaving UPenn for a teaching position at the University of California, Berkeley, she quickly and prominently rose to cochair of the Urban Design Program at the University of California, Los Angeles, that same year, later returning to the east coast with an appointment at the Yale School of Architecture.

Intrigued with automotive culture and the ways in which it had begun to shape the lifestyle and urban landscape of the Southwest— particularly in Los Angeles and Las Vegas— Scott Brown began examining the emergence of a new regional vernacular through studio courses she taught at Yale, to which she invited Venturi to join as coinstructor. Their landmark analysis, *Learning from Las Vegas: The Forgotten Symbolism of Architectural Form* (MIT Press, 1972), coauthored with Steven Izenour, grew out of the insights culled from the course and documented the design of the Las Vegas Strip—an unconventional subject for architecture's staid academics. An ideological thorn in the side of modernism, the controversial text irrevocably signaled a sea change for twentieth-century architecture.

Working in academics, architecture, and city planning, Scott Brown and Venturi are championed as leading postmodernist thinkers, and have helmed their Philadelphia-based firm, Venturi, Scott Brown and Associates, as equal partners since 1989, organizing exhibitions, lecturing, teaching, and realizing built projects of worldwide influence. A prolific writer on architecture and urban planning, Scott Brown is the author of numerous texts—one of which is actively in progress—and remains hard at work.

Denise Scott Brown in the studio, Philadelphia, Pennsylvania, c. 1984.

What are you currently working on?

Since turning fifty, my writing has tended to be more autobiographical. You want to sum up your life and understand it. But there are other reasons, too. When I was teaching, I learned that architects don't want to read; they don't want to absorb information. But I found if I told them anecdotally how I had learned to do that, they felt braver about studying it. I learned to write autobiographically so that my students would want to read what I had to say.

One of the things I've done over the years is take photographs. Now I've digitized them all—there are thousands—and begun writing a new book.

You were born in Zambia and traveled extensively in Europe. You've worked in New England, California, and now Philadelphia, where your firm has been based for quite some time. How has travel informed your understanding of architecture?

We were taught in school that it's no use looking at pictures of things; you have to go see the buildings. I was a child during World War II, and arrived at university when the war had ended, and all of us felt very cut off from things, including the architecture we were studying. I studied at Witwatersrand and the AA in London. While in Europe, I traveled every chance I got; I went to Spain, Yugoslavia, Germany, Switzerland, Sweden,

and Denmark. We had lots of books on modern art at home, but I went and saw it in galleries and museums. I paid particular attention to composition, and I was very intrigued, for example, by Kazimir Malevich's painting *White on White*. It is anti-composition, which is interesting if you love architecture and your training is in orthogonal and Cartesian relationships, particularly with the influence of Mies van der Rohe. I saw Japanese forms of composition, and the work of others who were also of that orthogonal tradition trying different things.

While traveling with a group of students, I also met a photographer who was very interested in war photography, which of course doesn't have any composition. You just take what you can of what is happening while it is moving. I talked to him a lot and that occupied my mind, too. It was a lot of that kind of thinking and studying.

Do you remember when you first became interested in architecture?

Bob's mother wanted him to be an architect before he was born. He was programmed, you could say, from birth. There was never any question for him.

With me, there wasn't much question either, because my parents began building an International Style house when I was two; we moved in when I was four. I remember the blueprints distinctly. My mother had studied architecture, and was at university the year modern architecture arrived. Students then were trained to follow what Le Corbusier did, and she was one of those students.

I have these very specific memories of that beautiful 1930s house, very much in the Le Corbusier tradition. I remember playing on the flat roof, and the sun shining through the porthole window—that porthole shape crossed the west-facing wall of my parents' bedroom as I lay in there watching it. The door handles were the height they put them in modern houses—straight handles, not round ones—and I was five before I could reach them and open the doors. I remember my grandmother's shoes—she had slippers with high heels on them—clacking on the black-and-white tiled stairway steps.

It's wonderful to hear about architecture being tied to such joyful memories.

When I think of the joys of being an architect, there are many. Arthur Korn, one of my teachers at the AA, said there's joy in being on the site, in the smell of the paint and wood. Other people say it's the beauty of the building you've made. As for me, I love how a building is made up of so many different dimensions, intellectual challenges, and theoretical challenges—the challenge of aesthetics, of how it gets put together. If you know about land economics, if you know about transportation, now you begin to design with many other strings to your bows aside from, "What did Le Corbusier do?" or, "How does it look?"

When I look at something that I've designed, putting together an intellectual challenge, making it physical, making it aesthetic, making it beautiful—there's a huge joy in seeing it being used the way I thought it would, and a fascination in seeing it used differently than I had thought.

What do you mean by that?

For example, I designed a complex at the University of Michigan. There were three buildings, and I planned them along a street designed to follow "desire lines" between the main campus and the medical campus. During the construction I got a letter from one of the planners, and he said,

"I think you will enjoy knowing that even though we still have the construction fences up around the three projects, the students have discovered your intended route through them and across to the medical center, and they've broken down our fences and are riding their bicycles through. I think that will make you happy." And it sure did.

People are sitting where I hoped they would sit. An architect may design a public space and the public never goes there, for good reason: there is nothing there for them, no way to get there, no crossing of paths to activate use. Architects never study those things.

You began your lifelong collaboration with Bob [Venturi] in the 1960s. What brought you to the University of Pennsylvania, where you first met?

I went to Penn because Peter Smithson said, "The only place you should go is where Louis Kahn is." If you were a good architect in England or Europe, you studied planning as well as architecture, because of all the urban renewal. So we entered the city-planning program because it seemed logical. Little did I know that in America, they think architects go into planning when they can't design. In England and Germany and France, you went into planning because Le Corbusier did—you wanted to be a *good* designer.

Planners at that time were coming from the social sciences. The federal government was putting a lot of money into urban renewal and urban research. And architecture schools all had planning departments, so suddenly, architecture school planning departments were all filled with social scientists. They looked around and said, "My god, I can't believe how naive these architects are." They started saying to the architects, "How can you think the way you do? You're all so arrogant, and you don't know what you think you know. Why don't you go and see what makes people actually go to public places? Why do people go to Las Vegas and not to, I don't know, *any* public urban renewal project *anywhere*?" We were very much encouraged to go to Las Vegas, and the West in general. The automobile cities were then developing in the West.

Left: Scott Brown in Debrovnik, former Yugoslavia, c. 1955.

Below: Scott Brown's International Style childhood home in Johannesburg, South Africa.

Bottom: Housing incorporating Western references in a Mapoch Village outside of Pretoria, Gauteng Transvaal, photographed by Scott Brown while traveling with her first husband, Robert Scott Brown, 1957.

Left: Denise and Robert Scott Brown in Venice, Italy, 1956.

Below left: Photograph taken by Scott Brown of road signage in Los Angeles, c. 1968.

Below right: Denise Scott Brown and Robert Venturi with colleagues at their studio in Philadelphia, Pennsylvania, 1991.

The trouble with urban renewal in America and Europe is that architects do too much navel gazing. To learn about cities, they ask, "What did Le Corbusier do?" instead of, "What's the sociology of a place? What are the forces that form its settlement patterns?"

As an African, I also went west to explore wide spaces different from those in Europe, and to understand how the automobile makes space and compare that to space generated by other technologies of movement—trains, carriages, and pedestrians. Form is determined not only by function, but by forces as well: economic forces, environmental forces.

Learning from Las Vegas was quite controversial and unconventional when it was first published in 1972. Was it intended as a direct rebellion against the modernist orthodoxy that dominated the architectural scene at the time?

I'm a modernist. American modernism had, at that stage, gotten very far away from what modernists really stood for. We were going back to the beginning, to the real challenge, trying to be relevant to what was really needed and redefine it with new technology. As I said then, there's nothing more reactionary than an old revolutionary. It was the 1960s, and I knew that if you wanted to capture students' attention, their imaginations, and get them to want to work, you had to do something pretty revolutionary. I'm not through with adolescent revolt yet myself; I'm still a rogue, rebellious adolescent in some ways. I got stuck there and I'll probably never leave it.

In architecture at Penn, there was a lot of discussion about the doctorate. There were two kinds of doctorates: a scholarly doctorate, which you got by studying history (and then you were going to teach architectural history) or structures; and there was a professional doctorate, where you became an expert in a building type, such as hospitals. That's what research was all about. Now, research is like translational research for getting from basic knowledge to design. That's what we introduced, and now, that's what research looks like. For example, one student in *Learning from Las Vegas*, in order to do a study on social patterns in different kinds of housing, read forty-four books on sociology—happily, I might add—and then translated that into different kinds of housing. She described various kinds of families, and showed pictures of how they organize themselves, what their living rooms were like, and so on. We really tried to make the transition from book learning to the physical environment, which is a very difficult thing to do.

There had also been a lot of discussion about the book as a design object itself, with its experimental visual direction. Why was its original design, by MIT Press art director Muriel Cooper, such a point of contention?

Muriel betrayed what we were trying to do with what she was doing. People said, "You're both revolutionaries." But she was a revolutionary from an old revolution, the one we were fighting against. We battled over graphic design. I then did the redesign [published by MIT Press in 1977]. Its paperback format made it cheaper and more convenient, though in many cases the pictures were bigger. In order to save space, I allowed them to separate the topic descriptions from the research itself. They run parallel now, among several other revisions to the text.

Muriel's version did show the study of communication, signs, and graphics very well, but it didn't show the study of southwestern automobile urbanism. That got lost. No architects have wanted to read that then or now. It's a shame because the whole thing about understanding urban structure and how it works was lost; it's still lost.

That project was an extension of a studio course you taught with Bob at Yale. How did the experience shape your approach to teaching?

I taught studio in South Africa, and in London at the AA. In America architecture schools were, to me, authoritarian places where big senior people tried to help you get up to their standards, but made you feel that you'd never learn it all.

When I went to planning school, everything was done in teams. The teacher was like a coach who played in the studio with us. The instructors were as keen on the projects as we were—and made sure people could shine as individuals, too. Today, many schools have a visiting studio like Las Vegas almost every semester. We essentially turned around the culture of research and design in America. Now there are many, many team studios. Before, there were none. In fact, it was just the opposite.

From design history to writing and even popular discourse, you and Bob are credited with laying the foundations for the postmodernist movement in architecture. Would you agree?

There's lots of spoofing in what we do, and lots of fun. There are puns in our writing. Sometimes it's difficult to get students to realize they're allowed to laugh. Bob is on the record as saying, "I am not a postmodernist and I have never been a postmodernist." He meant it very strongly, but it was partly a spoof on the House Un-American Activities Committee, where people were made to declare, "I am not a Communist and I have never been a Communist." [*Laughs*]

Then I began to think we were wrong to declare that, because, indeed, there was a movement

Top: The vernacular architecture of
the Las Vegas Strip, photographed by
Scott Brown in the 1960s.

Above left: First-edition book cover
of *Learning from Las Vegas*, coauthored
by Robert Venturi, Scott Brown, and
Steven Izenour, 1972.

Above right: Snapshot of Venturi and Scott
Brown's view of Las Vegas from the car,
photographed by Izenour, 1968.

Scott Brown in Las Vegas, photographed by
Venturi, 1966.

called postmodernism that came out of World War II with statements such as, "After the Holocaust, there can be no innocence." And that's very much part of what we stand for. We stand for no innocence. Looking at things like Las Vegas, you have to know why they are happening, and understand them.

A few years later, we applied our studies from the Las Vegas project as the basis of *Signs of Life,* which was a very dense exhibition; we thought nobody would ever read all the text. But apparently Philip Johnson read the whole thing. Out of that came *his* postmodernism. But his is not our postmodernism. His is pomo. There's a difference.

What are some of the distinguishing traits?
We were trying to understand the social origins and the forces behind things: how they get to be that way, where the pressures are. Trying to go along with pressures doesn't mean you become supine. Architects think of themselves as the captain of the ship, steering. I think you're better off thinking of yourself as a surfer—catching the waves, hoping the tides will take you somewhere near where you're trying to go. That's a better position to be in.
We understand commercial pressures and try to work with them to a certain point, but we will also stand against them. If you want to make water run uphill, you can. But you can't do it too often, and you have to understand the various forces at work. There's only one Central Park in New York, not six of them.

In recent years, you've become somewhat of a figurehead for dissent on gender equality within the profession. What was your reaction to the petition started by two students from the Harvard Graduate School of Design to retroactively include you as part of Bob's 1991 Pritzker Prize?
When the petition happened, that was a gift to me in my old age. Twenty thousand people all across the world called me Denise. I don't need the Pritzker Prize; my Pritzker Prize was that petition.
Whenever prerogative is lost, the old regime becomes very bitter. Boy, did you hear it in these

threads. The people I call the Sad, Old White Men—I've come across them particularly in politics—said things like, "Well, you know, she wasn't there when Bob designed his mother's house. She only married him in 1967." But Bob and I started working together in 1961 formally, and informally by 1960, seven years before we were married. In that time, a *lot* happened besides the six versions of the Vanna Venturi house that Bob designed, and the seventh that she built. In that time our collaboration over the two theories courses we taught grew closer and closer, and through me ideas from Penn's planning school influenced the plan of the last version of the Vanna Venturi House. But they don't know about that.

In your essay "Sexism and the Star System in Architecture," you refer to social injustices as "petty apartheid" and state that "architects cannot afford hostile critics." Do you think there's a brighter future ahead for female practitioners?
Isn't this the moment? Young women in the 1970s were very feminist, in the 1980s they were turning away. Now, in the petition, there are personal accounts of young women living under oppression in architecture offices; oh boy, do they feel persecuted. It's a very interesting social document. Very poignant. I call it "Mayhew's Architecture." Henry Mayhew was a British journalist who wrote a book called *Mayhew's London,* around 1850. The Industrial Revolution was just starting and people were living in dreadful conditions. He recorded and published their personal accounts; it was the source for Dickens's *Oliver Twist.* Here we have personal accounts of young women living under oppression in the early years of architecture offices, right now, as recent as in 2013.

What were your early professional experiences like as a young practitioner and teacher?
When I came to America, my first husband, Robert Scott Brown, had died, and I didn't expect to go into teaching, but I also didn't want to leave Penn. I'd done very well. The first course I taught at Penn was an introduction to urban design for non-architects. It gave them a taste of studio. I was

Drawing by Robert Venturi illustrating two central ways in which buildings embody iconography—the "duck" and the "decorated shed"—an idea he developed with Scott Brown, 1968.

twenty-nine. The students walked in the first day and said, "Where's the professor?" as I was younger than a lot of them. I remember an occasion when one of them complained that I'd scored him too low on a test, and he said, "You'll never be a professor. I can tell you that now." I stood firm but when he left, put my head down on my desk and burst into tears, professor or not. And a motherly female student found me and took me out for a drink at a local bar, Smoky Joe. Those were my kinds of experiences as a very young teacher.

Later, I was teaching my theories course and Bob and I were collaborating by sharing material and critiquing each other's work and teaching programs. Eventually I ran the seminars and researched and wrote the work topics and exams for both of our courses. Various faculty members, including me, gave "this I believe" lectures in my course, but Bob gave his own. They were the basis for *Complexity and Contradiction* and they were stupendous. I would go into the studio at night and over their drawing boards discuss with students how the lectures and work topics might connect with what they were designing. It was such a good way to make the connection. When Bob and I left and they stopped doing this, performance in studio went down.

We really had a close collaboration. I was as interested in mannerism as he was, coming from the New Brutalists, who were very into mannerism. We had lots to think about and discuss together.

Did the media attention surrounding the petition affect your working relationship with Bob?

When the Pritzker committee called Bob and told him he'd won the prize, he said, "It should go to Denise as well." They said, "We'll get back to you." So we waited, and waited, and waited, and finally the phone call came: "No, we're not doing that." We talked about it, and we agreed that our firm was not well enough established to say no to that prize. I had to say, "No, I can't do that to you. We have to do it. We need that."

Princeton gave him a prize at the same time, too, and the same thing happened. I have records and accounts of certain projects in which I was involved, but no one wants to believe those records. In many of those projects, the parti is mine. Architecture is such a complicated thing—the parti is just the beginning.

When Bob and I work together, our buildings are better. In some, he's gotten very little from me, and in others I've done the majority and he's done very little. When you work together, there's a ping pong of ideas, and many people can have important roles. At the same time, every architect thinks they invented things, because that's what you want to do as an architect—probably more so as a man, I think. Men want to say, "It was all me, and I did it all for you." Women like to say, "It was sharing, we all did this." But even they want to say, "I invented that."

We were once doing this building, a stadium. They were adding six extra rows of seating and it was a very complex problem. Sitting with the board, I whispered to Bob my proposed solution, and he said, "You tell them." So I did. Later, the project manager pointed out to me that by the end of the meeting, our clients were referring to it as Bob's idea.

Left: Scott Brown and Venturi in the studio, Philadelphia, Pennsylvania, 1968.

Below: Venturi and Scott Brown (center) with students at Tsinghua University, Beijing, 2004.

That's so frustrating.

The project manager did add, "While you two were whispering about it, I was having the same idea." And then Bob said, "Denise, while you were talking, I was having the same idea." So it's unavoidable. We make so much of the value of the design idea.

You've continued to be a prolific writer and a critical voice concurrent with your practice at the firm. How do you personally balance theory with practice?

I write to clear my mind. I get essential things down on paper so I can get on to the next thing. I didn't come from the tradition where you wrote as a scholar. When I first started teaching, all my writing was for studio. Scholars were writing academic articles and texts but no one wrote for studio, producing all the books that the students would use, like *Learning from Las Vegas*. I did, for all of my studios, and I ran many of them. That was the writing I did.

In planning school, people would tell me, "You better start writing." I didn't understand that you don't get promotions if you don't write scholarly texts. I had done some writing, but not very much, though it was all getting published. Then I got to UCLA and they told me I would be an assistant professor, while another guy— younger than me, with less of a record—was made a full professor. His father was an important Los Angeles architect, and they wanted him to run the department. I was just furious. I said, "Look, I didn't expect to be associated with an institution where they took 'publish or perish' so seriously." The dean of appointments bridled when I said that. You should have seen him. He later gave a talk called "Publish or Perish," a spirited defense. I listened, and he had some points.

I began publishing like crazy after that. But I also ran my studio and I made plans to run the next one on Las Vegas, and I invited Bob to come lecture to my students at UCLA. We were doing an urban design studio on the shorefront of Santa Monica, and its hippie culture, which intrigued the students.

Throughout your career, you've been very candid and honest about the injustices within the discipline, including your own firsthand experiences. How have you dealt with such instances of adversity?

If you like making things, then it's the making of things that keeps you in it, the gathering together. When I stopped practicing, I realized I'd become addicted to practice. But I love writing, I love photography, and bringing our ideas together on a project. And seeing the results in use makes me as happy as finding them beautiful.

The research side has its own creativity, too—you can be just as creative about analysis as you can about design, and you need both.

What would you consider your greatest triumph?

One of my triumphs now is this petition. People wrote things like, "Now I realize that my professor who assigned *Learning from Las Vegas* as a kind of warning had the book all wrong; he hadn't understood the book." Things like that are a triumph.

The National Gallery was also a major triumph for us. We got that job out of sheer nerve. I went to the clients and said, "I don't think you know about us, or that we're doing museums." I'd been studying in England, I knew what would interest them and I knew about the site. They already had a committee in New York, and they had us meet the committee after they'd interviewed everyone. And as a result we were allowed to join the competition.

Then the job became very difficult. The National Gallery had a terrible system for making decisions, with everyone on the board voting even when they hadn't been listening. So we resigned. I couldn't believe it; it was the job we wanted more than anything in our lives, and we resigned.

Clients! We really badly need a school for clients. Every time I say that to a university, they put it in the business school and make it a school for understanding the economics of development, which is a part of it but surely misses the point.

Most architectural commissions are now zwon through competitions. How has this affected or limited the practice?

Young architects see it as an opportunity. But there are so many disadvantages to competitions. First of all, many of them are fake. You're forced to jump through hoops. The competition runners want a good show. But often the winning designs are what someone thinks will be good for fundraising. And at the very time when you should be on whispering terms with your clients, when you should be getting to know them, listening for the contradictions between their words and their music, you can't talk with them. Of course, there's the possibility of breaking the wiring. Maybe they'll like your design so much they'll forget who they originally wanted, but that's not very likely.

What issues most interest you in architecture today?

Social concern in architecture is a very big deal for me. Understanding not only the needs of the poor, but the way people need to use architecture. This is the stuff I can't get people to read. The sad thing is, if you're really keen on housing and you come into the field, you come out not an architect, because it isn't really the architecture that gives people the housing they need in the end; it's the financial program (among other things). I was amazed when we were in Pakistan, there was an architect there who told us the story about how the low-income housing problem in Karachi was solved through graft—meaning the building of enough housing had nothing to do with architects designing houses. Architects can still be architects, but they have to think of other ways in which they can help the project.

How do you think technology is changing the field?

With technology, it's the same thing. There are pieces of Western technology that can help build houses in mud, for example. A little bit of pre-stressed concrete might be a good idea for the roof, if the roof is a part they have difficulty with. Understanding the level of technology that will work for your particular case is important, too. What might work in Karachi won't always work in Mexico City.

What is a typical workday for you?

I've worked from home for some years now, and I love it. We run a care organization for ourselves,

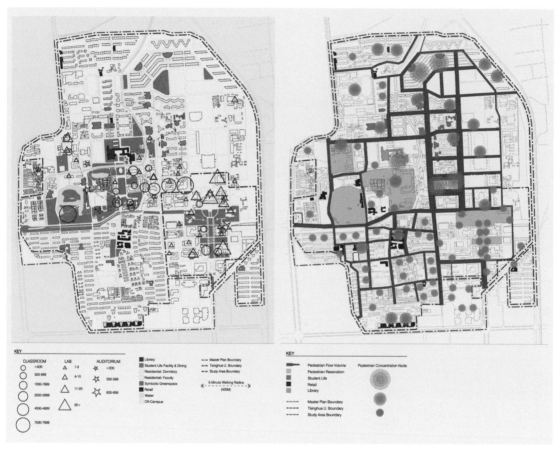

Area planning studies for the Tsinghua University campus in Beijing showing existing patterns of academic spaces (left) and existing bicycle volumes and pedestrian areas (right), 2005.

which is made up of what I call our mini university, people who help me do my work. They work part-time for me and part-time for the office, which is now owned by Dan McCoubrey. And a couple of people work for me and help care for Bob. I've become the HR person for this little group.

I try to get started at work before breakfast if I can. Then Bob goes off to the office and does nothing, and I stay here and work all day. Then I have lunch, and then this little dog makes me get up and have supper; otherwise I wouldn't.

Who's been your most important mentor?

I had all these German refugees as influences in my very young life. I had a marvelous structures professor, Manfred Marcus. I had my first studio when I was seventeen, and my teacher was probably twenty-four. Marcus was wonderful at finding out what our questions were when we were too naive to even frame the question. Any student could bring a sandwich to his office and he'd give them an extra class as they ate their sandwiches together. Of course, he gave us advice about life, too. I told him I loved Bach but just couldn't enjoy Brahms. And he said, "Don't try to enjoy Brahms. One day you'll suddenly find that you do." I never forgot that.

Arthur Korn was another. He'd argue for why a scheme should go a certain way and you'd argue for something else, and he'd say, "Stick to your guns, madam, stick to your guns." And then he'd pat you on the back and say, "God bless you, my boy. God bless you." Which meant you'd done something he liked very much.

It's hard to think of all the good advice right at this moment—but when I need something, I remember it.

What is your advice for emerging architects, writers, and critics?

There will be coherence in your life, but you have to be patient. At a certain age, I felt there was no structure in my life. When I left South Africa and went to England, I found a group of people and we were all searching. I said to Arthur Korn, "I have a need for structure in my life." I was living alone and worried. I think he sensed I was having some kind of a nervous breakdown, although I probably wasn't. He took me for coffee once a week until I was on my feet again. Somehow it helped us both. When you're trying to see if things are getting better, you have to learn to look backward to see how they were before.

What are you currently reading?

I don't have the time to read. I'm reading what I'm writing. I'm writing like crazy to get my book done. I'm putting things in this book that should be in other books because I may not have the time to write those other books. When you're eighty-three, you could die, or you could go on to ninety-five. What you must do is make the most of it.

Deborah Sussman

Graphic Designer
1931—2014

As a young college student just credits shy of her undergraduate degree, Deborah Sussman landed her dream job, working as a graphic designer in the office of Charles and Ray Eames. A Brooklynite by birth, she had long admired the pioneering California modernists and, as it turned out, would extend her stay in Los Angeles well beyond her decade-long stint at their venerable studio. Years later she would be touted an "L.A. Woman" in her own right in a titular *Creative Review* article written on a 2013 retrospective of her early work. The exhibition, aptly titled *Deborah Sussman Loves Los Angeles*, was but a small indication of Sussman's indelible mark not just upon the city but also on the wider design community.

The daughter of a successful commercial artist, Sussman was drawn to a creative path from an early age. A diligent student, she matriculated at a string of progressive art schools—the Art Students League, Black Mountain College, Bard College, Institute of Design in Chicago, and the Ulm School of Design—and continued to live a life of learning, traveling widely within Europe, as well as to Mexico and India.

Her time with the Eameses was perhaps her most significant educational experience: through her work at the studio, she honed a fluency with multiple mediums, collaborating on key projects, including the House of Cards picture-card deck, the 1957 film *Day of the Dead*, and countless illustrations for packaging, toys, and advertisements, as well as displays for museum installations and furniture showrooms.

Sussman opened her own practice in 1968, later forming Sussman/Prejza & Co. in 1980 with her husband, Paul Prejza, an architect and urban planner. Together the multidisciplinary duo specialized in urban and environmental branding, soon emerging as pioneers of "supergraphics"—a term Sussman insists has strayed from its original meaning but with which she has become associated nonetheless. With the firm's monumental work for the 1984 Summer Olympic Games in Los Angeles, her immersive, wildly colorful graphics and environmental designs came to embody the look and ethos of California New Wave. The large-scale branding effort included graphics, signage, and sculptural building installations with effusive, oversized images and shapes in a palette of prismatic monochromes. Punchy, era-defining motifs that would reemerge as hallmarks of her style in the comprehensive identity projects she designed for clients ranging from the Joseph Magnin department store to Universal Studios, the City of Santa Monica, and the Museum of the African Diaspora in San Francisco.

The longtime Angeleno continued to work until her passing from breast cancer in 2014. From publications, posters, exhibitions, and signage to immersive installations, facades, and entire structures, Sussman's works brim with a sense of joy that was matched only by her vibrant, larger-than-life personality.

Deborah Sussman, 2014.

You were born and raised in Brooklyn, New York.

In Flatbush! My Brooklyn was very different than your Brooklyn. It was like another planet.

And your father was a commercial artist. How has that early exposure to the arts influenced you?

I inherited my father's capacity for drawing, so I loved to do that. However, he was old school. I have some of his drawings and watercolors, which are fantastic, but they are on the realistic side, and I, at a reasonably young age, was not. I was into modernism, which was encouraged in the schools I went to, such as P.S. 99 in Brooklyn. My parents encouraged my art, and my acting, and we all took dance lessons. The girls all played piano and the boys all took the violin, so it was very cultured. My parents gave me every opportunity that they did not have in the old country. There were other first-generation people who were also pushed to achieve, and to achieve meaningful work. I grew up thinking I could be an artist.

You've studied and attended a formidable list of schools: the Art Students League, Black Mountain College, Bard, the Institute of Design in Chicago, and your Fulbright at the Ulm School of Design (Hochschule für Gestaltung Ulm). You must have been an excellent student.

I *was* an excellent student! I had scholarships all along. When I was young, I went to the Art Students League in New York, where my father had some connections. I studied watercolor and life drawing, among other things. The high school I went to was also very progressive. We had an art department and we published a magazine called *Patterns*, and because I was the design editor I had free tuition.

There's a strong history of pioneering— and a lineage of Bauhaus—in the institutions you attended.

Among all these schools, Ulm was neither progressive nor Bauhaus. It was restrictive, repressive, and sort of group-think. I received the Fulbright when Max Bill headed the school, and the day I arrived there, he was deposed. It was so far from my dreams and my needs at the time (and I'm not alone saying this). Many people who went there feel exactly the same way as I did.

It wasn't the second coming of the Bauhaus?

The Bauhaus was a place where people gathered who could express and make real their creativity. It wasn't dogma, it was a way of advancing and of creating new material: new art, new dance, new clothing, new everything. At the Bauhaus, it was all about opening new doors. In Ulm, every workshop, and every room was locked at night. You were supposed to toe the line. Even though I made lifelong friends, it was really the opposite of what I was interested in. Personally, I was interested in exploring and broadening, and they were interested in reduction. Ulm was so opposite to schools I went to; it was like prison.

Was it because they were trying to push functionalism?

One language, one style of dressing, one product system all over the world. *Ganzeweis*, which means all white, and *ganzenow*, which means all straight or all right. Whereas the rest of my life had been quite the opposite.

In comparison, what were your experiences like at the other schools you attended? Did you consciously seek out the most cutting-edge design institutions?

Well it was different in each case, but my experiences at the other schools, especially in Chicago, were wonderful and profoundly affecting.

I went to Bard straight from high school, focusing on art, acting, and the French language. And some piano and literature. Bard was very cultured and very unstructured. It also had lots of problems, as Mary McCarthy wrote about in *The Groves of Academe*. The student body was eccentric, bohemian, and very mixed. It was like a new world. Our poetry teacher, James Merrill, used to drive some of us to New York in his little MG, and when we got to Manhattan, we would always eat at this special Viennese place. Years later, when I finally came out to California, I had to have an MG.

Black Mountain College was just for the summer, but everybody was there. I had heard about Black Mountain, and about their scholarship program, and I of course had to go there, too. I studied dance with Merce Cunningham, and painting with Franz Kline. My best friend was Francine du Plessix Gray, and Remy Shahn was part of the group. Rauschenberg and Cy Twombly were doing their thing. So just being around these people.

What led you to the program in Chicago?

At Bard, they had a junior year program—which many schools did—where you could do something else for that third year. I decided to go to the Institute of Design in Chicago, which I had heard all about and was very intrigued by. It really helped form the direction my life was going to take. I loved design. I loved Chicago, even though I was almost penniless. I lived for the first year in the German northside in a fourth-floor flat where there was no heat. I thought it was so cool. The faculty included the photographers Harry Callahan and Aaron Siskind, and we used to pal around with Aaron, who owned a jazz club a block away. The school was in an old building, and we had all kinds of workshops. The Eameses came to visit the school and they asked Konrad Wachsmann to recommend somebody to come and help that summer, and Konrad recommended me. So that's how I got to the Eames Office. I think the school wrote a letter, but it was Konrad's words that meant so much to them.

So that was your ticket to California?

Yes. I didn't go to be in California, I just went to work.

Were you aware of the explosion of California modernism at that time?

Working at the Eames Office, how could you not be? We knew some of the famous people. These were the golden years for artists, musicians, writers, poets, designers, and photographers in Los Angeles. There were all kinds of cultural programs in the evenings, but the world was so much smaller. Now it's very compartmentalized.

Who were some of your colleagues at the Eames Office?

At the beginning, it was very small. The major people were Don Albinson, Parke Meek, Charles Krakow, and Jill Mitchell, who was a friend and colleague of the Eameses from Cranbrook. Then there was a bookkeeper and a secretary. I recently discovered stationery that was printed sometime during my four years there and that I was involved in designing—even though it's not designed at all, which was what Charles wanted. It said, the Office of Charles Eames, and underneath that it said Ray Eames, a hairline space, and then it said Don Albinson; it had three names, and mine.

There is also a letter that Charles wrote on my behalf to the school in Chicago, indicating how important I had become to the office—he didn't use the word "indispensable," but made it sound like that—and could I please get credit for working at the Eames Office? And the school said no! But there was no choice. Who would choose to go back?

Left to right: Eli Noyes, Ray and Charles Eames, Sussman, Glen Feck, and Eliot Noyes, photographed at the Eames Office, Los Angeles, 1960s.

Sussman outside the Eameses' Case Study House in the Pacific Palisades, California, mid-1960s.

Even though I loved Chicago, how could I give up the Eames Office? So I stayed. And four years later, I went to Europe, on my Fulbright.

What was it like working with the Eameses, at a time when the size of their studio was still rather small?

I loved it. Though in the beginning I was really scared. I thought, how could I live up to any of this? But soon, Charles and Ray and I became friends. In those early years, they would even take off in the evening and go to the movies, and they would take me. They always had picnics; we would go to the beach and eat lunch together.

The thing about Charles was that if anybody walked in the door, he somehow sensed their Achilles' heel, and he would make them do something they couldn't do or they weren't good at. My first assignment was the instruction sheet from the small House of Cards deck. I was in love with paper and sculpture, so I made these wonderful foldings that I thought would be just dynamite in the box. Charles looked at them and said he couldn't imagine a machine that would fold them. So I did an accordion fold, but my Achilles' heel was I had to draw the cards in perspective with a ruling pen, the most hated tool for both of us. It wasn't freehand—I could draw almost anything if I was looking at it, especially with a soft pencil— and it was torture. You would rule down this black

line and it had to be perfectly straight, holding this instrument in your hand and leaning against a ruler or a T square. And then the ink would leak, so then you had to put white-out on it, and then the white-out would leak into the black, so then you'd have to go back to the black. Now in a nanosecond you can get the results that took me weeks.

Later you worked in Milan and Paris. Did you find the same sense of community there?

I had a love affair with Milan. That's where all the great modern design was happening, and I was also very fortunate to meet all the right people— or the right people for me. I met Bruno Munari, who liked me and introduced me to Jacqueline Vodoz. In the late 1950s, they were in the middle of the Italian design renaissance. Munari and all these wonderful people became like family. I was working at Studio Boggeri, and during that period I also met Richard Sapper. I've since watched his children grow up, and we're still in touch. People make all the difference.

I always wanted to go and live in Paris. My mother was very linguistic and literary, and she read a lot. She taught us French before my sister and I were four, and so Paris was always a dream of mine. When I went, I did some freelance work, and I worked at a design atelier at Galeries Lafayette headed by Jean Vidmer, an important Swiss-born

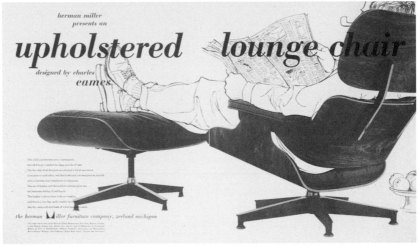

Top: Sussman (center) with the Eames Office all wearing "Independent Shades," paper cut-out glasses she designed in 1965 as an invitation to a Fourth of July beach party.

Bottom: Advertisement for the Eames Lounge Chair, featuring an illustration by Sussman, c. 1956.

graphic designer. We had a group that was international, and we all hung out together. When I think of what city in the world I would want to live in, it wouldn't be Rome, it wouldn't be New York—but Paris. I have this love like so many others. All you need to do is walk. Walking the streets of Paris and hopping into a cafe . . . it's heaven.

You've traveled, studied, and lived in many cities. How do you think these varied urban experiences have informed your practice?
Enormously. Before I had my Fulbright and went to Germany, one of the last projects I worked on at the Eames Office was the film *Day of the Dead* in Mexico. I did some of the photography in the film, and the film titles, and I fell in love with Mexico. That has been a great influence on my work.

What drew you back to California? Did you return directly after Paris?
I loved Paris, but I wasn't sure I wanted to spend the rest of my life there. And my sister was pressuring me to come back. Would I stay in New York, where my family was, or go to California? I did some freelance work in New York, and at that time the Eames Office was sort of exploding, and Charles invited me back. I was also offered a job at *Harper's Bazaar*. So I sweated it out one hot summer weekend, at the end of which I decided to move back to California, where now I've sprung roots. Work with the Eameses was filled with deep friendships and wonderful projects, and I wasn't sure how I would fit into the magazine world. But I think I made the right decision—because my work was so dimensional, and a magazine is flat.

It must have been such an amazing time in California during that period—the explosion of *Arts and Architecture* and the Case Study House Program.
Yes, yes. Well, I came at the end, toward the latter part of that particular culture, but I do remember when I was at the Eames Office and I had my nice little space with my drafting table. One, day Pierre Koenig came by. He was one of the designers of the Case Study Houses and he created that celebrated house that is always featured in photographs

and films—with the living room and glass looking out over Los Angeles from the Hollywood Hills. He was a rising star, and when he came to visit the Eames Office, I started showing him around as though he was nobody! I didn't know! [*Laughs*] But then we became friends.

What's your perspective on modernism today? Do you consider yourself modern?
One of my greatest mentors used to say "ism" is "think small." I don't like to be part of an "ism" and I don't think it's so easy to characterize the work with a word like that. It certainly isn't retro. What would the alternative to modernism be? What would another word be?

How was modernism discussed or referred to at that time?
When you're in the middle of it, you don't always discuss it so much. You *do* it. But it's hard for me to summarize. My work is very, very influenced by the culture of whatever I'm designing for. My work has always been passionate, strong, loud. Everything is colorful—even if it's all white, it's still in color. I am intuitive, and Paul Prejza, my husband and partner, is analytical. He goes from A to B to Z, and I go from W to G to M.

How did you first meet Paul, and when did you decide to start working together?
I won a competition to do a symbol for a program that was run by the City of Los Angeles's planning department. He was working there, and heard about me. He offered to bring my competition entries back, and that's how we met.

Me and my work are one. So naturally he was drawn into what I was doing, and he had intellectual rigor, enormous knowledge, and very critical facilities. There's probably nothing he doesn't know about. He's sort my opposite, and I thought that was very helpful, especially in the beginning.

Is that around the same time you began working with supergraphics and really pioneering that as a new medium?
"Supergraphics" is a misnomer. The word was

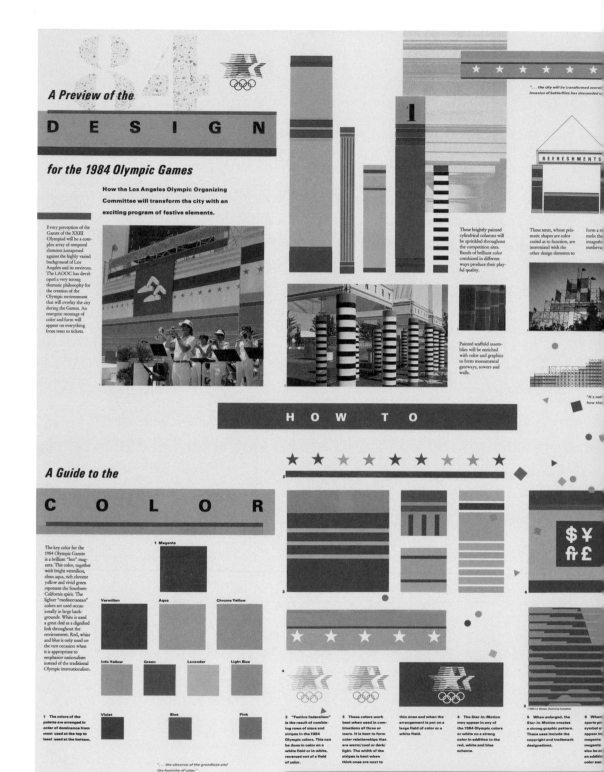

A Preview of the

DESIGN

for the 1984 Olympic Games

How the Los Angeles Olympic Organizing Committee will transform the city with an exciting program of festive elements.

Every perception of the Games of the XXIII Olympiad will be a complex array of temporal elements juxtaposed against the highly varied background of Los Angeles and its environs. The LAOOC has developed a very strong thematic philosophy for the creation of the Olympic environment that will overlay the city during the Games. An energetic montage of color and form will appear on everything from tents to tickets.

These brightly painted cylindrical columns will be sprinkled throughout the competition sites. Bands of brilliant color combined in different ways produce their playful quality.

Painted scaffold assemblies will be enriched with color and graphics to form monumental gateways, towers and walls.

These tents, whose prismatic shapes are color coded as to function, are intermixed with the other design elements to

form a m ment th imageab medieva

"... the city will be transformed overni invasion of butterflies has descended u

REFRESHMENTS

"It's not how the

HOW TO

A Guide to the

COLOR

The key color for the 1984 Olympic Games is a brilliant "hot" magenta. This color, together with bright vermilion, clean aqua, rich chrome yellow and vivid green represent the Southern California spirit. The lighter "mediterranean" colors are used occasionally in large backgrounds. White is used a great deal as a dignified link throughout the environment. Red, white and blue is only used on the rare occasion when it is appropriate to emphasize nationalism instead of the traditional Olympic internationalism.

1 Magenta

Vermilion   Aqua   Chrome Yellow

Info Yellow   Green   Lavender   Light Blue

Violet   Blue   Pink

1 The colors of the palette are arranged in order of dominance from most used at the top to least used at the bottom.

2 "Festive federalism" is the result of combining rows of stars and stripes in the 1984 Olympic colors. This can be done in color on a white field or in white, reversed out of a field of color.

"... the absence of the grandiose and the festivity of color."

3 These colors work best when used in combinations of three or more. It is best to form color relationships that are warm/cool or dark/light. The width of the stripes is best when thick ones are next to

thin ones and when the arrangement is put on a large field of color or a white field.

4 The Star-in-Motion may appear in any of the 1984 Olympic colors or white on a strong color in addition to the red, white and blue scheme.

5 When enlarged, the Star-in-Motion creates a strong graphic pattern. These uses include the copyright and trademark designations.

6 Whe sports p symbol appear in magenta also be ex an additio color sur

© 1984 L.A. Olympic Organizing Committee

$¥ fr£

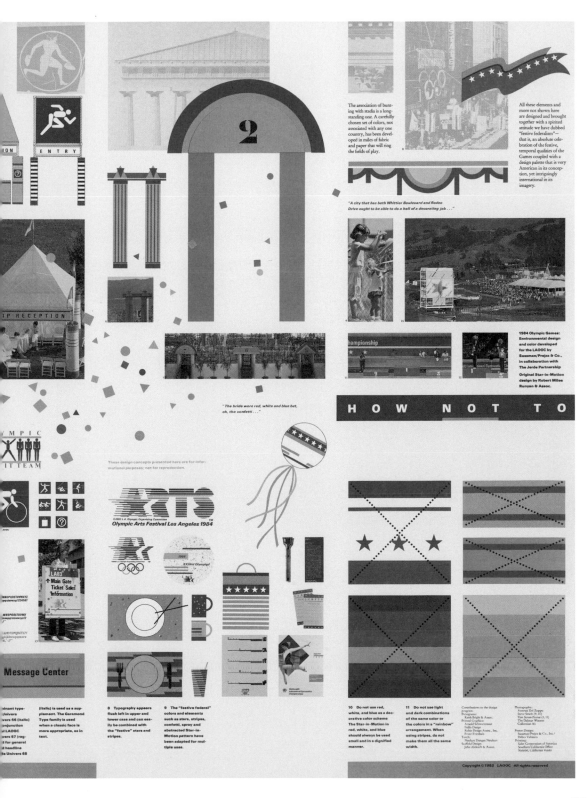

The association of bunting with stadia is a long-standing one. A carefully chosen set of colors, not associated with any one country, has been developed in miles of fabric and paper that will ring the fields of play.

All these elements and more not shown here are designed and brought together with a spirited attitude we have dubbed "festive federalism"— that is, an absolute celebration of the festive, temporal qualities of the Games coupled with a design palette that is very American in its conception, yet intriguingly international in its imagery.

"A city that has both Whittier Boulevard and Rodeo Drive ought to be able to do a hell of a decorating job . . ."

1984 Olympic Games: Environmental design and color developed for the LAOOC by Sussman/Prejza & Co., in collaboration with The Jerde Partnership

Original Star-in-Motion design by Robert Miles Runyan & Assoc.

"The bride wore red, white and blue but, oh, the confetti . . ."

HOW NOT TO

These design concepts presented here are for informational purposes; not for reproduction.

Olympic Arts Festival Los Angeles 1984
©1983 L.A. Olympic Organizing Committee

↑ Main Gate Ticket Sales Information

Message Center

...minant type—Univers... ...vers 66 (Italic) ...njunction ...al LAOOC ...vers 67 (reg- ...d for general ...d headline ...d Univers 68

(italic) is used as a supplement. The Garamond Type family is used when a classic face is more appropriate, as in text.

8 Typography appears flush left in upper and lower case and can easily be combined with the "festive" stars and stripes.

9 The "festive federal" colors and elements such as stars, stripes, confetti, spray and abstracted Star-in-Motion pattern have been adapted for multiple uses.

10 Do not use red, white, and blue as a decorative color scheme. The Star-in-Motion in red, white, and blue should always be used small and in a dignified manner.

11 Do not use light and dark combinations of the same color or the colors in a "rainbow" arrangement. When using stripes, do not make them all the same width.

Contributions to the design program:
Pictograms:
Keith Bright & Assoc.
Printed Graphics:
Arnold Schwartzman
Follis Design
Robin Design Assoc., Inc.
Franz Evenhuis
Torch:
Nathan Design Newland
Scaffold Design:
John Aldrich & Assoc.

Photography:
Annette Del Zoppo
Steve Swartz (9, 10)
Tim Street-Porter (1, 11)
The Delmar Watson Collection (6)

Poster Design:
Sussman/Prejza & Co., Inc./
Debra Valencia

Printing:
Sales Corporation of America
Southern California Office
Stanton, California 90680

Previous: Visual identity guidelines for the
1984 Summer Olympic Games in Los Angeles,
designed by Sussman/Prejza.

Top: Escher-like pattern graphics designed
for Standard Shoes, 1970 (top).

Above: Interior of a Standard Shoes store,
Los Angeles, designed in collaboration with
architect Bernard Zimmerman.

invented in the late 1970s by C. Ray Smith, an architect who wrote a book called *Supermannerism: New Attitudes in Post-Modern Architecture*. Smith used "supergraphics" to mean that the graphics had an identity severed from the architecture. For example, you didn't have to paint the ceiling one color and the wall another color, you would paint the ceiling in a color and make it drop down the wall into some shape. That's the most primitive description I can think of. People now use the word "supergraphics" all the time to mean just big graphics. And while I do make graphics, "supergraphics" is not the correct term.

If there were a single word that could describe your work—other than "supergraphics"— what would it be?
That's the questions I've never been able to answer. It's a marriage of graphics, messages, words, and the built environment. Going through my archives, we've found some tiny little drawings that I made. Most of my work, however, is big, involved, and

flashy—I think California has something to do with that. Maybe because it's horizontal. Or it was more horizontal when I got here. I could do all these big sweeps and gestures that I couldn't do in Manhattan.

Perhaps California provided a better canvas?
Yes, yes. Now we've worked in many places in the world, including New York and Racine, Wisconsin, which is one of my favorite programs that we've done within the last six years. So much is being written about me and Los Angeles—the *New York Times* captioned a photo of me as "L.A. woman." [*Laughs*] I guess that's what I am, although I think of myself more as "international woman."

Jane Thompson

—

Planner, Designer, Editor
b. 1927

At the entrance to Jane Thompson's studio in Cambridge, Massachusetts—home to Thompson Design Group, the interdisciplinary firm she's helmed since 1994—visitors are greeted by eight-foot-tall neon red letterforms reading *DR*. The studio devotes its practice to revitalizing neglected corners of cities, reclaiming waterfronts and industrial parks as habitable public spaces, while the massive sign is an homage and artifact of Design Research, the pioneering retail store she owned with her late husband and lifelong collaborator, the architect Ben Thompson. Vibrant and bold as the Marimekko prints she introduced to the American market in the 1960s, Thompson has defied categorization for nearly six decades. A planner, designer, entrepreneur, and urban advocate, she has always preferred to cut her own path.

An explorer by nature, Thompson moved to New York the day after her college graduation to secure a position in the Museum of Modern Art's then-nascent architecture and design department under Philip Johnson. An eager twenty-something, she led public tours of Marcel Breuer's *House in the Museum Garden* (1949) and enthusiastically embraced the modern thinking of the friends and mentors who surrounded her. Thompson credits the job with providing a postgraduate education and sowing the seeds of her lifelong advocacy—to promote design as a way of thinking, working, and living.

She left MoMA in 1949 to join the editorial team at *Interiors* magazine, and soon after became the founding editor of *Industrial Design* (later *I.D.*), a magazine devoted to the burgeoning profession. With deeply researched articles, technical information, and a cultural awareness about the end users of household products—predominantly women—Thompson's five-year tenure emphasized design over styling and criticism over fluff. Color foldouts and illustrations by well-known graphic designers, plus the efforts of art director Alvin Lustig, resulted in a richly beautiful magazine that continued to influence the field for fifty-five years.

When family life pulled her to Vermont in the early 1960s, Thompson spearheaded curricular and architectural planning for a new local high school. The endeavor led her fortuitously to Bauhaus founder Walter Gropius, whose interests in teaching and learning paralleled her own. Their friendship unfolded over many years, as Thompson interviewed Gropius and all the living *Bauhausler* to document the motivations and concepts behind their progressive institution.

A self-professed "architect without a portfolio," Thompson has advised on many successful civic spaces, including Boston's Faneuil Hall, Chicago's Navy Pier, and Governors Island and South Street Seaport in New York. Dedicated to solving complex planning problems, she is resolutely focused on celebrating local vendors and returning city streets to the public.

Do you remember the moment when you first became interested in design?

My first interest was music. As a kid, I just wanted to play the piano. We didn't have a piano, but my mother was quite musical. When I was nine years old, a German refugee became our neighbor. She was a dancer, and she sought out opportunities to teach local children to dance. She was marvelous in every way that she went about it. We learned to *move*, and I don't mean ballet—I mean modern dance. She made that very clear: "This is the new world, folks. Here we don't ruin our feet by standing en pointe." She started me dancing, gave me every opportunity, and even took me to dance performances in New York.

Not only did she take me to Martha Graham and her almost-premiere performance—*Letter to the World*—she immersed me in this. I can still see it. It wasn't her intention to educate our whole souls, but that is what happened. I had this completely accidental immersion in music, rhythm, dance, and costume design. Then she sent me off to college when I was seventeen.

What did you study in college?

I was an english and dance major at Vassar College. John Malcolm Brinnin was my key teacher. Everybody else was teaching Jane Austen, but then here came along this comprehensive modernist. It wasn't just T. S. Eliot's *The Waste Land*; we also went to see Billy Wilder's *Double Indemnity*. "Look up this artist," he would say. He taught us to see that modernism was in every art. Howard Moss was another teacher; he later became the poetry editor of the *New Yorker*. He taught us other sides of modern literature, like Djuna Barnes. I completely flipped when I read *Nightwood*.

What was your first job?

I went to the Museum of Modern Art right out of college. I had spent a summer as an intern researching in the theater and dance department for a production I was making for my thesis at Vassar. I decided that *that* was where I wanted to be: this is modern, this is new, this is everything.

Portrait of Jane Thompson (then Jane Fiske McCullough) for *Charm*, to accompany her article "Working in a Man's World," November 1957.

I was raised modern—not because of my parents, but because of the imaginative people that I came in contact with.

In those days, if you wanted to work at MoMA and you weren't already a curator, you had to get in through the secretarial pool. During my senior year, I studied shorthand for six months, then I went to MoMA to apply. They gave me a test and said, "Okay, you're in." Then they gave me my first assignment: "There's a man down the hall who wants you to take a letter, his name is Philip Johnson." I didn't know Philip Johnson; I didn't know much about architecture. In any case, I went and I did the letter and I guess it was okay, because the next day he asked me to come to the architecture department to be the secretary. To be a fly on the wall there and see everything that was happening—everybody who came and went, the exhibitions that were being made—it was an absolutely great education.

Who were some other figures working at MoMA at the time?

Ada Louise Huxtable was assistant curator,

and when she got a Fulbright scholarship, they asked me to take her job. So I was essentially a curator there for about a year, which I had no right to be, or at least not by academics standards. But by then I'd learned quite a lot, particularly working with the photo files: I pulled photographs for publishers, which taught me everything about what was being built or published. I got a pretty good education there in emerging modernism.

Alfred Barr was the genius of that museum. He took a year off from Wellesley, where he was teaching art, and went to Europe, Russia, and parts of Asia to find out who the modern painters really were—this was in 1927. At the end of his trip, he went to Dessau to visit the Bauhaus for four days, met everybody, and came away saying, "This is it, this is the menu of modernism. We've got film, music, costume, workshops of every kind, graphics, and painting. This all the arts; this is the comprehensive art statement of our time." Then he wrote that program for the new MoMA, and it was the menu from the Bauhaus. I thought all museums were like that, but there's none other. It really has made the multidisciplinary difference in our whole art world, and I certainly think in schools.

Did you feel any trepidation, being thrust into the design world?

I wasn't smart enough to be scared. I was just curious, and it was a very nice group. At the time, Philip Johnson decided to build a modern house, by Marcel Breuer, in the garden. He built the house and then assigned me to be the docent. It was a formative experience. People came in and said, "What's this about? Open space, no walls? No doors on the bedroom?" Well, there's a reason for that, and let's think about it. It made me realize how boxed in we were by our architecture, and if you'd never seen it before, modern was really weird. But people warmed up to it, very enthusiastically. Open space just makes you feel a lot better, doesn't it? It lifts your horizons.

What job or assignment has most affected your path?

In the early 1960s, I was finished with *Industrial Design* magazine and I had transitioned to home

life in Vermont. From 1959 to 1966 I was on the board of a foundation called the Kaufmann International Design Award, started by Edgar Kaufmann, the historian who had been design curator at MoMA in the office next to me. He started the foundation to give awards to designers. He asked me to be on the committee, which was pretty weird because there weren't women on committees in those days. We selected the juries. The first three years, the juries picked Charles and Ray Eames, Olivetti, and Walter Gropius (for innovation in design education). Edgar wanted books written about these winners; he appointed me the publications director and asked me to write three books. I didn't think I could write three books, so I gave Ralph Caplan one assignment, I gave another to a different editor, and I decided to work on Gropius because he was of interest to me, as I was in the process of building a school.

Fortunately I had access to Gropius, and he filled me in over the eight years I worked with him. He'd tell me where to go to see Marcel Breuer and Max Bill, and all these Europeans who had been in the Bauhaus. I went to Germany, and saw both the Dessau and Weimar schools. I interviewed everybody. Then I went across the United States to find Americans. I ended up with quite a lot of knowledge about the Bauhaus—more than anybody else—because no one else was very interested in German art at the time.

What was Gropius like?

Gropius was a total original. He wanted the nineteenth century to be over with, and he walked into the Bauhaus with no resources and no money: "We're going to find out what modernism is." He didn't say, "I've got a school, follow me." He said, "I'm a teacher and we need to experiment with making things useful, possible to manufacture, and true to the materials. We have to build for the public. Industrial design is here; if we don't master it, it's going to turn the world into crap." That was really his philosophy—both art and technology working together.

How did your relationship change after all those years of interviewing him?

Covers of *Industrial Design* issues two and three, 1954. Thompson served as founding editor in chief of the magazine.

Gropius was the most generous, uncomplicated person. He was very sweet, very friendly, never critical. He didn't spend his time talking about how bad everybody was. He was very clear about what he set out to do, what the conditions were, and who did what. He praised everybody who worked with him; he even sent me to them to get the details. He answered every question I ever asked him. He gave me books from his library to help explain what had happened and how it had happened. He was very idealistic; he wanted to help humankind. And God knows how many architects feel that way. He really was concerned for the welfare of society, with the quality of goods that were made.

The Bauhaus has been a big piece of my life; it was so real for me. And what they did was just astonishing—even more so under the circumstances, because it was a horrible time in Germany, with depression and postwar despair, poor resources, and the growing Nazi party.

How did your position at *I.D.* begin?

When I was working at *Interiors*, our publisher, Charles Whitney, came to me and said that he also owned *I.D.* When he bought *Interiors* it was part of the estate, but he didn't know what *I.D.* was all about. Fortunately George Nelson had an office upstairs, and had been made a contributing editor. So Charles said, "The time has come for industrial design." This was four or five years after the war, and all the factories were turning out cars and refrigerators, and all those products that needed chrome. So Charles asked me to be the founding editor and pick my team and go to work. I had one colleague at *Interiors*, Deborah Allen, who'd just done an absolutely marvelous issue on the television era. So Deborah agreed to be my coeditor. She had a very good background and a family in publishing, so she knew a lot of things I didn't. We'd also been given Alvin Lustig for our art director. And we sat down and said, "What should this magazine be?"

We wanted what we were doing to be beautiful and dramatic and wonderful. We worked very hard and did a lot of research. There wasn't a puff piece by any means. We knew every product designer in America and they all wanted to be published, because it was the only magazine on industrial

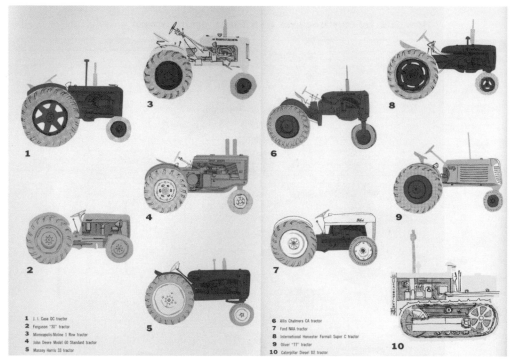

1 J. I. Case DC tractor
2 Ferguson "30" tractor
3 Minneapolis Moline 1 Row tractor
4 John Deere Model 60 Standard tractor
5 Massey Harris 33 tractor
6 Allis Chalmers CA tractor
7 Ford NAA tractor
8 International Harvester Farmall Super C tractor
9 Oliver "77" tractor
10 Caterpillar Diesel D2 tractor

Illustration by Andy Warhol for Thompson's article "Prime Mover: The American Tractor," featured in the second issue of *Industrial Design*, 1954.

design. We also did stories on design centers; the first one was Detroit. I went to Detroit and got swallowed up in the car studios, Harley Earl (GM's then-head of design), and the architecture. Then I moved on to Chicago and interviewed the designers there. The whole pattern was really great.

How was it collaborating with Deborah Allen?

Deborah was raising five children at the time, so we had a special way of getting our editorials written. I would go to Deb's house on Saturday night after the kids were asleep, and her husband, who was an editor at *Life*, was at work. We'd sit and write. It worked. What should we write about now? What's bugging us? She would write a sentence or two. Then we'd play hangman. I'd sit down and write the next sentence or two, because I knew what she was thinking. And we went through and wrote the editorial all the way through. I wrote some, she wrote some; a true collaboration.

How did you find design writers for the magazine when the field was so young?

People suggested things all the time, and we got special writers: George Nelson, for instance, and other good designers. And then Ralph Caplan started, and we had another writer who was actually a poet from England. That was the way it was. If you came in and you had ideas, it didn't really matter. We hired historians and architects to write, too.

Deborah and I decided we weren't going to be the people to tell readers how to make a new mold for plastics or something, but we had people who could. We made sure we had a lot of technical information. Our job was to really stress the qualities of the products and the reviews of the products. We were very prominent in publishing foreign goods, beautiful designs, and great department stores, none of which existed in the United States.

Jane and Ben Thompson, 1965.

There were amazing stories that got told. I remember there was a foldout piece on tractors in our second issue. A guy came by saying he'd like to illustrate something. I think at the time he was drawing shoes and working for a big department store, and was a graduate of Carnegie Tech (now Carnegie Mellon University). I said, "Okay, you should be able to do something." I gave him a sketch of all the processes in agriculture: seeding, haying, mulching. There was one tractor that was doing all those things. He said, "Sure, I can do that." I gave him my sketch, and he came back with this beautifully articulated thing. His name was Andy Warhol! He was just starting out in his career. Then Ben Thompson, who would later become my husband, opened the store Design Research. Within a few years, it came to us as a story. I had shopped in the store, but I wrote two pieces on Design Research before I ever talked to him.

How did your collaborations evolve once you were married?

We completely merged. Complete symbiosis. We both thought the same way, and we never stopped working. At Ben's firm, Benjamin Thompson Associates (BTA), they were thinking bigger. They'd think about the building, and how the building sits on the site. Ben had a universal view: how things should be designed and what the environment should be like. Pretty soon we were doing a whole campus, a whole college. Suddenly I understood that this amount of space could be mastered.

Ben used to say, "People in Boston don't drink and they don't eat. They put a plate of food in front of you, and before you've eaten they're asking if they can take it away." He was pointing out that there was no pleasure. As far as he was concerned, joy and pleasure were it. That's what he was about. Once I was liberated to feel that way, I completely agreed. But I also connected it to how your senses were used in your creative life. And if they're not, then you do one thing; you're restrained. I think that sensory input is essential to our lives.

Did you collaborate with Ben on Design Research?

I helped him out enormously at Design Research, although we eventually lost the store in a hostile takeover by Ben's financial partner. Buoyancy is the secret. You just take it, it's life. You fought the battle and the other guy won. You want something new and positive. We'd always find another way to do it.

What was it like being a leading woman in a predominantly male field?

I never saw a woman in a design office in all those years. Except maybe Betty Reese, who was a PR person for Raymond Loewy. Design was amazingly devoid of women. Mary Roche, the editor of *Charm*, asked me to talk about this in an article titled "Working in a Man's World," but I have to say I've never had any problems dealing with a totally male population, at any level or job.

Left: Design Research flagship store, Cambridge, Massachusetts, Benjamin Thompson Associates, 1968–1971.

Opposite: Design Research interior, Cambridge, 1970s.

Why do you think your experience was different, in that it was relatively free of difficulties?

I think because I was talking about things men wanted to talk about: the magazine, the field. I met them on their level, and I knew a few things they didn't. No one was aware that women were having a problem breaking in because they just weren't around; the women's magazines all had women staff concentrated on domestic design.

Later I did take a position on women with respect to design. Women know more than men, and they can see more than men, but they must apply their senses: their sense of family, and their sense of relationships. Because these count in the way you design.

How has your position as an outsider—a critic, a woman, a self-described "architect without a portfolio"—informed your work?

I prefer that role, and I've played it all along. The outsider perspective is something most architects don't have. That's what we did with the magazine: we showed products and things that we loved that designers didn't know about. For example, when we wrote about pots and pans, we didn't write about how pretty they were, but we said this one has good, even heating. And the handle works, too. We evaluated the actual performance. We didn't do it scientifically, but we used the damn thing.

Was there one person you would say was a mentor?

There were several. I'd say Ada Louise Huxtable when I was working with her at MoMA. She realized that I needed a little bit of coaching from time to time. And Mary Barnes, too. Peter Blake was a colleague I used to collaborate with. When I got to *I.D.*, George Nelson was delivered on a platter. He was with us from the very beginning. I worked with him the longest of my life. George was a generalist, and he was the most fun. Low key. He knew everything, but he wasn't about to pile it on you; he was always unraveling ideas, always thinking about the experience of design. The best thing was having lunch with George— you'd ask a question and then we'd be off. He didn't want to be a mentor—that was George's idea of too much work. He was more in the mode of, "Let's just have fun in our sandbox, and get everybody else in there." He really loved collective ideas, among all progressive designers.

How would you characterize your approach to projects and so-called 'frontier jobs'?

I like to start things. I don't care where we are; let's make a new cut. Where are we going? I've been starting things all my life. The Mount Anthony Union High School I started was certainly a big one. And *I.D.* It just seems like second nature to me. Nobody said, "We've got

Thompson Design Group oversaw master planning and development guidelines for the City of Long Branch, New Jersey, 1994–2000.

Thompson directed planning and programming for the redevelopment of Chicago's Navy Pier, Benjamin Thompson Associates, 1991–1995.

to change our world." But it looked like that opportunity for me.

Everyone in my family—my cousins, parents, my grandparents—every one of them was a PhD or a professor. They're all brains. I loved that, but I didn't want to be an academic. The demands of academia, the precision, and the small footnotes and details weren't attractive to me. I wanted to do something more visible. My father was also an inventor, always coming up with something.

Education has been a consistent thread throughout your life, from your interest in Gropius and the Bauhaus to your work in schooling in Vermont and the Aspen International Design Conference. What are your thoughts on the evolving state of design education?

Because there are so many teachers in my family, early on I got into questions of how you think about creativity, how your mind works. In design, you use your hands and therefore you're considered a tradesman. In art, you use your brain and therefore you're an artist. And that's just totally wrong! Your hand is the biggest conductor of information to your brain. If you feel the material you're not a tradesman, you're infusing your brain with the material you're going to use. Your senses are important.

All the education that I've done—for the school in Vermont, and in studying the Bauhaus—was about sensory training: you're going to touch this

material, you're going to form it, figure it out. That's how you're going to understand your medium. You can communicate with color, and with form, but not if you aren't used to using your eyes.

How does social responsibility inform your practice?

It informs everything at Thompson Design Group, whether it's new or old. When we were hired to do the Grand Central District Master Plan around 1986, it was a competition. We beat the other firms because they were doing buildings, and we were doing streets. Everywhere you are, there's infrastructure that's holding you back, or something built already. But that was a real kick for me—to take some of these dark alleys and get the circulation going, even keep it alive at night. I see things from the street level. In my urban planning projects, I act like the user: What can you see? Where can you sit? That's been the motto of what I do.

We invented the illumination of Grand Central, and it had to be done from the roofs of surrounding buildings. That took some doing. Now the entire terminal is illuminated, really changing the aura of Grand Central. People began walking around again, not just passing through to get away. The whole thing involved a social program as well. Through the partnership office, we made arrangements with the church next door, which had facilities for the homeless. We helped people get

The Grand Central District planning and improvement program, directed by Thompson, transformed forty-four blocks of Midtown Manhattan into desirable retail space, and a safer, more pedestrian-friendly urban environment for New Yorkers, Benjamin Thompson Associates, 1986–1996.

rehabilitation if they needed it, and then we hired them back to take care of the streets. It's a very important job. Their eyes on the street are what keep the crime down. That's worked marvelously.

What advice would you give yourself at the beginning of your career?

Wake up sooner. You think you can take another ten years because you've got all your life, but it'll get away from you. You need those years to figure out what you're going to do, find out about it, and get started. Learning something early gives you a sense of competence, control of some sort. You are learning how to deal with your environment, with what you're making, with people and how they live their lives. There's so much distraction. We once thought television was going to make everybody more visual, but it's not true. They're not *seeing*, really; they're substitute-seeing. That was the big myth of our youth.

Now it's a visual world, but only if you're looking at something and figuring it out and putting it in your brain. That's my feeling. Get somebody interested, be an apprentice—it's the way you discover yourself. You find yourself by testing many different things.

What are your biggest motivators?

I find longevity proves something. Accomplishing any change in a city—other than a developer coming in with a billion dollars and ripping everything down—really making it work, takes long-term energy. The long-term aspect lets me think much more deeply about what truly needs to be done. That's been the scope of my career. People are so limited in their ideas of what they're capable of. You have to make a battle plan for everything you're doing in order to get through all the obstacles. And there are a goddamn lot of obstacles.

Stanley Tigerman

—

Architect, Educator
b. 1930

An enfant terrible of Chicago's design scene, architect, educator, and critic Stanley Tigerman is known to deliver iconoclastic statements with a dose of tough love. Believing that one's greatest influence takes root in his or her hometown, the born-and-raised Chicagoan has never practiced outside of the city. Studies took him briefly to the East Coast and MIT, but he dropped out after only a year. He later resumed at the Yale School of Architecture, earning his bachelor's and master's degrees under the tutelage of Paul Rudolph, whose famously severe teaching approach instilled within him a rigorous work ethic and critical outlook.

Upon graduating from Yale, Tigerman returned to the Midwest and established his own practice in 1965. He became a founding member of the Chicago Seven, a group of architects, who, like the New York Five a few years before them, convened to write, debate, and organize lectures and exhibitions. Independent of his practice and collaborative work, he also produced a considerable body of collages and "architoons" offering utopian schemes and provocative speculations. In his infamous 1978 photomontage *Titanic*, Tigerman depicts Mies van der Rohe's Crown Hall, home to Illinois Institute of Technology's school of architecture, stern aloft, sinking into Lake Michigan. Tigerman mailed copies of the image—a critical statement on his colleagues' blind admiration of the modernist canon, rather than of Mies himself—to members of the architectural community, also offering a one-way ticket on the *Titanic*, in a cheeky move befitting his alternative approach.

Spanning five decades, Tigerman's diverse body of work has come to define its own brand of postmodernism, with widely varying forms and approaches emphasizing agility over adherence to a given aesthetic style or dogma. His built works include the Illinois Holocaust Museum and Education Center in Skokie; Saint Benedict's Abbey, in Benet Lake, Wisconsin; the Anti-Cruelty Society building in Chicago; the Chicago Children's Advocacy Center; and his largest project to date, the Five Polytechnic Institutes in Bangladesh. Devoted to his local community, Tigerman is also known to mentor the city's emerging talents, and in 1994 cofounded an alternative architecture school, Archeworks, with interior designer Eva Maddox.

After all these years, Tigerman continues to guide the architectural community with his wry, sharp wit. In 2015 the inaugural Chicago Architecture Biennial borrowed its theme, "The State of the Art of Architecture," from an influential conference Tigerman organized in 1977, in which leading American designers were invited to the city to assess the state of the field. Never shy to argue for a strong detour, Tigerman remains a public conscious for the architecture community, and today helms Tigerman McCurry Architects with architect Margaret McCurry, his wife and creative partner of more than thirty years.

You've built more than 175 works, plus created a large body of speculative and critical texts, cartoons, sketches, models, drawings, and exhibitions. How do the two sides of your practice—the conceptual and the built projects—relate, or perhaps even feed into each other?

It's not conceptual *versus* built work. It's actually teaching that led to both the conceptual and built work. To teach—which means to make yourself vulnerable to students, who are very critical—and to build are two opposite considerations. And everything feeds into everything else. I'm always cautious about architects who don't teach or write. Or, frankly, who don't think. But then, I'm also critical of people who critique, teach, write, and theorize, but don't build. I've always either taught a course titled "Ethics and Architecture," or wrote. When you posit something in a classroom or on the page, you need to make sure you behave in your work in a way that is consistent with that.

Your firm has never grown larger than ten or twelve people. Has that been intentional?

Yes, it has. I enjoy being hands-on with the work. I think that *not* being hands-on—being a supervisor or making generalist decisions—doesn't do much for the work. Mies said that "God is in the details," and he was right. You can't get involved in the

details of something if you're working on gigantic projects or if you're working all over the world. Much of the work that satisfied me the most was right here in Chicago, because I could control it.

How did you go about starting your firm?

I returned from Yale in 1961, and then went into a partnership with Norm Koglin. So for two years it was Tigerman and Cogland. And then we had a falling out, as sometimes happens. It became Stanley Tigerman, then, and ultimately, Tigerman McCurry. My wife, Margaret McCurry, is an architect and a partner in my practice. We tend to work independently—she has her clients and I have mine—but from time to time, we do collaborate. We're working on an education center right now for a botanical garden society in southwestern Michigan.

Your work combines many different architectural styles. What are some of the historic and aesthetic influences that inform your approach? Would you consider yourself a postmodernist, for example?

No. I'm the kind of architect who, whenever somebody comes to me—which is the only way we get work, since we don't market—what they get is where my head is at at that moment, as well as what they want. My early influences included

Stanley Tigerman (far left), Michael Abbot, Robert Fugman, and Deborah Doyle at his first office, at 920 N. Michigan Street in Chicago, 1980.

Tigerman, c. 1990.

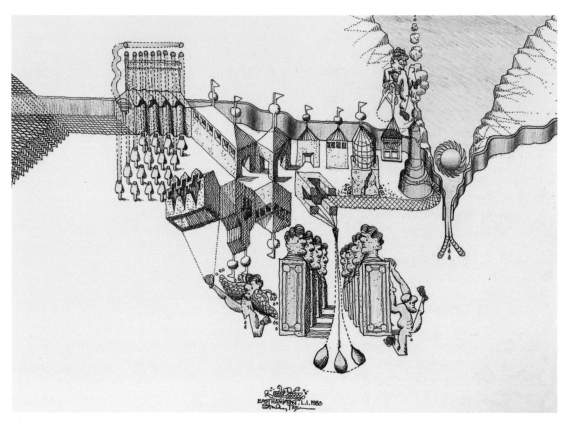

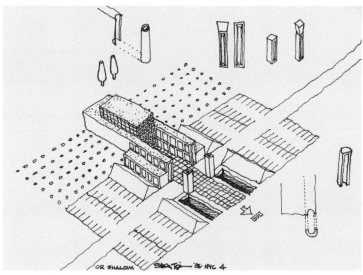

Top: One of Tigerman's "architoons,"
a genre term he coined to describe
his body of satirical architectural
sketches, 1983.

Bottom: First concept sketch for
Or Shalom Temple, 1986.

Mies van der Rohe, who I knew even before I went to Yale. He had a huge impact on the way I approached work. Paul Rudolph, because he basically invented me out of whole cloth. And my first employer, George Fred Keck. He was the first solar-passive architect in the United States; way ahead of his time. John Hejduk because of his soulful approach to architecture. We were incredibly close; we spoke every week until he died in 2000. He was a huge influence on me, and I like to think I was somewhat of an influence on him. Peter Eisenman, no question about it. Muzharul Islam, my master's classmate at Yale, with whom I worked on Five Polytechnical Institutes in Bangladesh for the World Bank. Islam was an utterly ethical being, sometimes to his own detriment, and he had a major impact on my thinking and my spirit. And my parents also.

One of your most famous collage works, *Titanic* (1978), depicts one of Mies's iconic designs—the Illinois Institute of Technology's Crown Hall—sinking into Lake Michigan.

That wasn't done antagonistically toward Mies. If I ever felt any antagonism, it was toward his descendants, the sycophants, the acolytes, in Chicago, largely, who added nothing to the language but just ripped him off at every opportunity. That was troubling to me. That's why we started the Chicago Seven—to open Chicago up to other influences, people from the Ivy League, UCLA, and so on—and create a more multivalent atmosphere here.

You were one of the original Chicago Seven. What were some of the core missions and discussions that took place in that group?

It began earlier than the Seven. There were four of us originally: Ben Weese, Stuart Cohen, Larry Booth, and me. We did a book, *Chicago Architecture*, and an exhibition, which opened in 1975 at Cooper Union through the good auspices of John Hejduk, and then came to Chicago the following year. The purpose of the original four, and then expanding to seven by bringing in Tom Beeby, Jim Nagle, and James Ingo Freed, who was then the dean at IIT, was to foster multivalence. We had nothing in

common stylistically or ideologically—if, that is, you had any ideology. Some of us had none.

In what kinds of ways did the group collectively act to expand discourse?

We did exhibitions, we did books, we sat on juries, we talked. I think every one of the seven talked, six of the seven full-time. What we portrayed was diversity, as opposed to the monolithic approach that Mies's descendants decided upon (not Mies himself, although Mies did say, "I taught them how to do it.").

What prevented you from attending the reunion of the Chicago Seven in 2005?

I had nothing in common with those people. I didn't in the beginning, and I didn't at that point, either. We only joined together for the reasons I already explained, and by 2005 we had long since succeeded. I'm much closer to Peter Eisenman, Frank Gehry, and Bob Stern, who are not in Chicago—maybe precisely because they're not in Chicago—than I am with people in Chicago. I don't have a lot of close friends here, just colleagues, and some of them I don't particularly respect.

Why is that?

Very few of them are really good architects. Stuart Cohen is a good architect; he has a more contextual approach. And of course Ingo Freed was a fabulous architect. But the rest of them are weak. So I never saw them socially. I'm exaggerating a bit; I just had dinner the other night with Larry Booth, for the first time in four years. Beeby is presumably a good friend of mine, but he never calls. I've always been sort of an outsider, which I cherish. I'm a Jew, so by definition, in a Christian country, I am an outsider. I've played upon that, consciously, for years to retain my position as an outsider.

What are the advantages to being an outsider, in your opinion?

Being an outsider in combination with not marketing means that I've always retained a very small practice. I like not being in the mainstream, observing from a distance. I'm a bit of a voyeur, and I'm also a bit of a bricoleur. My work and the drawings critique the architecture; the architecture expands thought, the drawings, writing, and text—they all do.

I've always taught and/or written. I've authored six or seven books, and edited another fourteen. That hasn't left a lot of time for other things. Le Corbusier once said how lucky he was to paint five hours a day, write five hours a day, and do architecture five hours a day. And that's basically what I do. All three pursuits somehow support or challenge each other continuously. Margaret and I are both loners. We see some people, but mostly her family. All of my family is deceased except my son and grandchildren, who are here in Chicago, and I see them all the time.

If you don't actively market your firm's services, does that also affect how clients approach your practice?

When clients come to me, they don't know what they're going to get, because I don't have a signature style. You could say that Richard Meier dips everything in white; Bob Stern, you know what he does; you know what Eisenman does; you know what Frank Gehry does. But nobody knows what I do, because it changes all the time, and I mean literally, not just figuratively. It's what's on my mind. And Margaret's work is very different from mine, though we do collaborate. No two architects are alike, and so it is with a husband and wife. We're different people.

It was very different back when I was an employee at Skidmore, Owings & Merrill, before I went to Yale. There, I was shoehorning every project into preconceived notions.

When you say "shoehorning," do you mean working within the style of the firm?

They had no different styles, they had one style, which was Miesian. Period. This was in the 1950s. My first assignment at Yale, given by Paul Rudolph, was a sketch prompt for a townhouse somewhere in New York. I did a Miesian kind of collage thing. And I flunked. I realized that that wasn't going to fly at Yale. So I quickly adapted. I became open

to other things, listening to critics, listening to the project's demands, to the brief.

When I got back to Chicago, I left SOM and tried to focus on what was in front of me. I'd start with a clean slate, nothing in my head, so that when a client came in, I didn't try to adapt them to my preconceptions, I adapted myself to the client. But as time passed, I realized I had certain ideas as well. It became a sort of fencing match between the preconceived notions that I was developing, and my ethical belief that an architect should be at the service of a client. It was a struggle, and it's still a struggle. Having a *tabula rasa* sounds fabulous, but it's very hard to keep your mind open to new possibilities every time out of the gate.

You practiced as an architect before pursuing formal studies at Yale. Do you feel this gave you an edge over your classmates?

Perhaps not so much an edge as a different approach. When I arrived at Yale, I was a bit older than everyone else in the bachelor's thesis class, although we'd all been in the service; I'd spent four years in the navy. But I was already a registered architect, and I'd worked for quite a number of architects. When I was twelve years old, I read *The Fountainhead,* and it had a gigantic impact on me. I identified with Howard Roark. I knew I didn't want to make money per se; I didn't want to embalm myself in success. I wanted to be an independent soul. A lot of detours resulted from that kind of behavior and thinking.

You grew very close to Paul Rudolph, who has said you were probably his best student at that time.

I did, even though he ate students for breakfast, and flunked them out left and right. The people who survived—Norman Foster, Richard Rogers, Tom Beeby, Bob Stern, Jack Robertson, Charlie Gwathmey—are all incredibly different types. Rudolph was a great teacher because he didn't bring anything to the table; he *created* you and your work. On a personal as well as a professional level, he was a bitch, a tough guy, but ask any of those who survived—there was a guy in my class who committed suicide, and a number of people who

Above: *Titanic*, Tigerman's critical 1978 photocollage depicting Mies van der Rohe's Crown Hall for the Illinois Institute of Technhology sinking into Lake Michigan.

Left: Tigerman with studio classmates gathered around his bachelor's thesis model at Yale University, April 1960. Pictured, left to right: Robert Engman, Tigerman, Will Reimann and Catherine "Kitty" Austin.

Above: Chicago Seven exhibition, pictured, left to right: Helmut Jahn, Tom Beeby, Tigerman, and Stuart Cohen, all members of the Chicago Seven, at the Townhouse Competition they organized and juried, 1978–79.

Right: Tigerman playing tennis with Richard Meier, Charles Gwathmey, and Peter Eisenman during a conference and lecture series in Boca Raton, Florida, 1979.

had to get counselors—and you'll find that they thrived. He was drastic in his approach to teaching, and I'm not saying that the end justifies the means, but I owe Paul Rudolph. I'll never pay off the debts that I owe people who have had an impact on me. Rudolph had a gigantic impact and he changed my life. You wouldn't know Stanley Tigerman from beans if it hadn't been for him.

Was he a mentor figure, or was your relationship with him more personal?

He made me grow up. Not on a personal level, but on an architectural level. As I said, with my first project at Yale, he flunked me. Two years later at a master's thesis crit, he publicly threatened to flunk me again. So I proceeded to work my ass off. When I got the MArch, he wanted me to come work for him. But I couldn't do it anymore, I had to go home. That was the hardest two years of my life, no question about it.

Did you continue to stay in touch after you moved back to Chicago?

Absolutely. I saw him whenever I went to New York. For me, he was a great role model because he lived architecture. He lived, breathed, ate, slept, and shit architecture. He was the ultimate, totally consumed architect. And the best teacher I ever had. He really spent a lot of time with students and supported them—*if* they performed.

Did the two of you share any particularly memorable meetings?

I'll tell you a story. I was in Dhaka working on a project with my ex-classmate Muzharul Islam. Louis Kahn, who had been one of our critics at Yale, was also there building a fabulous complex at Dhaka; it might as well have been a return to Piranesi's *Carceri* series, just incredible. We were both going there four or five times a year, and since there was only one hotel, whenever our visits coincided, Lou and I would meet and have breakfast or dinner. One time I was on my way to Dhaka from Chicago, and he was on his way back to Philadelphia from Ahmedabad, and we intersected at Heathrow. We had tea and a sandwich and talked. As he was leaving, he said to me how much he admired Paul Rudolph. Paul had been very mean to him at Yale. When I got to Dhaka, I read that Lou had died in New York in that awful way in the men's room at Penn Station. I sent a cable to Paul, asking to have breakfast with him at the Plaza, which we regularly did. I told him about Lou Kahn and how much he'd admired him and his work. Paul looked at me like I was nuts and said nothing.

In other words, architects are not great at supporting each other.

You've openly criticized architects for not being supportive of one another, for being too competitive, and for not mentoring others. How have you tried to remedy that situation, to the extent that any one person can?

I like successive generations, I like the young. I've always supported Jeanne Gang, John Ronan. They're terrific architects. But I told them both: "As long as I consider what you do good, I'll support you. If you do shit, I will not support you." And their work has been, by and large, good. Ronan has not done anything that has bombed. Jeanne unfortunately has, because success, public adulation, and exposure came to her too early. It spoiled her a bit. But she's a brilliant, fabulous architect.

In what ways do you give your support?

First of all, as they will tell you, I've never bad-mouthed them behind their backs. I've always recommended them. I'm honest to a fault. Another reason my practice is small is because I have a big mouth and say what's on my mind.

Have others supported you in return?

I only have a problem with adults of my own generation. When I was the director of architecture at the University of Illinois at Chicago, I was really harsh, because that's what my training had been under Paul Rudolph. That's what I understood, what I knew. And the students hung me in effigy.

What prompted them to do that?

It was a reaction to a jury in which I took a student's drawing and burned it. The drawing really was that bad. But students over the years—all the students at

UIC, and then Archeworks, et cetera—have always come back and supported me. It sounds bad, my burning a drawing, but there are architects and non-architects who sit on juries and are not interested in the students whatsoever. They talk to the other jurors, who they're trying to impress. I really resent that they are approaching the opportunity as a networking event rather than a teaching one.

What were some of the main ideas you sought to instill while at the UIC?
It's simple. I wanted to bring it into a more theoretical stance. Chicago is a great architectural city, unquestionably. People here always refer to Mies's apocryphal saying, "Build, don't talk." But the Midwest is a problem. It's very right-wing, Baptist-Fundamentalist, anti-intellectual. So I'm an outsider. Whenever I talk to Peter Eisenman, which I just did this morning, each of us tries to one-up the other, like, "Who's more of an outsider?"

Who won today?
This morning, he said, "I heard you're not coming for my jury next week." I said, "Who the hell told you that? Of course I'm coming for your jury." He and I are equally insecure.

It's surprising and humbling to hear that.
Being insecure is very liberating. It frees you to rethink propositions that you may have mistakenly made and not seen earlier. So I have no problem at all with being insecure. I'm not type-bound, and I'm not bound to some preconception. In fact, it's more of a contrarian decision, freeing me to question everything, including myself.

You've crafted this public perception of being one of Chicago's most critical voices in architecture. You were born in the city and have lived there nearly your entire life. What is your relationship to the city, and how has it evolved over time?
When you get older, young people come to you and ask, "When should I start my practice?" My answer is always the same: "Not when you inherit money

from your mother. Not when you have a client already. Open your practice when you are no longer qualified to work for others, when you think that anybody who tells you what to do doesn't know his ass from a hole the ground."

People also ask me, "*Where* should I open a practice?" And my answer, again, is always the same: home, where you come from. Because no matter which side of the tracks you were born on, that's where you have the greatest longevity, the longest tenure, the greatest influence. I was born in Chicago, and I've always supported Chicago. As a result, Chicago has always supported me. If you flit from one city to another, as many architects do, you can't invest the time required to develop loyalty. You need tenure, you need a life commitment to a place. Actually, you don't have to go back to the place where you were born, but you should go to one place and stay there your whole life.

How do you feel about the growing cult of the starchitect?
Without mentioning names—well, I will mention Zaha Hadid, who is a great friend of mine. I'm very fond of her, because she's a loyal human being. If you're friendly to her, she's friendly to you. But when Zaha said that it's not her job to pass judgment on the governments of the places where she works, even if they're less than ethical, that was a mistake. She has such a potent position that, were she to challenge or reject working for such countries, it could have a huge impact.

You've frequently spoken about the ethical responsibilities facing architects. What is the ethical framework you believe they should be working in? And are there ways in which you're reflecting this in your own practice?
You have to build what you speak. You have to walk the talk. I'm an old guy, I'm eighty-four years old. I come from a time when the AIA code of ethics was very clear. You couldn't displace another architect before you wrote him a letter explaining that this client, who was originally his client, approached you; you ask if he was paid in full, and so on. I still behave that way. I'm virtually the only architect who does. If you read the AIA code of

ethics today, you'll see, right off the bat, that you can now market, you can now undercut another architect's fees, you can now displace architects without notifying them. That's not the AIA I signed up for. So I have a problem with that.

How did you react when the AIA presented you with the AIA/ACSA Topaz Medallion for excellence in architectural education in 2008, and the Lifetime Achievement Award in 2013?
When I got the Topaz Medallion, my opening words were about how appreciative I was to receive the award, particularly because sixty years earlier, I'd flunked out of MIT. It meant a great deal to me. And I'm delighted that the Chicago chapter of the AIA gave me their Lifetime Achievement Award.

I love it when people feel compelled to honor someone. So I'm very thankful, but I also will continue to say the truth about my feelings on architecture, education, and ethics. Ethics loom very large for me—larger than design. I think ethical behavior is what you learn as your mommy feeds you. If you don't learn it there in the beginning, you never do. Architects who are payroll-driven, who need higher and higher fees, and do more and more work no matter what— I have a problem with them. In a way, not to my credit, I'm like Jack the giant-killer. Or Don Quixote. I do things and behave in a way that doesn't clearly, and is not meant to, make friends or influence people. I realize that makes me a dinosaur.

Top: The Five Polytechnic Institutes in
Bangladesh, completed in 1975 by Tigerman
and architect Muzharul Islam, a friend and
colleague from Yale.

Bottom: Tigerman (right) with Islam in
Gulshan Thana, a suburb of Dhaka,
Bangladesh, c. 1965.

Urban Matrix, a utopian city proposal for a modular "total-environment" formed by buoyant, tetrahedral mixed units, 1967.

Axonometric image of *Kingdom of Atlantis*, a hypothetical, unbuilt concept for a floating development, 1968.

The architecture critic Blair Kamin once characterized you as a "Chicago design maven who can spit venom like a snake." Do you agree with that? What are some issues you're fighting for at the moment?

My main agenda right now is starting a school of architecture at the University of Chicago. I'm on the visiting committee for the Divinity School, and my wife is on the women's board. The University of Chicago is arguably the only place between the mountain ranges that has a clear intellectual network. It's a great university, like Harvard, Yale, and Princeton. Probably better than Princeton.

How would this new school be different? What would it hope to achieve and introduce to the community?

It would start out with a doctoral program in architecture—which means there's history, criticism, and theory—then work backward, like Princeton did, to include an MArch. Because I am a booster of the city of Chicago, I want to see publications emanate from Chicago, about Chicago, and have a ripple effect on the rest of the country. So that's an aspiration of mine that I will or will not be able to achieve.

I'm not really interested in handling such a program; I'm interested in *starting* such a program, of causing and influencing it to begin.

I continue to write about ethical issues. I build for whoever walks in the door. I love people who walk in the door and want to build something with us.

You've now been practicing for more than fifty years. How has the profession evolved over that time, particularly with respect to technology?

Architecture has changed dramatically and will continue to change. 3D printing, for example: it's great, absolutely spectacular, and it's clear to me, as it must be to you, too, across our generations, that ultimately buildings will be built that way. But even if we're moving in a direction where the old-fashioned ways of producing architecture will not be there, the ethic, I hope, will still be.

I have very strong feelings, but they are more philosophical than architectural. What God really wants is for you not to speak it, but do it, live it, be it. To make things. One of the antagonisms that I have with Peter Eisenman, constantly, is that I hate deconstructivism: It's like pulling wings off flies. Architecture is an optimistic pursuit; it's about life. I believe in the constructive pursuit of making things. And that is architecture: writing about it, building it, making it. To make something requires a great sense of optimism, because everything conspires against you: building and zoning codes, city officials. They're all against change.

Drawings of *Instant City*, Tigerman's
avant-garde proposal for multi-use
megastructures built over expressways, 1966.

Illinois Holocaust Museum and Education Center completed by Tigerman in Skokie, Illinois, 2009.

Do you think technology has taken away from the aura of architecture? That drawing has become a lost, or less spiritual, art?

Yes. But I must say, the computer is fabulous. You can't have an architectural practice unless your office is entirely computerized. Margaret and I are the only people in our office who don't know Revit. I'm an old guy. I draw, then someone puts it on a computer, then I look at it, change it, then they input it again. I can work with the computer, but I like to draw because that's the way I was trained. I always wrote and I always drew, since before I went to Yale.

What are your hopes for Archeworks, the alternative architecture school you cofounded with Eva Maddox in 1994? Do you think it will continue to evolve as needs change along with the profession?

I hope it will, but history says that it won't. Already, it's weakening. Not because I'm not there, but because it's becoming rote. It's becoming something that we were antagonistic to in its founding. We were antagonistic to the lack of ethics being taught in architecture schools, antagonistic to the ways in which tenure was played out, weakening people as a result. And that's what it's becoming, so I left five years ago. I'm out but I wish them well.

Nothing is forever. Everything is a metaphor for life, which means everything changes, and then dies. The practice of architecture, the kinds of buildings we will be doing in fifty years, will all be sustainable. We will be building on other planets. It will be a whole different gig. All I want for the rest of my life is to influence others, to give clear consideration to ethical behavior, to respect others. When you don't respect others, you don't respect yourself. That's where my interests are. I recognize the value of massive change.

What advice do you have for young, emerging architects or critics today?

Be open. Be consistent as a human being. You are what you eat. Be open to change, because that's all you can anticipate.

After more than fifty years in the profession, what would you consider a dream project?

You want to know what my dream project is? The next one.

Beverly Willis

—

Architect, Planner, Philanthropist
b. 1928

Passion and self-possession have been leading forces in the life and career of Beverly Willis. Born in Tulsa, Oklahoma, during the Great Depression, Willis grew up during World War II and learned to fly a single-engine propeller plane as a rough-and-tumble teen, qualifying for the Women's Air Service. With the same industriousness and fearless conviction of her youth, Willis has continued to pursue new horizons ever since—as an architect, planner, and, above and beyond her call of duty, as a proponent for civic responsibility and gender equality in the field.

Initially training to be an engineer at Oregon State University, Willis transferred to the University of Hawaii in 1954 and earned a fine arts degree under the tutelage of artist Jean Charlot. Soon after, she opened her own studio, Willis Atelier, in Waikiki. With a focus on mural and fresco work, she devised an innovative technique for producing sand-cast mural panels, most notably used for the Royal Hawaiian Hilton's Shell Bar, a design commission that memorably served as the setting for the *Hawaiian Eye* television series.

Working on large-scale projects with site-specific conditions fostered Willis's growing interest in architecture, an apt combination of her training in fine art and engineering. By 1958 she had relocated to San Francisco and started a new venture, Beverly Willis Architects, specializing in historic preservation and reuse, as well as residential design.

An early adopter of digital technology, in the 1970s BWA developed CARLA (short for Computerized Approach to Residential Land Analysis), one of the first software programs to be used for large-scale planning and architectural projects. Now regarded as a key precedent for the profession's now-standard digital toolkit, the pioneering program arose out of necessity: Willis's firm was enlisted to design Aliamanu Valley, a 525-building military housing community in Honolulu, a site too large to comprehend at scale.

In recent years, Willis has increasingly turned her attention to advocacy and philanthropy. A founding trustee of the National Building Museum in Washington, DC, and founder of the Architecture Research Institute, a public urban policy think tank, Willis is dedicated to both preservation and innovation. In 2011 she rallied hundreds of designers, professionals, and residents behind Rebuild Downtown Our Town, a research initiative geared toward revitalizing lower Manhattan in the aftermath of 9/11.

She has also acted as a powerful proponent for gender equality in the profession, organizing national symposia and programs through the Beverly Willis Architecture Foundation. In 2009, at the age of eighty, she released *A Girl Is a Fellow Here: 100 Women Architects in the Studio of Frank Lloyd Wright*, a documentary film that marked her first foray into writing and directing. Having once denounced the fact that "historically important women designers are still not in the history books," Willis has spent several decades on actively expanding this history, leading by example and a self-effacing generosity of spirit.

You're a self-made woman who has pioneered many initiatives: first an art atelier, then an industrial design firm, an architecture firm, a think tank, and a foundation. What drives your passions?

I was not a person who knew what they wanted to do at a very early age. My ambition in life was to be independent. I read this wonderful book as a child, the title of which escapes me, but the author's background felt similar to mine. She didn't like the situation she was in (nor did I), so she found something that she could do: in her case, catching butterflies, which she sold to people in her neighborhood to earn money to become able to do what she wanted. I figured, I've got to find something like that; maybe I could make things with my hands. Once I discovered art—painting, drawing—it was everything. I became completely absorbed in it.

You first began working in art, then later transitioned to design. Do you distinguish between the two?

Willis on-site, 1982.

I don't. I think there's design in everything—even a good program, like a roundtable, takes a lot of what I consider design. All aspects of design are important and useful. The most successful people are good designers, even though they may not be in art or architecture.

When did you first become interested in design?

I was born in Oklahoma, and the only environment I knew before the age of six consisted of oil fields, which were grim places. There was no landscaping—just barren and totally flat. Very few sidewalks, no parking regulations, no organized streetscape.

This was also the era of the rise of the industrial designer, when everything was perceived as needing design work, whether it was a teakettle, or salt and pepper shakers, or a chair. I was really bothered by the lack of design in Oklahoma. Why? I don't know. I hadn't experienced designed things, hadn't been to Europe. But for some reason, I perceived Oklahoma that way and hated it. It was only much later that I thought I could do something about it.

You had an adventurous youth, becoming a licensed solo pilot by the age of eighteen. How did growing up during wartime influence you?

The era in which I was born gave me a fearlessness, and to some degree an aggressiveness, that came from being instilled with the idea that you might have to fight for your life. I was in high school during World War II, and the government wanted everybody to learn survival skills because there was a great sense—at this point I was in Portland, Oregon, a big ship-building city—that we were going to be invaded. They wanted us as individuals to be equipped: not necessarily to fight the enemy, but to survive. I built a radio. I learned wiring and welding. These were things I practiced as part of the war effort. So I had a very early and robust introduction to a lot of tools that actually had to do more with architecture than painting or art.

Fresco for United Chinese Society, completed in Honolulu in 1954.

It seems to have greatly shaped your work ethic.

Also as a result of growing up during this time, I became adept at rallying and creating organizations. I am a cofounder of the Women's Leadership Council of the Association of Collegiate Schools of Architecture, for example. All I had to do was make two telephone calls to create that.

Creating the National Building Museum, on the other hand, took five years. There were many people involved in that project. What motivated me was a feeling that carried over from the war: I looked around the world and saw that four or five other nations had such a museum. Why shouldn't we also have a facility dedicated to celebrating the work of artists and designers, architects, engineers, and urban and transportation system planners, not to mention builders and laborers? They're the ones who are actually out there with the tools, building the buildings. To create a place where they would be honored or represented struck me as a huge national need.

How would you describe your approach to work?

I'm a believer in research. And I have an ability to connect the dots, which some people do and some people don't. These two aptitudes continue to inform my approach to anything. Also remaining fairly current on what's going on. I may not know how to use a particular software program, but I'll know *about* it—what it does and how it fits in.

You were one of the first architects to experiment with computer-aided programming. CARLA (Computerized Approach to Residential Land Analysis) was custom-developed by your firm. Were there other similar software programs in use at the time?

Not in architecture or planning. CARLA had its genesis in World War II. The government developed a little piece of 3D software for the bombers on planes that actually drew the bombing site, to improve accuracy. We picked up that software and adapted it for the placement of housing concepts on land.

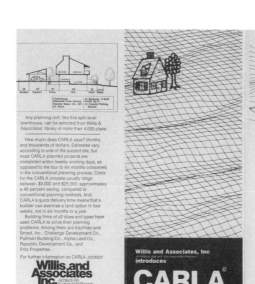

Top left: A 1974 brochure featuring Computerized Approach to Residential Land Analysis (CARLA), a digital software for land planning developed in-house by Willis and Associates in 1971.

Top right: Aliamanu Valley Community for Military Housing, a 525-acre site adjacent to Pearl Harbor in Honolulu, completed by Willis and Associates in 1978.

Above: River Run Residence and Vineyard, designed by Willis as her own residence, Napa Valley, California, 1983.

How did the development of the software come about?

We were motivated by need: How do you plan a building site that's a hundred or even a thousand acres? When I entered into the architecture and design world, all the firms were essentially one person with a couple of drafting assistants. Even a firm the size of Skidmore, Owings & Merrill only had, maybe, twenty people. It was because the projects were relatively small. A skyscraper in those days was twelve stories high; that was a huge building that cost a million dollars. A site was never larger than, say, a block. So you could walk around it, and indeed, that's what you were taught in school: to walk around a site to get a sense of it. That was considered good design.

But you can't walk and memorize a hundred-acre site. The postwar suburbs were on the rise. Developers were acquiring five hundred acres of farmland at a time and building whole clusters of housing units. We felt we needed a tool to help us analyze the land.

At the same time, we were reading stories in the newspaper about people's lives and houses being lost because of mudslides and flash floods that were in part a result of builders moving land around. That's not done anymore; we've become smarter and wiser. But back then, that was one of the big issues. I had the idea that if I could put together an automated system that enabled us to analyze the topography, we could then easily decide where to put things. The whole point was to minimize the cutting and filling. The less you move, the safer it is, and the more money you save.

I knew Harvard and MIT were playing around with computer concepts, so I approached one of the people at Harvard, hired a consultant, and found the graphic software program at Kansas State Geological School. We put it all together. Suddenly we could do six months of work in fifteen days, with greater accuracy than anybody else. So when the military wanted to build a new town of 11,500 people in Hawaii, we beat out all the big firms in the United States because we were the only ones who could get the approvals to do the job on five hundred acres of unstable soil.

Technology seems to develop ever more quickly these days. How do you think the widespread use of digital tools in architecture has affected the practice?

Being an architect, as I understood it and practiced it, was along the lines of being a master builder. We did everything: we not only designed, we did construction documents, specifications, the costing, construction supervision. Whatever needed to be done, we did it. As the years have gone by, architects have given up cost estimating, they've given up specification writing, environmental impact queries—all of these pieces of a practice that I was taught were essential.

So what remains, then, for the architect to do after fifty years of giving up so many parcels of the master-builder environment? Designing on the computer. I think it's narrowed the profession. Engineers are taking over. Arup is now doing architectural design, whereas it was previously known as a structural engineering firm. IBM and Google are moving into the field, because underlying the sophistication of what gets built today are mutations, and people in the software business have the capability to do that work. Architects don't.

The scale of the work is also changing. Big firms exist today because their clients want, for instance, a city for a million people planned, designed, and set up. We have fewer than ten cities that big in the entire country. So you have these huge firms of over 50,000 people. Anybody coming into the field today has to be very technologically savvy. And the people who take those courses tend to emerge with similar capabilities. Robotics are being introduced via software. Ten years from now, there will be a lot of robots.

Design education continues to evolve as the tools and means of the profession shift and develop. How do you think architectural education has changed, and where do you see it heading?

Architectural education has changed to keep up with the times, but it's still behind the times and has a lot of catching up to do. Much of it is simply a matter of scale. It's no use to send a bunch of

Top: Willis leading a staff meeting, 1979.

Above left: Interior of the National
Building Museum in Washington, DC,
of which Willis is a founding trustee.

kids out to work on a community project for five hundred people when their future jobs are for cities of a million people.

We have to remember that what an architect does—or what any other professional does—is driven by a client need. So, what are people paying for? What is the need? If the need is cities that house a million people, then you better be teaching students to design that. That's why IBM can step in with its Smarter Cities program, because that's the core of such an assignment. From my viewpoint, the profession is facing a tremendous transformation. It's already happening, and it's going to accelerate in the next decade. Unless certain people rise to a leadership level, the whole idea of a master builder will disappear.

As an active member of the architectural community, you've been a public advocate for women's rights. What are your views on the profession's longstanding gender imbalances?

Those of us who had practices before the women's movement—that is, before the late 1960s and early 1970s—had a totally different experience than the young ones now coming up. The big women's movement in architecture happened when a substantial number of women graduates couldn't get jobs because the male-run firms wouldn't hire them. We went through a horrible period where they were finally hiring one woman, and then a second woman, and then playing the two of them against each other. It was awful, and it took a few years to break through that.

In my experience, the construction people loved me, and I loved construction. There were no gender considerations involved. But after my practice grew enough for me to compete for larger projects, that's when I felt it. Male architects would say, "Oh, we can't hire her firm because women just can't design as well as men can. Everybody knows that." At that point in history there was still overt discussion about how women were innately incapable of design. The same prejudices existed in music, art, and other creative fields.

How did you face that kind of blatant bias and stay motivated?

I never dwelled on it. As in anything I wanted to do in my life, when I could see a solid wall in front of me, I'd approach it with the mindset that I'd climb over it or go around it—whatever I had to do to get to the other side. I could always figure out something.

Did you have mentors to help guide you along the way?

Early on, right out of the university, Jean Charlot, who was my professor, introduced me to his patrons and they became my patrons. Then I worked right off the bat for Henry Kaiser, who was one of the country's biggest industrialists during World War II, and he had a very "find a need and fill it" mentality. He created everything from chemical plants to aluminum plants to the Hoover Dam. That really impressed me. He was very quiet, and able to do all of these things with no background and only an eighth-grade education. I realized that I also could do all kinds of things without an important background or a lot of formal technical education.

What would you consider your biggest professional triumph?

The San Francisco Ballet building, no question. We asked the dancers what they wanted, and they said, "We don't know, nobody's ever asked us that before. What can we tell you?" Not having a ballet background myself, I had to get a feeling for it, sort of by osmosis. It was a wonderful experience and very challenging from the beginning to the end. It took eleven years—the longest I've ever worked on any one project.

And your biggest setback or challenge?

I think the biggest challenge that I've faced—and it happened with my own firm—is that all of the key partners and associates have moved on professionally. At that point in my career, in the 1970s and 1980s, I didn't have strong management skills. My background was art and design, not how to grow a firm and take on larger and larger projects and more and more staff.

Entry view of the San Francisco Ballet
Building, completed in 1982.

I could probably do it today, though. The wonderful thing about being my age is that I get to use all of the things I learned along the way. Younger people don't have the same context, the ability to see relationships and connect the dots. But I've "been there, done that," so nothing is all that difficult. I like to think big, and take on big projects. I really enjoy challenges.

What advice would you give someone just starting out?

What I say to scholars and students is that each generation faces a different set of issues from what their parents faced, or their grandparents, or their great-grandparents. The world is changing very rapidly, and you have to make an effort to understand what's going on in your world, and how that interfaces with your life and your work. You can't depend on the past to help you. You are required to be inventive.

People have to follow their passions—don't do what everybody else does. Follow your instincts, follow your heart, follow your passion, and things will work out better than you ever dreamed.

Below: Preliminary section view of the San Francisco Ballet Building, the first major building in the United States to be designed and constructed for use by a major ballet institution.

Chronologies

Ralph Caplan

—

1925 Born in Sewickley, Pennsylvania · **1942** Graduates from Kiski after being kicked out of Ambridge High School in Pennsylvania · **1943** Enlists in the US Marine Corps; trains as a radio operator but is assigned to an entertainment unit and performs comedy at military bases in the South Pacific · **1944** Participates in the invasion of Guam, where he serves until World War II ends · **1946** Attends Earlham College in Richmond, Indiana · **1950** Receives his MA from Indiana University and begins teaching, first at Penn State, then at Indiana University and Wabash College · **1957** Joins the staff of *Industrial Design* (later called *I.D.*) magazine, eventually becoming editor in chief · **1963** Leaves *I.D.* to work on his novel, *Say Yes!* (Doubleday, 1965); begins consulting for corporations and design studios, notably the office of Charles and Ray Eames, Chermayeff & Geismar, and Herman Miller · **1968** Becomes a member of the board of directors of the International Design Conference in Aspen, Colorado · **1976** Publishes *The Design of Herman Miller* (Whitney Library of Design) · **1978** Publishes *Attention, Connection, Tension, and Omission* (in-house publications by Herman Miller Inc.) · **1982** Publishes *By Design: Why There Are No Locks on the Bathroom Doors in the Hotel Louis XIV and Other Object Lessons* (McGraw-Hill) · **2004** Revised edition of *By Design* (Fairchild) · **2005** Publishes *Cracking the Whip: Essays on Design and Its Side Effects* (Fairchild) · **2010** Receives a National Design Award in the Design Mind category · **2011** Awarded an AIGA Gold Medal

Seymour Chwast

—

1931 Born in the Bronx, New York · **1946** Attends Abraham Lincoln High School; joins the school's elite Art Squad under the tutelage of Leon Friend · **1948** Publishes his first illustration, in *Seventeen* magazine, with art direction by Cipe Pineles; attends Cooper Union to study drawing and painting; meets future partners Milton Glaser, Edward Sorel, and Reynold Ruffins · **1951** Joins the staff of the *New York Times* as a junior designer in George Krikorian's promotions department, followed by short stints at *Esquire*, Sudler & Hennessey, and *House & Garden* · **1954** Forms Push Pin Studios with Glaser and Sorel (Ruffins joins the group shortly thereafter) · **1957** Launches the *Push Pin Monthly Graphic*, a freeform publication used by the studio as a vehicle for experimentation and self-promotion; in 1961, "monthly" is dropped from the title · **1970** A retrospective of Push Pin Studios, *The Push Pin Style*, is the first exhibition of graphic design at the Musée des Arts Décoratifs in Paris · **1972** Receives the Augustus Saint-Gaudens Award from the Cooper Union · **1975** Joins the Alliance Graphique Internationale as a member; becomes the sole director of Push Pin Studios after Glaser leaves to pursue his own interests · **1977** Launches the Push Pin Press with J. C. Suares · **1980** Produces the last issue of *Push Pin Graphic*, ending its twenty-three year run · **1982** Forms Pushpin Editions with Steven Heller; publishes books on art and design; briefly joins forces with Alan Peckolick

to form Pushpin Lubalin Peckolick, though the partnership only lasts a few years; later renames the studio Pushpin Group · **1984** Inducted into the Art Directors Club Hall of Fame · **1985** Publishes his first monograph, *The Left-Handed Designer* (Harry N. Abrams) · **1985** Receives an AIGA Gold Medal for Lifetime Achievement · **1997** Publishes his first issue of *The Nose*, a thematic publication designed to investigate social (and trivial) issues; receives the Masters Series Award from the School of Visual Arts · **2004** Publishes *The Push Pin Graphic: A Quarter Century of Innovative Design and Illustration* (Chronicle Books) · **2005** Named Honorary Royal Designer for Industry by England's Royal Society for the Encouragement of the Arts · **2009** Publishes *Seymour: The Obsessive Images of Seymour Chwast* (Chronicle Books) · **2012** *Double Portrait: Paula Scher and Seymour Chwast, Graphic Designers* opens at the Philadelphia Museum of Art; receives the Collab Design Excellence Award · **2015** Launches a digital archive of his work; the Modern Graphic History Library at Washington University in St. Louis acquires the complete Seymour Chwast poster collection

Bob Gill

—

1931 Born in Brooklyn, New York · **1948** Studies design and drawing at the Philadelphia Museum School of Art · **1951** Attends the Pennsylvania Academy of Fine Arts · **1952** Returns to New York; attends the City College of New York; begins work as a freelance designer and completes his first job, a cover for *Interiors* magazine · **1955** Receives an Art Directors Club Gold Medal for his title design on the sitcom *Private Secretary* · **1956** Begins teaching at the School of Visual Arts, and later at Pratt Institute in Manhattan · **1960** Moves to London on a whim; works briefly for Charles Hobson · **1962** Forms Fletcher/Forbes/Gill with Alan Fletcher and Colin Forbes on April Fool's Day; with Fletcher, Forbes, and several others, establishes the British Design & Art Direction (now D&AD) awards; F/F/G opens a second office in Geneva · **1963** F/F/G publishes *Graphic Design: Visual Comparisons* (Van Nostrand Reinhold); the books sells over one hundred thousand copies · **1967** Leaves F/F/G and resumes work as freelance designer; designs the cover of George Harrison's soundtrack album for the film *Wonderwall*; teaches at Central School of Art and Design in London · **1968** *Bob Gill's Portfolio*, a solo exhibition of his work, opens at the Stedelijk Museum in Amsterdam · **1970** Begins teaching at the Royal College of Art in London · **1971** Writes *I Keep Changing* (Scroll Press) and *Bob Gill's New York* (Kynoch Press) · **1974** Publishes *Ups & Downs* (Addison-Wesley) · **1975** Returns to New York after fifteen years in London; writes and produces the Broadway musical *Beatlemania* with Robert Rabinowitz; directs the porn film *The Double Exposure of Holly* · **1979** With Rabinowitz, stages a thirty-minute "sound-and-light spectacle" to celebrate the Lincoln Center's twentieth anniversary · **1981** Writes and designs *Forget All the Rules You Ever Learned About Graphic Design, Including the Ones in This Book* (Watson-Guptill); teaches at Parsons School of Design · **1991** Inducted into the New York Art Directors Club Hall of Fame · **1992** Publishes *Graphic Design*

Made Difficult (Van Nostrand Reinhold) · **1999** Presented with the Lifetime Achievement Award by D&AD · **2001** Publishes *Unspecial Effects for Graphic Designers* (Graphis) · **2003** Publishes *Graphic Design as a Second Language* (Images Publishing Group) · **2004** Publishes *Illustration* (Images Publishing Group) · **2006** Publishes *LogoMania* (Rockport Publishers) · **2009** Publishes *Words Into Pictures* (Images Publishing Group) · **2011** Publishes *Bob Gill, So Far* (Laurence King); retires from teaching · **2013** Instructs the online Skillshare class "Design as Idea"

Milton Glaser

—

1929 Born in the Bronx, New York · **1947** Graduates from the High School of Music and Art · **1954** Graduates from Cooper Union, having attended the Academy of Fine Arts in Bologna, Italy, on a Fulbright Scholarship; cofounds Push Pin Studios with Seymour Chwast, Edward Sorel, and Reynold Ruffins; directs the group with Chwast for more than twenty years · **1967** Illustrates a poster for Bob Dylan, which is inserted into more than six million copies of Dylan's *Greatest Hits* LP · **1968** Founds *New York* magazine with Clay Felker, acting as president and design director for nine years · **1970** Push Pin Studios is the first American studio to be featured at the Musée des Arts Décoratifs in Paris with the exhibition *The Push Pin Style*; the show travels throughout Europe and to Brazil and Japan · **1972** Receives an AIGA Gold Medal · **1974** Establishes Milton Glaser, Inc., in New York, which works on print collateral, branding, environmental and interior design, illustration, and publishing · **Mid-1970s** Collaborates on the comprehensive redesign of the American supermarket chain the Grand Union Company over the course of a fifteen-year collaboration · **1975** Solo exhibition at the Museum of Modern Art in New York · **1976** Designs the "I ♥ NY" logo, commissioned by the state of New York · **1977** Solo exhibition at the Centre Pompidou in Paris · **1981** Designs Sesame Place, an educational play park in Pennsylvania · **1983** Forms WBMG with Walter Bernard; the publications design firm collaborates with newspapers, including *The Los Angeles Times*, *The Boston Globe*, and *The Dallas Times Herald*, as well as magazines such as *TIME*, *Adweek*, *Golf Digest*, and many others · **1984** Solo exhibition at Cooper Union's Houghton Gallery; designs the logo for Brooklyn Brewery · **1987** Leads the interiors and concept design for "World Cities and the Future of the Metropolis," the Triennale di Milano International Exhibition in Milan; designs the World Health Organization's International AIDS symbol and poster · **1990** Leads the concept and interior design of New York Unearthed, a museum in Lower Manhattan; serves as president for the International Design Conference in Aspen, Colorado; the documentary *Milton Glaser: To Inform and Delight* premieres · **1991** Creates an exhibition in tribute to the 500th anniversary of artist Piero della Francesca, commissioned by the Italian government · **1993** Designs the identity and poster for the Pulitzer Prize–winning play *Angels in America* · **1997** Japan's Suntory Museum mounts a retrospective of Push Pin Studios · **2000** A major retrospective at the Fondazione Bevilacqua La Masa in Venice · **2004** Receives a National Design Award for Lifetime Achievement · **2006** The School of Visual Arts opens the Milton Glaser Design Study Center and Archives to the public · **2009** Awarded the National Medal of the Arts, making him the first graphic designer to receive the honor · **2011** Receives the Lifetime Achievement award from the Fulbright Association

Michael Graves

1934 Born in Indianapolis, Indiana · **1952** Attends the University of Cincinnati · **1959** Graduates from Harvard University with a master's in architecture · **1960** Works briefly for George Nelson; awarded the Rome Prize, travels to Italy and studies for two years; later becomes a trustee of the American Academy in Rome · **1962** Begins a thirty-nine-year teaching career at Princeton as the Robert Schirmer Professor of Architecture · **1964** Establishes an architecture practice in Princeton, New Jersey · **1967** Designs the Hanselmann House in Fort Wayne, Indiana · **1969** Together with Peter Eisenman, Charles Gwathmey, John Hejduk, and Richard Meier, now known collectively as the New York Five, arranges a meeting and critique at the Museum of Modern Art; the event later inspires a book on the work presented · **1972** George Wittenborn publishes *Five Architects* · **1975** Oxford University Press publishes the second edition of *Five Architects*, to greater acclaim · **1977** Designs the Plocek Residence in Warren, New Jersey · **1979** Named an AIA Fellow · **1981** Designs a dressing table for the Memphis Group · **1982** The Portland Building opens in Oregon; awarded the Humana headquarters commission in Louisville, Kentucky · **1985** Creates the best-selling 9093 kettle for Alessi; proposes an addition to the Whitney Museum of American Art in New York; after several revisions, plans for the Whitney expansion are eventually dropped; designs Disney's Burbank, California, headquarters · **1999** Partnership with Target begins, as the national retailer's first guest designer; receives National Medal of the Arts · **2000** Designs scaffolding to sheath the Washington Monument during its restoration · **2001** Awarded the AIA Gold Medal · **2003** Paralyzed by a spinal cord infection; spends time in eight hospitals over the course of a three-year recovery · **2010** Inducted into New Jersey Hall of Fame · **2011** The National Park Service adds the Portland Building to the National Registry of Historic Places · **2012** Ends his relationship with Target after eighteen years and two thousand products; begins working with JCPenney · **2014** Michael Graves School of Architecture opens at Kean University in New Jersey; an exhibition at the Grounds for Sculpture, *Michael Graves: Past as Prologue*, celebrates the fiftieth anniversary of his firm, Michael Graves Architecture & Design · **2015** Receives a National Design Award for Lifetime Achievement; dies of natural causes on March 12 at his home in Princeton, New Jersey

Charles Harrison

—

1931 Born in Shreveport, Louisiana · **1937** Relocates to Texas, where Charles Harrison Sr. teaches at Prairie View A&M University; the family later moves again, this time to Arizona · **1943** Attends George Washington Carver High School in Phoenix, an all-black institution that closed in 1954 after segregation was ruled unconstitutional; the former high school is now a museum and cultural center · **1947** Graduates high school at age sixteen, and moves to San Francisco to attend San Francisco City College; earns an associate's degree and decides to pursue further study in industrial design · **1949** Attends the School of the Art Institute of Chicago; SAIC is one of only five colleges accredited for industrial design · **1954** Earns a bachelor of fine arts degree; meets lifelong mentor Henry Glass; drafted into the US Army and serves as a cartographer in a topography unit in Germany · **1956** Returns to SAIC to pursue graduate studies; later transfers to the Illinois Institute of Technology, to complete his master's in art education · **1957** Freelances for Sears, Roebuck & Company; begins working for Henry P. Glass & Associates, and Ed Klein & Associates · **1958** Begins working at Robert Podall Associates; while there leads the team that designs the View-Master stereoscope; the toy sells with only minor changes for more than forty years · **1961** Becomes the first African American executive at Sears, Roebuck & Company; eventually becomes head of design · **1966** Designs a plastic garbage can, the first of its kind · **1993** Retires from Sears to teach part-time at the University of Illinois at Chicago · **2003** Teaches product design at Columbia College in Chicago · **2006** Publishes his memoir, *A Life's Design: The Life and Work of Industrial Designer Charles Harrison* (Ibis Design); receives a Lifetime Distinguished Service Award from the Industrial Designers Society of America · **2008** Receives a National Design Award for Lifetime Achievement · **2009** Awarded an honorary doctorate of fine arts from his alma mater, the School of the Art Institute of Chicago

Richard Hollis

—

1934 Born in London, England · **1952** Begins Arts and Crafts coursework at Chelsea School of Art; later transfers to Wimbledon School of Arts following two years of military service · **1956** Leaves Wimbledon, opting to take night classes at the Central School of Art and Crafts while running a silkscreen studio in his apartment and working as messenger to a photo engraver · **Late 1950s–early 1960s** Travels to Cuba, Zurich, and Paris, cultivating interests in left-wing politics, Concrete art, and film; begins a career as an independent book designer to several publishers, including Penguin Books, Anvil Press, Pelican Books, and Pluto Press · **1963** Works as a designer in the art department of Parisian department store Galeries Lafayette · **1964** Returns to Britain and begins teaching lithography and design at London College of Printing and Chelsea School of Art; cofounds the School of Design at the West of England College of Art with friend Norman Potter; begins designing the quarterly

journal *Modern Poetry in Translation*, which he continues to design for forty years · **1965** Becomes the art director of *New Society*, a social sciences and general weekly · **1970** Creates the visual identity for Whitechapel Art Gallery, beginning a fifteen-year collaboration · **1972** Designs *Ways of Seeing* (Penguin Books), a groundbreaking paperback adaptation of John Berger's BBC television series; collaborates on the design of Berger's Booker Prize–winning novel *G.* (Weidenfeld & Nicolson) · **1974** Becomes the production director at Faber and Faber · **1975** Designs *A Seventh Man* (Pelican Books), written by Berger and Jean Mohr · **1994** Writes and designs *Graphic Design: A Concise History* (Thames and Hudson) · **2005** Elected Royal Designer for Industry by the Royal Society for the Encouragement of Arts, Manufactures, and Commerce · **2006** Writes and designs *Swiss Graphic Design: The Origins and Growth of an International Style, 1920–1965* (Yale University Press) · **2012** Independent British publisher Occasional Papers releases *About Graphic Design*, a compilation of his writings, letters, and lecture outlines; Gallery Libby Sellers in London hosts a retrospective survey of his work, which later tours to ECAL in Lausanne, Switzerland; Centre Pompidou in Paris; and Artists Space in New York

Phyllis Lambert

—

1927 Born in Montreal, Canada · **1948** Receives a BA from Vassar College; relocates to Paris to pursue art and study architecture · **1954** Writes a passionate, eight-page letter to her father, Samuel Bronfman, head of the Seagram Company, after reviewing the unremarkable proposal he selected for the company's headquarters in New York; moves from Paris to New York; oversees research to select a new architect for the building; becomes the director of planning for the Seagram Building and works closely with Mies van der Rohe and Philip Johnson through design and construction; consults for the Seagram Company until 2000 · **1957** Purchases the stage curtain Pablo Picasso painted for the legendary ballet *Le Tricorne* for the Four Seasons restaurant at the Seagram Building · **1963** Studies architecture at Yale University, then transfers to the Illinois Institute of Technology from which she receives a master's in architecture · **1967** Designs the Saidye Bronfman Centre for the Arts (now the Segal Centre for Performing Arts) in Montreal · **1975** Forms the preservation group Heritage Montreal · **1979** Forms Society for Milton-Parc to renovate seven hundred not-for-profit housing cooperatives in downtown Montreal; founds the Canadian Centre for Architecture, a research center and museum; drafts article 26 of the Seagram Building lease to protect against unwanted changes · **1989** The Seagram Building exterior, its plaza, its lobby, and the Four Seasons restaurant are designated as New York City landmarks · **1990** Receives an honorary doctor of fine arts from the Pratt Institute · **1992** Made officer of the Ordre des Arts et des Lettres de France · **1996** Creates the Fonds d'investissement de Montréal, a private fund to revitalize housing in medium- and low-income Montreal neighborhoods · **2006** Awarded the Vincent Scully Prize by the National Building Museum, Washington, DC; the Seagram

Building is added to the National Register of Historic Places ·
2007 *Citizen Lambert: Joan of Architecture*, a documentary
film on her civic advocacy, premieres · 2014 Receives the Golden
Lion for Lifetime Achievement at the 14th Venice Architecture
Biennale

Lora Lamm

—

1928 Born in Arosa, Switzerland · 1946 Attends the Kunstgewerbeschule (School of Arts and Crafts) in Zurich and studies
graphic design under the direction of Johannes Itten, Ernst
Keller, and Ernst Gubler · 1952 Works for various agencies,
including Atelier von Romain Sager · 1953 Moves to Milan; joins
Studio Boggeri, where well-known designers Max Huber, Xanti
Schawinsky, Carlo Vivarelli, Walter Ballmer, Aldo Calabresi,
and Bruno Monguzzi had all worked at various times; takes
on small assignments such as designing wrapping paper and
packaging for Motta · 1954 At the urging of Huber, who
designed La Rinascente's logo and visual identity, joins the
Italian department store as a graphic designer in the advertising
and communications department; works on catalogs, posters,
advertisements, packaging, and promotional materials for the
store · 1956 Designs promotional materials for *Il Giappone*,
an exhibition held at La Rinascente · 1958–62 Promoted to head
of La Rinascente's creative department; carries out independent
assignments for other Italian companies such as Pirelli, Niggi,
and Olivetti · 1963 Returns to Zurich; begins freelance career ·
1964 Starts work at the advertising agency of Frank C. Thiessing;
later becomes partner · 2000 Retires · 2013 *Lora Lamm, Grafica
a Milano 1953–1963*, a solo exhibition of her work, opens at the
m.a.x. museo in Chiasso, Switzerland · 2015 Receives the Swiss
Grand Award for Design from the Federal Office of Culture;
Lora Lamm: La vita è bella, an exhibition of her posters, opens
at the Museum für Gestaltung Zürich

Jack Lenor Larsen

—

1927 Born in Seattle, Washington · 1945 Attends the University
of Washington and studies architecture · 1946 Begins weaving
and develops an interest in furniture design; moves to Los
Angeles to concentrate on fabric · 1951 Earns an MFA from
Cranbrook Academy of Art; relocates to the East Coast
and opens a studio in New York · 1952 Designs draperies for
the lobby of Manhattan's Lever House · 1957 Reports on the
Triennale di Milano for *Interiors* magazine · 1958 Designs
upholstery for Pan American World Airways; consults for the
US Department of State; advises on grass weaving projects in
Taiwan and Vietnam · 1959–62 Codirects the fabric design
department at the Philadelphia College of Art · 1962 Designs
and directs *Fabrics International*, an exhibition that travels
throughout Africa · 1963 Opens Jack Lenor Larsen International
in Zurich · 1964 Acts as design director and US commissioner
of the Triennale di Milano · 1966 Commissioned by Louis Kahn
to design fabric wall panels for the First Unitarian Church of

Rochester, New York · 1968 Awarded an AIA Gold Medal;
cocurates the exhibition *Wall Hangings* at the Museum of
Modern Art in New York · 1971 Publishes *The Dyer's Art: Ikat,
Batik, Plangi* with Dr. Alfred Buhler Bronwen and Garrett
Solyom (Van Nostrand Reinhold) · 1974 Establishes a furniture
division · 1975 Publishes *Fabrics for Interiors* with Jeanne Weeks
(Van Nostrand Reinhold) · 1979 Retrospective exhibition opens
at the Musée des Arts Décoratifs in Paris · 1989 Publishes
Material Wealth: Living with Luxurious Fabrics (Abbeville Press /
Thames and Hudson) · 1992 Establishes the LongHouse
Foundation (now LongHouse Reserve) in East Hampton, New
York · 1998 Publishes *A Weaver's Memoir* (Harry N. Abrams) ·
2000 Receives a Lifetime Achievement Award from the Museum
of Arts and Design in New York · 2001 *Jack Lenor Larsen: The
Company and the Cloth* opens at the Minneapolis Institute of
Arts; an accompanying online archive showcases the Institute's
collection of his work · 2009 Awarded the Smithsonian's
Archives of American Art medal · 2012 The exhibition *Jack
Lenor Larsen: 40 Years* opens at the New York School of Interior
Design · 2015 Receives a National Design Award in the
Director's Award category

Ingo Maurer

—

1932 Born on Reichenau Island, Germany · 1954–58 Studies
typography and graphic design in Munich and Switzerland ·
1960 Moves to the United States and works in New York
and San Francisco as a freelance graphic designer for clients
including Kayser Aluminum and IBM · 1963 Returns to
Germany and opens a graphic design studio; founds Design M,
a lighting design company · 1966 Designs his breakthrough
project, Bulb, a table lamp now in the permanent collection
of the Museum of Modern Art in New York · 1970s Travels
throughout Japan, meeting with fan maker Shigeki-san and
artist and designer Isamu Noguchi · 1973 Renames his company
Ingo Maurer GmbH · 1984 Launches his YaYaHo halogen
lighting system; installs custom versions at the Centre Pompidou
and Institut Français d'Architecture in Paris; and Villa Medici
in Rome · 1989 *Ingo Maurer: Lumière Hasard Réflexion* opens
at Fondation Cartier pour l'Art Contemporain in Paris; begins
producing special-edition works not intended for commercial
production · 1992 *Ingo Maurer: Working with Light* opens
at Villa Stuck in Munich · 1999 Designs a lighting concept for
Issey Miyake's Autumn/Winter 2000 runway show in Paris;
also designs the brand's London showroom · 2000 Receives
the Lucky Strike award from the Raymond Loewy Foundation ·
2002 Receives the Georg Jensen prize; *Ingo Maurer—Light:
Reaching for the Moon* opens at the Vitra Design Museum in
Weil am Rhein, Germany · 2005 Appointed a Royal Designer
of Industry by the Royal Society of Arts · 2006 Designs interior
lighting for the Atomium in Brussels · 2007 *Provoking Magic:
The Lighting of Ingo Maurer* opens at the Cooper Hewitt,
Smithsonian Design Museum in New York · 2011 Awarded
a Compasso d'Oro · 2015 *Collective Influence: Ingo Maurer*
opens at the Collective Design Fair in New York

Alessandro Mendini

1931 Born in Milan, Italy · 1959 Receives an architecture degree from the Politecnico de Milano; works as a designer in the offices of Marcello Nizzoli · 1970s Leads several groups within Italy's Radical Design movement, including the Global Tools Collective and, with Ettore Sottsass and Michele De Lucchi, Studio Alchimia, an experimental practice and predecessor of the Memphis Group · 1970–85 Becomes editor of *Casabella*, *Domus*, and *Modo*, each post lasting five years · 1974 Designs the Lassú, a sculptural chair that thwarts conventional function; he sets the piece on fire for the cover of *Casabella* · 1978 Designs the Poltrona di Proust armchair, manufactured by Studio Alchimia · 1979 Receives his first Compasso d'Oro (he receives two more, in 1981 and 2014) · 1982 Cofounds Domus Academy, a private postgraduate design school in Milan · 1988 Designs La Casa Della Felicità (The House of Happiness) for Alberto Alessi; becomes publisher and editor of *Ollo* for one year · 1989 Opens Atelier Mendini in Milan with his brother Francesco · 1990 Designs a bus stop in Hannover, Germany, as part of a citywide initiative to improve public transportation · 1993 Designs Alessi offices and factory in Omegna, Italy · 1994 Designs the Groninger Museum in the Netherlands; designs the Anna G. series of bar and kitchenware for Alessi · 2007 Designs the new Triennale de Milano brand in Incheon, South Korea · 2009 Designs a subway station in Naples · 2010 Returns to *Domus* for one year · 2014 Receives the European Prize for Architecture

Jens Risom

1916 Born in Copenhagen, Denmark · 1935 Begins studying design under Ole Wanscher at the Kunsthåndvaerkerskolen (formerly the School of Arts and Crafts, now the Danish Design School) in Copenhagen · 1937 Designs furniture for A/S Normina · 1938 Attends business school; works briefly for Danish architect Ernst Kuhn · 1939 Immigrates to the United States after a chance meeting with the American Ambassador to Denmark; works for interior designer Dan Cooper; commissioned by Edward Durell Stone to design furniture for *Collier's* "House of Ideas," a model home displayed at Rockefeller Center during the New York World's Fair · 1941 Begins working with Hans Knoll · 1942 Embarks on a four-month, cross-country road trip with Knoll to research the growing market for furniture design; first Knoll catalog is released; designs fifteen of the twenty pieces in the inaugural 600 Series of furniture · 1943 Serves in the US Army under General Patton · 1946 Launches Jens Risom Design Inc., serving as sole creative director for twenty-five years · 1952 Requests that Knoll remove his name from the company's designs to avoid competing against himself in the marketplace · 1954 Photographer Richard Avedon shoots a series of ads for JRD featuring the slogan, "The Answer Is Risom"; JRD sales increase · 1961 Featured in *Playboy* magazine alongside five other notable furniture designers: George Nelson, Edward Wormley, Eero Saarinen, Harry Bertoia, and Charles

Eames · 1970 Cedes control of JRD to the Dictaphone Corporation; a series of missteps and poor management by Dictaphone quickly leads to the demise of JRD · 1973 Launches the consulting service Design Control · 1976 Builds a summer home from prefabricated components on Block Island, Rhode Island; the house is featured in *Life* magazine; receives the Danish Knight's Cross from Margrethe II · 1997 Knoll reissues his designs from the 1940s and 1950s · 2005 Launches a new line of furniture for Ralph Pucci International · 2010 Works with Rocket/Benchmark to reissue furniture designs in Europe; the collection debuts in *Wallpaper* · 2015 Collaborates with Chris Hardy, a designer seventy years his junior, on a collection of modular storage for Design Within Reach

Richard Sapper

1932 Born in Munich, Germany · 1956 Begins his design career in the styling department of Mercedes-Benz after having researched the company as a student · 1958 Relocates to Milan, where he begins working in the offices of Giò Ponti and later as a designer for the Italian department store La Rinascente · 1959 Opens his own design office in Milan; collaborates with architect and designer Marco Zanuso for several years as a consultant to consumer electronics company Brionvega and produces a range of designs, including the TS 502 radio · 1972 Designs the Tizio task lamp for Artemide · 1976 Designs a series of watches for Swiss company Tag Heuer · 1979 Receives his first commission from longtime client Alessi; among his many designs for the Italian home and kitchenware company is the 9090 espresso maker; designs the Sapper Office Chair series for Knoll · 1980 Appointed principal industrial design consultant at IBM, beginning a longtime partnership with the company · 1984 Designs the Nena folding chair for B&B Italia · 1992 Designs the first ThinkPad 700C, followed by all subsequent models · 2009 Receives a Lifetime Achievement Award from the German Design Council · 2010 Designs Sapper™ Monitor Arm Collection for Knoll; receives an honorary doctoral degree from the University of North Carolina · 2012 Receives a Merit Cross from the Order of the Merit from the President of Germany

Ricardo Scofidio

1935 Born in New York, New York · 1952 Attends Cooper Union · 1960 Graduates from Columbia University with a bachelor of architecture · 1965 Begins teaching at Cooper Union · 1979 Forms a partnership with Elizabeth Diller; opens a studio in New York · 1981 Diller + Scofidio realize the Kinney Plywood House, a weekend residence in Westchester County, New York · 1986 Designs stage pieces for *The Rotary Notary and His Hot Plate, or a Delay in Glass* · 1987 *The withDrawing Room*, an installation The Capp Street Project in San Francisco · 1989 D+S installs *Para-Site* in the Poject Room at the Museum of Modern Art in New York · 1991 Designs Slow House for a site in North Haven, New York; it remains unbuilt · 1993 Video installation *Soft Sell* debuts in New York's Times Square; *Bad Press: Dissident Housework Series* begins, and is later acquired by the San Francisco Museum of Modern Art · **1999** Wins a MacArthur Foundation Award with Diller; the couple become the first architects, and the second married couple, to receive the honor · **2000** D+S designs Slither Housing as part of Arata Isozaki's master plan for government-subsidized residences in Gifu, Japan; redesigns Brasserie, a restaurant in the Seagram Building originally designed by Philip Johnson · **2001** *Travelogues*, a permanent installation in New York's John F. Kennedy International Airport, opens to the public · **2002** Realizes the Blur Building, a permeable pavilion made of steel and fog, for the Swiss Expo; the D+S–designed overhaul of Lincoln Center begins; the project is completed in 2013 · **2003** *Scanning: The Aberrant Architectures of Diller + Scofidio*, a retrospective of the firm's work, opens at the Whitney Museum of American Art in New York · **2004** Charles Renfro becomes a partner and the studio is renamed Diller Scofidio + Renfro · **2005** DS+R receives the National Design Award for Architecture from the Cooper Hewitt, Smithsonian Design Museum in New York · **2006** Realizes the Institute for Contemporary Art in Boston · **2009** The first section of the High Line, running from Gansevoort Street to West Twentieth Street in New York, opens; DS+R received the AIA President's Award and the AIA Medal of Honor · **2013** Publishes *Lincoln Center Inside Out* (Damiani) · **2014** Selected to design the expansion of the Museum of Modern Art; completed the third phase of the High Line · **2015** Benjamin Gilmartin becomes a partner of DS+R; publishes *The High Line* (Phaidon); the Broad Museum in Los Angeles opens to the public

Denise Scott Brown

—

1931 Born in Nkana, Northern Rhodesia (now Zambia) · **1948** Studies at the University of the Witwatersrand in Johannesburg · **1952** Travels to London and works for architect Frederick Gibberd; resumes studies at the Architectural Association School of Architecture · **1955** Marries her first husband, Robert Scott Brown; graduates with a degree in architecture · **1958** Relocates to Philadelphia to study planning at the University of Pennsylvania · **1959** Robert Scott Brown dies in a car accident · **1960** Completes her master's in planning and becomes a faculty member at UPenn; meets Robert Venturi in a faculty meeting and begins a longtime collaborative relationship · **1965** Leaves UPenn to take a post at the University of California, Berkeley; moves to the University of California, Los Angeles, rising to cochair of the Urban Design Program · **1966** Begins researching the Southwest; invites Venturi to attend her classes at UCLA and visit Las Vegas; Venturi writes *Complexity and Contradiction in Architecture* as a rebuke to orthodox modernism · **1967** Marries Venturi; returns to Philadelphia, joining Venturi's firm, Venturi and Rauch (renamed Venturi, Rauch and Scott Brown in 1980, then Venturi, Scott Brown & Associates in 1989), becoming principal-in-charge of planning · **1972** With Venturi and Steven Izenour, writes *Learning from Las Vegas: The Forgotten Symbolism of Architectural Form* (MIT Press), a collection of studies of the Las Vegas Strip conducted in research studios coinstructed with Venturi at Yale University · **1987** Designs the Center City Development Plan for Memphis · **1991** Venturi receives the Pritzker Architecture Prize (but not Scott Brown); protests and does not attend the award ceremony; realizes a new building for the Seattle Art Museum · **1995** Devises the Denver Civic Center Plan for Denver, Colorado · **1997** Begins a campus plan for the University of Michigan · **2004** Designs the Brown University Campus Life Plan · **2005** Designs a proposed update for the Tsinghua University campus, Beijing · **2007** Receives a National Design Award in the Design Mind category with Venturi; accepts the Athena Award from the Congress for the New Urbanism, and the Vilcek Prize from the Vilcek Foundation · **2011** Publishes *Having Words* (Architectural Association), a collection of essays · **2013** Women in Design, a student group at the Harvard Graduate School of Design, starts a petition calling for Scott Brown to retroactively receive joint recognition of Venturi's 1991 Pritzker Prize · **2015** Awarded, with Venturi, the AIA Gold Medal

Deborah Sussman

—

1931 Born in Brooklyn, New York · **1948** Takes classes at the Art Students League; attends summer school at Black Mountain College · **1950** Receives a bachelor's in visual arts and acting from Bard College · **1953** Becomes a designer in the offices of Charles and Ray Eames in Los Angeles; works for the Eameses for ten years · **1957** Receives a Fulbright Scholarship to study at the Hochschule für Gestaltung in Ulm, Germany · **1968** Establishes her own practice · **1961** Returns to Eames Office · **1972** Meets urban planner Paul Prejza; marries him later that year · **1980** Sussman and Prejza form Sussman/Prejza & Co. in Culver City, California, specializing in urban branding and environmental design · **1983** Designs the visual identity, signage, and wayfinding for the Summer Olympics in Los Angeles · **1987** Cofounds the Los Angeles chapter of AIGA with designers Saul Bass, April Greiman, and others · **1987** Elected to the Alliance Graphique Internationale (AGI) · **1988** Becomes an honorary member of the American Institute of Architects; receives an Honorary Doctorate of Humane Letters from Bard College · **1996** Designs the comprehensive identity program for the city of Santa Monica, California · **2004** Receives an AIGA Gold Medal · **2005** Designs the identity and print collateral for the Museum of the African Diaspora in San Francisco · **2006** Receives the Golden Arrow Award from the Society of Environmental Graphic Design · **2012** Named a Laureate of the Art Directors' Global Hall of Fame in New York · **2013** *Deborah Sussman Loves Los Angeles*, a retrospective of her early work, opens at Woodbury University's WUHO Gallery in Hollywood · **2014** Dies of breast cancer at age eighty-three in Los Angeles, California

Jane Thompson

—

1927 Born in Champaign, Illinois · **1947** Graduates *cum laude* from Vassar College · **1948** Completes graduate courses at New York University's Institute of Fine Arts; joins the Museum of Modern Art in New York as a secretary and is promoted to assistant curator of architecture · **1950** Leaves MoMA to become architecture editor at *Interiors* magazine, contributing regularly to the industrial design section · **1953** Founds *Industrial Design* (later called *I.D.*) as the magazine's editor in chief · **1959** Joins the board of directors of the Kaufmann International Design Award · **1961** Chairs the building committee for Mount Anthony Union High School in Bennington, Vermont · **1965** Joins Benjamin Thompson's Cambridge, Massachusetts, retail venture, Design Research; marries Thompson four years later · **1966** Begins work on Faneuil Hall Marketplace in Boston · **1967** Becomes a planning associate at Benjamin Thompson & Associates · **1971** Serves as a board member, program chair, and occasional speaker for the International Design Conference in Aspen, Colorado; holds the position for twenty-nine years · **1975** Opens Harvest Restaurant in Boston's Harvard Square with Benjamin Thompson · **1986** Begins work on the planning and revitalization of a 44-block site near Midtown Manhattan's Grand Central Terminal · **1988** Becomes a partner at BTA · **1991** Plans Chicago's Navy Pier as the acting BTA partner in charge on the project · **1994** Opens Thompson Design Group as principal and owner; begins a coastal beach master plan for an oceanfront site in Long Branch, New Jersey · **1997** Receives a Lifetime Achievement Award from the American Society of Industrial Designers · **2001** Awarded the Knight First Class, Order of the Lion of Finland and is bestowed with the nickname "Sir Lady Jane" · **2010** Receives a National Design Award for Lifetime Achievement; publishes *Design Research: The Store That Brought Modern Living to American Homes* (Chronicle Books) with architecture and design critic Alexandra Lange

Stanley Tigerman

—

1930 Born in Chicago, Illinois · **1948** Begins studies at MIT but drops out during his first year; serves in the US Navy · **1949** Becomes a draftsman and designer for several Chicago firms, including Keck & Keck; Milton Schwartz; and Skidmore, Owings & Merrill · **1960** Receives a BArch from Yale University · **1961** Receives an MArch from Yale University · **1964** Establishes Stanley Tigerman and Associates Ltd. (now called Tigerman McCurry Architects, managed with his partner and wife, Margaret McCurry) · **1965** In collaboration with Yale classmate Muzharul Islam, designs Five Polytechnic Institutes, an educational institution in Bangladesh · **1973** Elected to the College of Fellows of the American Institute of Architects · **1976** Revives the formerly defunct Chicago Architectural Club, assuming the role of president; cofounds the Chicago Seven; among the group's critical output is the exhibition *Chicago Architecture,* which opens at the Cooper Union and later travels to the Museum of Contemporary Art, Chicago; selected to

represent the United States at the Venice Architecture Biennale (and again in 1980) · **1978** Designs the Illinois Regional Library for the Blind and Physically Handicapped · **1985** Serves as director of the School of Architecture at the University of Illinois in Chicago, occupying the post for eight years · **1980** Cofounds Archeworks, a progressive, socially oriented design school in Chicago, with Eva Maddox · **2008** Receives the Topaz Medallion for Excellence in Architectural Education from AIA/ACSA · **2001** Publishes *Designing Bridges to BURN: Architectural Memoirs by Stanley Tigerman* (ORO Editions) and *Schlepping Through Ambivalence: Essays on an American Architectural Condition* (Yale University Press) · **2009** Designs the Illinois Holocaust Museum and Education Center in Skokie · **2012** The Graham Foundation organizes *Ceci n'est pas une rêverie*, a retrospective of his illustrated and built works; Yale acquires and transfers his drawing archive to its Manuscripts and Archives repository · **2013** Receives a Lifetime Achievement Award from the AIA · **2014** The Art Institute of Chicago organizes the exhibition *Architecture to Scale: Stanley Tigerman and Zago Architecture*

Beverly Willis

—

1928 Born in Tulsa, Oklahoma · **1943** Learns to fly a single-engine propeller plane, qualifying for the Women's Air Service Pilots (WASP), but does not serve; moves to Portland, Oregon · **1946** Studies engineering at Oregon State University · **1954** Earns a BFA from the University of Hawaii, studying under artist Jean Charlot; opens Willis Atelier in Waikiki · **1956** Pioneers a technique for creating sand-cast mural panels · **1958** Relocates to San Francisco, opens Beverly Willis Architects (BWA), which ultimately grows to a staff of thirty-five · **1966** Becomes a licensed architect · **1971** BWA pioneers the development and use of CARLA (Computerized Approach to Residential Land Analysis), one of the first computer software programs for large-scale land use · **1979** Leads the design for the Aliamanu Family Housing Development in Honolulu · **1980** Joins the board of the National Building Museum in Washington, DC, as a Founding Trustee · **1982** Completes the San Francisco Ballet Building · **1988** Closes BWA and relocates to New York; completes the Manhattan Village Academy, her final architectural commission · **1995** Founds the Architecture Research Institute · **2001** Through ARI, founds R.Dot, Rebuild Downtown Our Town, a public initiative for the rehabilitation of Lower Manhattan in the wake of 9/11 · **2002** Founds the Beverly Willis Architecture Foundation, a nonprofit organization focused on documenting and expanding knowledge of women's contributions to the built environment · **2008** At age eighty, makes the documentary *A Girl Is a Fellow Here: 100 Women Architects in the Studio of Frank Lloyd Wright*

Acknowledgments

To Alice Twemlow, for introducing us to the field of design criticism
and each other; to Alexandra Lange, for helping us grasp the
responsibility of this assignment, and for her ongoing encouragement;
to Adam Harrison Levy, for teaching us the true art of the interview;
and to Judith Ramquist, for her warm friendship and enthusiasm
for our project.

Thank you to Michael Carabetta, Kevin Lippert, and Jennifer
Lippert for entrusting us with this book, and to Paul Wagner for first
presenting the idea, as well as designing the book's pages; and to
Megan Carey, Tom Cho, Jenny Florence, Marielle Suba, and Lindsey
Westbrook for their editorial support and guidance in shaping this
project. We are also grateful to Jenn Miller and Lauren Palmer for their
tireless assistance.

For the many gracious colleagues and friends who helped us track
down, connect with, or lead us closer to our twenty interviewees,
our thanks to: Emily Alli, Nicoletta Ossanna Cavadini, Rob Giampietro,
Kind Company, Sheila McCullough, Polimekanos, Vera Sacchetti, Paula
Scher, Jonathan Stephenson, Scott Stowell, Joeffrey Trimmingham,
Chris Wu, and the team at Project Projects.

To Peg Bull, Helen Risom Belluschi, and Henny Risom of the
Risom family for welcoming us with open arms, and introducing us to
their family mantra: "If you're going to do a job, do it right."

Thanks also to the numerous individuals who aided in our visual
research and image selection: Eliza Alkire, Anna Ballard, Dan Bates,
Alessia Contin, Greg D'Onofrio, Luca Farinelli, Beatrice Felis,
Sal Forgione, Marissa Glauberman, Angela Guevara, Thomas Happel,
Katherine Herzog, Isabelle Huiban, Alexis Hyde, Mark Jespersen,
Vicki Matranga, Claude Maurer, Camille Murphy, Mary Kate Murray,
Nancy Nguyen, Roberta Prevost, Carola Sapper, Dorit Sapper,
Olga Viallet, and Taber A. Wayne.

To our partners, Brad Engelsman and Josh Primicias, for their love
and support, as the project filled our extra hours, nights, and weekends
over the past two years.

Not least of all, our utmost and immense gratitude to our
interviewees—Ralph Caplan, Seymour Chwast, Bob Gill, Milton Glaser,
Michael Graves, Charles Harrison, Richard Hollis, Phyllis Lambert,
Lora Lamm, Jack Lenor Larsen, Ingo Maurer, Alessandro Mendini, Jens
Risom, Richard Sapper, Ricardo Scofidio, Denise Scott Brown, Deborah
Sussman, Jane Thompson, Stanley Tigerman, and Beverly Willis—
for offering their time, interest, support, and sage wisdom, and without
whom this book would not have been possible.

Image Credits

—

Michael Pateman photo, published in United States by Thomas Y. Crowell, Publishers 13

Herman Miller 14

Fairchild Publishers, by permission of Bloomsbury Publishing Inc. 14 (2)

Courtesy Ralph Caplan 17, 18 (4)

Courtesy of Alvin Lustig Archive. ID Magazine, An F+W Publication 17, 183 (2), 184

Alvin Lustig Archive 17

Greg Preston photo 21

Courtesy of Seymour Chwast 23, 24, 25, 27 (3), 28, 29, 30 (2), 31, Harry N. Abrams 24, © Seymour Chwast, 2011, Used by permission of Bloomsbury Publishing Inc. 24

Penguin Random House LLC 29

Courtesy of Bob Gill 33, 35, 37 (2), 38 (3), 41, John Cole photo 33

Logo used with permission by the New York State Department of Economic Development 43

Milton Glaser 44, 46 (3), 48 (2), 49, 51 (3), Michael Soronoff photo 46

Brooklyn Brewery 48

New York Media 48

Courtesy of Michael Graves Architecture & Design 53, 54, 55 (2), 56 (3), 59, 60 (2), 61, 63 (2), Target Corporation photo 60, Peter Aaron/OTTO photo 61

Courtesy of Charles Harrison 65 (2), 67, 68 (2), 71, Joeffrey Trimmingham photo 71

Richard Hollis 73, 76, 77

Pelican Books 75

Courtesy of Whitechapel Art Gallery, Whitechapel Gallery Archive 77 (2)

Modern Poetry in Translation 78 (2)

Indiana University Press 80

Pluto Press 80

African National Congress 80

Fonds Phyllis Lambert, CCA, Montréal 83, 84, Ed Duckett photo 87, © United Press International 89, The House of Patria, December 1956 89

© Canadian Centre for Architecture, Montréal 83, Ezra Stoller © Esto 88, © Naoya Hatakeyama 90, Gift of the artist on the occasion of Phyllis Lambert's 80th birthday © Naoya Hatakeyama 91

© Italo Rondinella. Courtesy: la Biennale di Venezia 90

Courtesy of Lora Lamm 93

Leonard Zubler photo 93

Zürcher Hochschule der Künste, ZHdK / Museum für Gestaltung Zürich, MfGZ / Plakatsammlung 94, 95, 96–97, 98 (2)

Courtesy of LongHouse Reserve 106 (3), 107 (3), 108 (2), Dorothy Beskind photo 101

Balthazar Korab photo 103 (2)

Courtesy of the Western Pennsylvania Conservancy, Christopher Little photo 105

Ingo Maurer GmbH 111 (2), 112, 113 (3), 114, 115, 116 (2), 118 (2), 119, Tom Vack, Munich photo 115 (2), Engelhardt Sellin, Munich photo 116 (2)

Courtesy Cooper Hewitt, Smithsonian Design Museum, Tom Vack photo 117 (2)

Atelier Mendini 121, 122 (2), 123 (2), 124 (3), 125, 126, 127

Carlo Lavatori photo 127

Courtesy of Jens Risom and the Risom family archives 129 (2), 134, 135 (3), 136 (3)

Knoll, Inc. 130, 136

© Richard Avedon photo 131

Courtesy of Marvin Koner Archive, Marvin Koner photo 132–133

Courtesy Richard Sapper 139, 140 (3), 141, 142 (2), 143 (2)

Serge Libiszewski photo 140, 141, 143

© Aldo Ballo 141

Giorgio Boschetti photo 142

Courtesy of DS+R 147 (2), 149 (2), 150, 152, 153, 154, 155, Abelardo Morrell photo 145, Iwan Baan photo 151 (2)

Michael Moran/OTTO photo 147

Courtesy of VSBA 157, 160, 168

Denise Scott Brown 159 (3), 160, MIT Press 162 (2), 163, 165

Maria-Marcella Sorteni photo 160

MIT Press 162

George Pohl photo 166

Jim Venturi photo 166

Jiro Schneider photo for Riposte Magazine 171

Sussman/Prejza 173 (2), 174 (2), 176–177, 178 (3), 179 (2)

Courtesy of Jane Thompson 185, 186, 187, 188, 189, © Richard Pousette-Dart photo 181

City of Long Branch, NJ, photo 188

Kathy Pick photo 188

Tigerman McCurry Architects 191, 192 (2), 195 (2), 196, 199 (2), 200, 201 (2), 203

Margaret McCurry photo 196

Rafique Muzhar Islam photo 200

Balthazar Korab photo 202 (2)

Beverly Willis Archive 205, 206, 207 (2), 209, 212–213

Michael Kanouff photo 207

National Building Museum 209

Peter Aaron/OTTO photo 211